Ethics Matter

Burçak Çağla Garipağaoğlu

Ethics Matter

Unwrapping Ethics for Beginners in the Quantum Age

PETER LANG

Berlin - Bruxelles - Chennai - Lausanne - New York - Oxford

Library of Congress Cataloging-in-Publication Data
A CIP catalog record for this book has been applied for at the
Library of Congress.

**Bibliographic Information published by the
Deutsche Nationalbibliothek**
The Deutsche Nationalbibliothek lists this publication in the Deutsche
Nationalbibliografie; detailed bibliographic data is available online at
http://dnb.d-nb.de.

Funded by Bahçeşehir University

ISBN 978-3-631-91292-8 (Print)
E-ISBN 978-3-631-93046-5 (E-PDF)
E-ISBN 978-3-631-93047-2 (E-PUB)
10.3726/b22552

© 2025 Peter Lang Group AG, Lausanne
Published by Peter Lang GmbH, Berlin, Germany

info@peterlang.com - www.peterlang.com

Ethics Matter

No matter how much we would like it to be otherwise, there is no simple straight-forward solutions to moral dilemmas and no simple straight-forward way to think about ethical issues. Every ethical problem can be examined using several perspectives, and thus, the outcome may vary depending on the path chosen. For centuries, philosophers have been trying to find answers to fundamental issues such as "What does it mean to be a 'good' person?" and "What should the laws and norms be?". Although these questions led to nuanced and insightful discussions attracting the attention of people from diverse aspects of life, so far there has been no absolute success in resolving them. However, by adding the tools of quantum paradigm to those of conventional philosophy, we may be able to shine more light on such difficult questions. Drawing upon one of the most famous quotes attributed to Plato – "the right question is usually more important than the right answer"- the purpose of this book is not to find the "right" answers. Instead, this book intends to offer the kind of insight that is drawn from behavioral science and the wisdom of influential philosophers spanning centuries. The book is designed to guide you to think about ethics through some important philosophers, social psychological experiments, and codes of ethics. This book will ensure that what answers you might arrive at the end will be built on a better foundation than before. So, the purpose of this book is to inspire and encourage you to ask thoughtful and probing questions to gain a deeper understanding of ethical dilemmas until you come up with better questions that indeed make more sense.

Table of Contents

Part II. Normative (Prescriptive) Ethics

Part III. Meta-Ethics

Part IV. Applied Ethics

Editor's Preface

For most of the world, the "ethics" and what we mean by it is so much more elusive today. The Quantum age with its many crises and opportunities has posed several daunting ethical challenges to societies. Bridging the gap between ethics and decision-making has never been more difficult than today. To begin with, now what is ethical and not ethical seems to be much more complicated than it used to be. Therefore, sharpening our ability to detect ethical issues and improving our moral intelligence (moral IQ) are more essential than ever to navigate the complex moral landscape of the quantum age. In this context, the purpose of this book is, thus, to help us improve our moral IQ much the same way that children learn and understand about the world around them and present a set of resources to support a more moral society. First, we present some insightful and thought-provoking questions about ethics and then provide a little theory about the potential answers to those questions. And finally, there is a part explaining how we think or should think about ethical problems in the age of quantum. This book will help us better understand our ethical dilemmas and how to approach them. While it does not necessarily ensure us to make sound moral judgments, by making us more sensitive to moral matters this book aims to be a book of people who seek ethical counsel. By equipping us with an understanding of ethics and ethical principles, this book may cultivate a sense of moral awareness and develop skills needed to navigate ethical dilemmas and make ethically informed decisions in various contexts.

Now, more than ever we need higher ethical standards in every part of our lives. The proliferation of advanced technologies, the widening gap between those who have access to them and those who do not, and the rapidly evolving environment present us with a host of novel ethical dilemmas that often defy traditional solutions or "common wisdom." As technology advances, it introduces complex ethical issues that may not have clear precedents or established ethical frameworks. These challenges require us to adapt our ethical thinking and approaches to address emerging concerns effectively. There are many new important ethical issues that need to be re-considered. This re-raises the basic questions about ethics that philosophers have been trying to find answers to for centuries: "What principles drive our choices?", "What are we willing to do to ensure that ethical decisions are achieved?" and "What do we value ethics for?" Ethics from many aspects in our lives are still obscure. More and more people (teachers, students, employees, employers, and customers) are complaining that our generation and society suffers from immorality and amorality. To address more effectively the ethical implications of the new situations, ethics is gaining greater relevance in educational institutions and workplaces. To navigate more effectively in today's elusive ethical standards, we all need to understand what we and other people might think about what constitutes what is ethical or not.

The purpose of this book is to help (1) people re-imagine ethical issues and dilemmas with the new value propositions of quantum paradigm; (2) develop a new ethical contract for people and institutions (3) people challenge themselves to consistently learn, grow and advance more ethically to pursue a more meaningful and purposeful life; (4) leaders support common-sense ethical policy that invests in new ethical propositions of quantum paradigm. In this context, our book is thought to be important for practitioners, leaders, teachers, parents, employers, and for people who need some ethical guidance in order to navigate the harsh realities of ethical dilemmas presented by the Quantum world. In the light of the current and foreseen ethical dilemmas of the future, this book tries to relate traditional ethical paradigm and practice with the Quantum paradigm.

Acknowledgments

I would like to express my deepest love and gratitude to my children, Çağıl Garipağaoğlu and Işık Garipağaoğlu, and to my beloved parents, Fatma Tılı and my late father Sami Tılı, whose unwavering love and support have been my guiding light throughout this journey.

I would like to express my sincere gratitude to Prof. Dr. Esra Hatipoğlu, the President of Bahçeşehir University, and Enver Yücel, the chairman of the executive board at Bahçeşehir University, for their exceptional leadership and unwavering support throughout the process of writing this book. Their encouragement and the supportive environment they have fostered have been invaluable.

Additionally, I extend my heartfelt thanks to the publisher, Peter Lang, for their belief in this project and for agreeing to publish this book.

B. Çağla Garipağaoğlu, PhD Bahçeşehir University,
Istanbul, Turkey
April, 2024

Introduction

This book consists of four parts and eleven chapters regarding the field of ethics. Each part covers one of the main branches of ethics:

Part I, including three chapters, dedicated to behavioral ethics (why people act as they do) and explain factors that might and does influence ethical decision-making and behavior by the tools of behavioral psychology, cognitive science, and evolutionary biology. Thus, Part I focuses on descriptive (or comparative) ethics aiming to describe, compare and explore how people do think and behave about moral issues. The first chapter (Chapter 1) aims to provide some invaluable insights by describing and comparing people's moral beliefs, claims and behaviors in different cultures. The second chapter (Chapter 2), on the other hand, aims to explore the cognitive processes, emotions, psychological and sociological factors that influence moral decision-making. The third chapter (Chapter 3), on the other hand, attempts to understand ethical sensemaking by exploring various ethical decision-making models.

Part II, including three chapters, is dedicated to normative (or prescriptive) ethics attempting to discover which actions are in fact right or wrong. This part aims to seek answers to questions studied primarily by philosophy and theology such as "What should people do?", "What should they think?", "How should one act?", "What should the laws and norms be?" and "What is right and wrong?" It also attempts to discover "which action are in fact right or wrong", "which things are in fact good or bad", and "what it takes to be a good or bad person?" Since there is no straight-forward answers to these questions, and the answers depends on the approach chosen, each chapter focuses on different approaches. The first chapter (Chapter 4) is dedicated to virtue ethics and addresses questions such as "How should I live?", "What is good life?", "What kind of a life I want to pursue in life", "What are proper family and social values?", and "What kind of a person I want to be?". The second chapter (Chapter 5), on the other hand, focuses on deontological ethics (non-consequentialist ethics) which attempt to determine the right action in terms of a duty or set of duties or some intrinsic drive, motivation, intent of actions/or agents. The third chapter (Chapter 6) focuses on the teleological ethics (Consequentialist ethics) which suggests that the moral value of an action is determined by the goodness or desirability of its consequences. All these chapters present some insightful and thought-provoking ideas and more importantly prompt us to ask more questions.

Part III, including two chapters, provides a little theory about meta-ethics -a branch of moral philosophy that focuses on understanding the nature of moral language, moral knowledge, and moral truth and attempts to achieve a conceptual clarification when addressing questions such as "What's goodness?", "What does 'power', 'beauty', and 'money' represent to me?", "How can we tell what is good from what is bad?", and "How are moral propositions defended?" The chapters in this part focus on the origins of ethical principles and attempt to answer the questions studied primarily by philosophers such as "Whether moral values are eternal truths or simple human conventions" and "Whether moral judgements are universal or relative, of one kind or of many kinds". The first chapter of Part III (Chapter 7) focuses on non-cognitivism which is a philosophical position within metaethics that denies the cognitive status of moral judgments by proposing that moral statements are not propositions with truth values and not capable of being true or false as they are merely capable of expressing emotions, attitudes, or preferences. The second chapter (Chapter 8), on the other hand, focuses on cognitivism which is a philosophical position within metaethics that asserts the cognitive status of moral judgments and propose that moral statements express propositions that are capable of being true or false.

Lastly, Part IV, including three chapters, focuses on applied ethics. The first chapter (Chapter 9) offers a practical and widely used framework for ethical decision-making in various professional contexts (Principlism). The second chapter (Chapter 10) attempts to identify the correct course of action for real problems by case-based reasoning. Finally, the third chapter (Chapter 11) attempts to illustrate the role of a code of ethics in any industry, profession, or organization focusing on some selected professions.

Part I Descriptive (or Comparative) Ethics

Descriptive (or comparative/behavioral) ethics describe and compare moral beliefs, values, behaviors of individuals, and the ethical norms in different societies without prescribing what people ought to do. The primary goal of descriptive ethics is to describe, analyze, and interpret the moral landscape without making normative judgments. By documenting and understanding the diversity of moral beliefs and practices, scholars in descriptive ethics contribute valuable insights to our understanding of how ethics function in human societies. The primary contributions in descriptive ethics come from scholars who engage in empirical research, observation, and analysis of existing moral practices. Many contributions in descriptive ethics involve interdisciplinary collaboration, bringing together scholars from various fields such as anthropology, ethnography, sociology, psychology, and philosophy to provide a comprehensive understanding of moral phenomena. Philosophers engaged in descriptive ethics analyze and interpret moral practices, traditions, and beliefs by exploring the historical development of moral concepts and the ways in which ethical norms are embedded in cultural and social contexts.

By using the tools of cognitive science, evolutionary biology, cognitive psychology, behavioral psychology and neuroscience, behavioral ethics attempts to explain how people do think and behave about moral issues. Psychologists contribute by conducting experiments and exploring the cognitive processes, emotions, and psychological factors that affect moral decision-making. This includes research on moral development, moral reasoning, and the impact of situational factors. By studying diverse societies and documenting their moral norms, practices, and ethical systems, cultural anthropology helps us gain insights into how different cultures approach moral issues. By conducting experiments and exploring the social dynamics, structures, and factors that shape moral behavior within communities and institutions, sociologists help us understand how those factors contribute to the variations in ethical beliefs. By engaging in immersive fieldwork to observe and document the moral practices of specific groups or communities, ethnographers provide detailed accounts of how individuals navigate ethical dilemmas within their cultural contexts.

Cultural Ethics, as a subfield within descriptive ethics, explores how different cultures shape and influence moral beliefs and practices. It considers how cultural norms, messages, symbols, traditions, and values impact individuals' ethical decision-making. Behavioral ethics, as a subfield within descriptive ethics, on the other hand, focuses on the psychological and social factors that influence individuals' moral decision-making and behavior. It seeks to understand how people navigate ethical dilemmas, make moral judgments, and behave in moral situations. This includes studying cognitive biases, social influences, situational factors, and the role of feelings and our moral development level in shaping ethical choices. Instead of focusing on how people ought to behave, behavioral ethics studies "How people develop a moral sense and moral identity?" and "why and how people make the choices that they do".

Chapter 1 Some Valuable Insights From Cultural Ethics

Ethical language may vary across different cultural contexts and philosophical traditions. What is considered morally acceptable or unacceptable in one culture may not be perceived the same way in another. Interchanging words without considering these cultural nuances can lead to misunderstandings. Clearly defining key terms and concepts at the outset of ethical discussions can help establish common ground and prevent misunderstandings. Encouraging critical reflection on the use of language in ethics can promote awareness of potential ambiguities and inconsistencies, leading to more rigorous and meaningful discussions.

Cross-cultural studies compare moral practices across different societies by exploring commonalities and differences in ethical systems. These studies contribute to a more nuanced understanding of human morality by shedding some light on cross-cultural variations in ethical norms. Without going into much detail, in this chapter, we are going to delve into the ways in which ethical norms are embedded in cultural and social contexts by emphasizing some well-known differences in Western and Eastern culture.

Humans come to know and understand moral principles and values through a combination of innate predispositions, cultural influences, rational reflection, and social interactions. It's important to note that different individuals and cultures may prioritize these sources differently. Additionally, there is an ongoing philosophical debate about whether there exists a universal, objective foundation for morality, or if moral values are entirely subjective and relative to individual or cultural perspectives. Here are some key factors that contribute to our understanding of morality:

- Innate Predispositions: Some researchers argue that humans have an innate capacity for moral reasoning. This is often referred to as "moral intuition," which suggests that certain moral principles may be hardwired into our brains. For example, the idea of fairness seems to be a universal concept that is present in many cultures.
- Cultural and Social Influences: Much of our moral development is shaped by the society and culture in which we are raised. Different cultures have different moral frameworks, and individuals tend to adopt the values and principles of their cultural milieu. This includes religious teachings, legal systems, family values, and societal norms.

- Family and Upbringing: Families play a crucial role in instilling moral values in individuals. Parents and caregivers are typically the first moral guides for a child. They teach basic principles such as honesty, kindness, and respect. The family environment also influences the development of empathy and social awareness.
- Religious and Philosophical Beliefs: Religion has been a significant source of moral guidance for many societies throughout history. Religious texts and teachings often provide explicit moral frameworks and ethical guidelines. However, individuals can also derive their moral principles from secular philosophies and ethical theories.
- Education and Formal Instruction: Formal education, including schools, religious institutions, and other educational settings, plays a vital role in shaping a person's moral compass. It provides opportunities for learning about ethical theories, critical thinking about moral dilemmas, and exposure to different perspectives.
- Rational Reflection and Critical Thinking: As individuals mature, they engage in more complex moral reasoning. This involves reflection, deliberation, and the evaluation of different ethical perspectives. Philosophical thinking and moral philosophy provide tools for critical examination of moral issues.
- Empathy: Empathy, the ability to comprehend the feelings and perspectives of others, is a fundamental aspect of moral development. It allows individuals to take the impact of their actions on others into account and helps to foster a sense of responsibility towards fellow human beings.
- Social Interactions and Relationships: Engaging with others in social contexts allows individuals to learn about different perspectives and values. Interactions with peers, colleagues, and members of diverse communities contribute to a broader understanding of morality.
- Personal Experiences and Reflections: Life experiences, including successes, failures, and challenging situations, can shape an individual's moral outlook. These experiences provide opportunities for personal growth and can lead to shifts in one's moral principles and values.
- Media and Literature: Books, films, and other forms of media can influence moral thinking by presenting various scenarios and ethical dilemmas. They offer opportunities for reflection on complex moral issues and exposure to different moral viewpoints.

It's important to note that individual experiences and circumstances vary, and as a result, people may come to understand and prioritize different moral principles and values. Additionally, moral beliefs can evolve over time in response to new information, experiences, and shifts in societal norms.

Three Wise Monkeys' Ethics (Senses of Japanese Ethics)

Let's start with the simple example of three wise monkeys and then delve into the slippery meaning of it. The origin of "the three wise monkeys" can be traced back to the ancient China, but they are most famously known as a part of Japanese culture. The three monkeys, together, symbolize the proverbial saying, "See no evil! hear no evil! and speak no evil!". They are also known as the senses of Japanese ethics. The three wise monkeys -often depicted covering their eyes, ears, and mouth- are known as Mizaru, Kikazaru, and Iwazaru in Japanese. According to Buddhist teachings, the three wise monkeys are generally seen as a representation of avoiding or abstaining from engaging in evil actions. In some East-Asian world, their message goes a step further than that, and people may use the concept of the three wise monkeys to encourage discretion, politeness, and the avoidance of awkward, embarrassing situations. So, the message becomes a message about "saving face" which is often associated with avoiding public embarrassment or shame for others. In some cultural contexts, where "face" is highly valued, this expression might encourage a more empathetic and understanding approach to interpersonal interactions (Li, 2020). It suggests exercising caution and compassion when addressing the actions or mistakes of others. It advises recognizing that everyone has their own challenges and faults, and together the three wise monkeys represent the moral message of acting benevolently by turning a blind eye to the innocent wrongdoings of others to prevent embarrassment or loss of dignity on behalf of others. When interpreted from some East-Asian perspective, teaching of "the three wise monkeys" becomes to restrain oneself from putting the innocent wrongdoer into a difficult or embarrassing situation. So, this is simply a message of preserving one's reputation, dignity, or social standing by pretending as if no wrongdoing happened. The idea is to refrain from seeing, hearing, or speaking about negative or embarrassing matters to maintain harmony and respect in social interactions. The concern behind this modesty is empathy and is sparing other's from shame (Han, 2016). Thus, in Eastern culture, people may play "three wise monkeys" as a gesture of sympathy and support. When applied within the realm of Eastern culture, "playing three wise monkeys" aligns pretty well with the biblical expression, "Let he who is without sin cast the first stone" (Holy Bible, 2011, John, 8:7) in the sense that both sayings encourage empathy, and self-reflection to our own imperfections. Even though the biblical expression emphasizes more on the idea of refraining from passing judgment, criticizing others, and pointing out the shortcomings of others when one is not free from faults and flaws themselves, "the three wise monkeys" urges us to be mindful of the consequences of our own actions on the other person's reputation. Overall, the combination of the biblical wisdom and Buddhist wisdom with the cultural concept of "saving face" underscores the importance of humility, empathy, and thoughtful communication in navigating social interactions and relationships. Together, they encourage individuals to approach others with a spirit of understanding, forgiveness, and empathy and to acknowledge that everyone is susceptible to making mistakes.

In the West, the phrase "playing three wise monkeys", on the other hand, advise people "not to put themselves into trouble by talking about others" wrongdoings even if they witness them in-person, especially if doing so entails any trouble or hardship on the part of the revealer. It literally advises people to turn a blind eye to something morally or legally wrong to avoid any hardship and responsibilities of doing otherwise. It suggests ignoring evil if not doing so entails any hard-ship on your part. This version of the three wise monkeys aligns pretty well with one ancient Turkish wisdom claiming that "To live in peace one must be blind, deaf and dumb". The message is then very simple: "Pretend as if there is nothing wrong, save yourself from any fuzz or trouble and live a peaceful life without the heavy burden of taking any responsibility". The message claims that doing other-wise would make life impossible to endure. Or consider this Latin phrase which can be translated as "Hear, see, but be silent if you wish to live in peace". The mes-sage is quite similar. But does playing "Three Monkeys" as in the Western ver-sion invalidate the existence of any inappropriateness or evil? This is a question one might ask from a metaethics perspective (see Part III). In short, although the idea of three wise monkeys was born in the East, its other-oriented message transformed into a more self-oriented message in the West, where individualism has been the norm. The phrase "playing three wise monkeys" in Western culture is a colloquial expression that typically means remaining silent or turning a blind eye when observing immoral behavior and implies a moral muteness. It happens when people see unethical behavior and prefer not to tell or report anything to anyone. When we see others acting unethically, we often tend to look the other way, and avoid speaking out rather than risk paying an emotional and social cost for it because it is the easiest way. Studies indeed show that only a relatively small percentage of people who see wrongdoing speak up.

However, in many cultures, playing "three wise monkeys" as implied in Western culture is not a righteous way to live though it may be seen as a wise choice. As a wise man once said, "The only thing necessary for the triumph of evil is for good men to do nothing" or as most famously said in one Turkish proverb "He who keeps silent in the face of injustice is a mute devil." People wishing to be ethical generally strive to combat moral muteness in all areas of our lives. Indeed, in western culture when people say "do not play three wise monkeys" they aim to condemn people who avoid responsibility particularly when it comes to addressing any wrongdoing or confronting evil. This statement then becomes a harsh warning suggesting a commitment to accountability and ethical conduct, regardless of the consequences.

To sum up, three wise monkeys represent a perfect example of how one symbol can mean completely different things depending on the context. Visual representation of the three wise monkeys can be either positive or negative based on whether you're looking at it from an easterner's or a westerner's perspective. Whereas, in the East, the image of three wise monkeys is a reminder to follow a morally upright path by avoiding evil in any form (passive and active) and reminding one to be pure and virtuous by not engaging in negative and destructive behaviors, interestingly in the West, this symbol has very different and somewhat negative connotations. It must be noted that the message of "three wise monkeys" in the Eastern version has nothing like the Western message and surely does not entail avoiding being morally upright in the face of evil. Different cultures may adopt and adapt symbols like the three wise monkeys to convey messages that resonate with their values.

Let us consider the famous saying that "*if you have nothing nice to say, say nothing at all,*" whether it is good advice or not is highly debatable. What is the source of this advice? Is it just an oversimplification, really aimed at teaching manners (being pleasant and constructive) to small children who may blurt out "look at that fat person" or other unfortunate observations or is it a teaching aiming to teach people not to cause any unnecessary drama for themselves and just pay lip service to people to avoid any trouble? Life is very subtle and complicated and therefore here perspectives matter: One might choose to ignore the truth, not to see, hear or talk about it, by simply thinking "Why to create drama, for myself?" or thinking that "there is no need to be harsh on people" and play "Three Monkeys" or tell and reveal the truth no matter what.

Advice Ethics (Morality of Advice)

Consideration of cultural norms and contextual appropriateness is crucial in determining the morality of advice whether it is solicited or unsolicited. The morality of solicited and unsolicited advice depends on factors such as consent, intentions, respect for autonomy, manner of its delivery and cultural considerations. While solicited advice is generally considered more ethically sound due to the explicit request for input, the morality of unsolicited advice can vary based on the circumstances and the impact on the individuals involved. Sensitivity to the preferences and boundaries of others is essential in both cases. Solicited advice is generally considered morally acceptable in every culture, -of course, when it is delivered kindly- because it is given with the consent and willingness of the person seeking guidance -meaning that the person has actively sought assistance, indicating a recognition of their own need for input or perspective.

The approach and reception of advice, whether solicited or unsolicited, can vary between East and West due to cultural differences. It's important to note that cultural norms are generalizations, and individual preferences may vary. Here's a general overview of how solicited and unsolicited advice may be perceived in both cultural contexts:

In East Asian Cultures, solicited advice is often appreciated and considered as a sign of respect. Seeking guidance from elders or those with more experience is viewed as a kind of respect to the elderly or the superior (Feng, 2015). However, in East Asian Cultures, even when advice is sought, it should be delivered indirectly to avoid causing embarrassment or discomfort. The emphasis is often on maintaining face. East Asian societies generally place a high value on respect and politeness and preserving dignity of others (Hwang & Han, 2010). Criticizing someone openly or challenging their ideas in a confrontational manner can be seen as disrespectful (Hou, 2022). In East Asian cultures, open confrontation or criticism should be avoided to prevent causing embarrassment or loss of face for individuals involved (Xiaoxi & Stapa, 2022). So particularly, if the advice requires confrontation with some hurtful truths that are hard to admit, and process, Confucius societies generally tend to avoid it not to make the situation worse (more stressful and complicated) or awkward, even if the advice is solicited. Thus, advice that points out someone's mistakes or shortcomings, even if it is solicited, should be delivered with sensitivity, not to threaten one's face. Similarly, in Western Cultures, solicited advice is generally welcomed, especially in professional or collaborative settings. Seeking the expertise of others is often seen as a positive and proactive approach. However, in western cultures, advice is often given straightforwardly and directly, especially in professional settings where clarity and efficiency are often prioritized.

Offering unsolicited advice, on the other hand, is always morally questionable as it carries the potential of infringing on the autonomy of the individual. Offering advice without permission -even if the advice is given with good intentions and aims to genuinely help the individual- may be perceived as intrusive and disrespectful when it disregards the boundaries and preferences of the person receiving the advice. In some situations, or cultures, unsolicited advice may be more acceptable, while in others, it may be perceived as inappropriate (Feng, 2015). Unsolicited advice is generally unwanted in Western culture, whether it is well-intentioned or not, because westerners tend to perceive unsolicited advice as a challenge to their autonomy and may feel highly uncomfortable when they receive it. On the other hand, if the unsolicited advice is genuinely meant to help and docs not cause harm or discomfort, it is morally encouraged in Eastern cultures. Even if some Westerners may appreciate it as constructive input, in Western cultures unsolicited advice is less tolerated as Westerners often value individual autonomy more than Easterners. Thus, Easterners tend to give more unsolicited advice and have more tolerance to receive so, as well-intentioned unsolicited advice is morally acceptable and even encouraged in Eastern societies (Feng & Magen, 2016). In East Asian cultures, there may be a preference for indirectness and preserving harmony, while in Western cultures, direct communication is often more accepted. The nature of the relationship plays a role. In both cultures, close relationships may allow for more direct advice, but in general, cultural norms still influence these interactions. The context in which advice is given or sought matters. In professional settings, solicited advice is often expected and valued in both East and West. It is crystal clear that cultural awareness and adaptability are essential in navigating these differences. It's advisable to approach interactions with openness, understanding, and a willingness to adapt communication styles based on the cultural context at hand.

Here is another approach to ethics of offering advice from a quantum standpoint that may be helpful and seems to work almost in any culture: "*Before you speak ask yourself if what you are going to say is True, is Helpful, is Inspiring, is Kind, is Necessary -THINK. If the answer is no, maybe what you are about to say should be left unsaid*". The acronym "THINK" serves as a practical guide to help individuals assess the impact and appropriateness of their words before expressing them. It aligns with principles of effective communication, mindfulness, and ethical speech.

Truth? Is what you are about to say true for all people?

Helpful? Reflect on **what you are about to say** and ask yourself if it needs to be told. Is it helpful or inspiring. And maybe, there is no need to say anything at all, as usually people only listen to "helpful" advice when it's solicited.

Inspiring? Actions are more important than words, and we generally need a helping hand more than advice. If your words are uplifting and motiving, then go for it, otherwise it is better left unsaid.

Necessary? People are often their own harshest critic. Sometimes we already know what we need to hear. People are pretty clever, and we all know more than we say. Sometimes we are just not ready to hear it. So, if your advice is not going to change anything for the better, there is no need to be a smart ass and make the situation worse (or awkward) with unnecessary words.

Kind? If your words do not come from a place of love and compassion and if you aren't willing or able to support someone to act on what you have to say, then it's probably better left unsaid? Diplomacy, sensitivity, and emotional support may be more important here than telling the truth.

Morality of the Golden Rule

The Golden Rule is a principle that is found in many religions and moral philosophies. It is a moral guideline that suggests treating others as you would like to be treated. The Golden Rule is often expressed in various forms, but the essence is the same: to treat others with kindness, respect, and fairness, as we would wish to be treated ourselves. The Golden Rule can be found in many religious texts and traditions, including:

> Christianity: "Do unto others as you would have them do unto you." (Holy Bible, 2011, Matthew 7:12)
>
> Islam: "None of you [truly] believes until he wishes for his brother what he wishes for himself." (Eaton, 2008, Hadith of the Prophet Muhammad)
>
> Judaism: "What is hateful to you, do not do to your fellow: this is the whole Torah; the rest is the explanation; go and learn." (Cohen, 2013, Talmud, Shabbat 31a)
>
> Buddhism: "Hurt not others in ways that you yourself would find hurtful." (Rockhill, 2000, Udanavarga 5:18)
>
> Hinduism: "This is the sum of duty: do not do to others what would cause pain if done to you." (Vyāsa, 2020, Mahabharata 5:1517)
>
> Confucianism: "Do not do to others what you do not want them to do to you." (Confucius, 1979, Analects 15:23)

The Golden Rule is a fundamental principle of ethical conduct that encourages empathy, compassion, and understanding towards others. The underlying principle is about treating others with kindness and respect, regardless of the potential benefits or consequences for oneself. But the motive behind following the golden rule may vary depending on cultural, social, and individual factors. Some people may interpret the Golden Rule as a rule of reciprocity, where they treat others well in the hope of receiving similar treatment in return -by harnessing their gratitude. This interpretation can be seen as a form of self-interest, where individuals act in a way that benefits them in the long run. Others may interpret the Golden Rule as a way to avoid retaliation or revenge. By treating others with kindness and respect, individuals may hope to avoid conflict or negative consequences. Although, at its core, the Golden Rule is about empathy, compassion, and understanding towards others and it encourages individuals to consider the feelings and needs of others and to act in a way that promotes mutual respect and cooperation, self-interest or avoiding harm -harnessing gratitude or avoiding retaliation- may well be the factors in some interpretations of the Golden Rule.

Let's examine the interpretation of golden rule from the perspectives of different kinds of egoism (i.e., psychological egoism, ethical egoism, and enlightened egoism). Some ethical egoists argue that following the golden rule would be just foolish because we often can do better for ourselves by breaking the golden rule because this would be exactly what all other people do. However, enlightened egoists would argue otherwise and assert that this argument is not entirely correct because although this claim might be true only for short-term wins, it is not so for long-term wins. Indeed, enlightened egoists would argue that what we do for others' benefit may eventually benefit ourselves in the end and they advocate that genuine self-interest cannot be served without honoring the maxim, "You scratch my back, I scratch yours". So, as you have seen neither of those arguments backs up the original essence of "golden rule" as implied in ancient texts.

Let's examine the feeling of "gratitude" as a rule of reciprocity. Some people advocate that gratitude is a survival skill that must be nurtured for various reasons. Some say being grateful increases a person's resilience as it motivates you intrinsically (i.e., the power of being thankful) and some focus more on the power of earning the gratitude of others. Many anthropologists, including Marcel Mauss, suggest that gratitude elicits reciprocation. If someone does a favor to us, the assumption is that we are beholden to him/her. Cialdini (2006) explains that the innate principle of reciprocity or gratitude is so strong that even though you do not ask for any favor, if you are at the receiving end of it (even if it is uninvited), you feel obliged to deal with it (i.e., repay) eventually. Gratitude can be a weapon to harness future favors and might be used to manipulate people to gain unfair and undeserved advantages. Feeling of revenge or reciprocity can be examined in the same way. The fear of retaliation can be a significant deterrent for people who are considering treating others poorly. This fear is often based on the principle of reciprocity, which is the idea that people tend to respond to actions in kind. If someone treats another person poorly, they may fear that the other person will retaliate by treating them poorly in return.

"Turn the other cheek" Ethics

The phrase "turn the other cheek" is a biblical expression originating from the teachings of Jesus Christ, specifically found in the Gospel of Matthew (Holy Bible, 2011, Matthew 5:39). The complete verse delivers: "But I tell you, do not resist an evil person. If anyone slaps you on the right cheek, turn them the other cheek". This teaching can be either interpreted as an encouragement to respond to aggression and insult with nonviolent resistance or an encouragement to endure further mistreatment. Within the realm of second interpretation, "turn the other cheek," can be seen as a form of social control or pacification, according to Marx's (1843/1976) critique of religion as "the opium of the people" in his Critique of Hegel's Philosophy of Right.

While the specific cultural expressions and interpretations of "turning the other cheek" can be found in various forms and interpretations in different cultures, the underlying theme of responding to adversity with a commitment to nonviolence, forgiveness, and tolerance is a common thread. It reflects a universal aspiration toward peace, understanding, and the resolution of conflicts without resorting to further harm or retaliation. According to Rand, on other hand, the doctrine of turning the other cheek is a mistaken tactic of appeasement, altruism, or simple cowardice, and she defended that it is a sanction of the victim that allows evil to triumph, and thus it is a moral crime. Here are a few examples of similar ideas in different cultural and philosophical contexts:

Gandhian Philosophy (India): Mahatma Gandhi, a key figure in India's struggle for independence, was influenced from the biblical wisdom "turning the other cheek" within the realm of its principles of nonviolence. His philosophy encouraged individuals to respond to oppression with nonviolent resistance. Gandhi's principles of nonviolence left a lasting impact on various movements for social and political change (e.g., Gezi Park Protests in Turkey). The Gezi Park movement encompassed a diverse range of individuals and groups with varying political ideologies and methods of protest. While some participants advocated nonviolent resistance, others engaged in confrontations with the police, and the overall atmosphere was characterized by a mix of peaceful demonstrations and clashes. The ones who adhere to Gandhi's principles of nonviolence, showed history's one of the greatest examples of resisting with nonviolence and incorporating elements of humor to the biblical wisdom of "turn the other cheek" notion to convey their message.

Taoism (China): Taoist philosophy emphasizes the principle of wu wei, often translated as "non-action" or "non-resistance." The idea is to respond to challenges with a passive, non-aggressive attitude, akin to turning the other cheek.

Buddhism (Global): Buddhism teaches the importance of compassion, forgiveness, and non-harming. The practice of metta (loving-kindness) involves responding to negativity with kindness and understanding, aligning with the spirit of turning the other cheek.

Here are other potential ways to consider "turning the other cheek". Let's consider it from the perspective of ethical egoism. One may prefer to "turn the other cheek" to preserve long-term relationships, because doing so could be seen as beneficial to one's long-term self-interest. By avoiding retaliation or conflict, an individual may foster a harmonious social environment that contributes to their well-being over time. Choosing not to retaliate or seek revenge might be viewed as a means of minimizing personal stress and emotional strain. In the long run, avoiding negative emotions and conflicts could be seen as serving one's self-interest by promoting mental well-being. Ethical egoism acknowledges that one's reputation can influence personal success and well-being. Turning the other cheek could be a strategy for building a positive reputation, which may lead to better opportunities, cooperation, and support from others. An ethical egoist might also choose to "turn the other cheek" strategically, recognizing that aggressive or retaliatory actions may have negative consequences. Non-resistance in certain situations might be seen as a calculated decision to maximize one's overall benefit.

Cancel Culture Ethics

"Cancel culture ethics" refers to the ethical principles and values associated with the phenomenon known as "cancel culture." Cancel culture is a term used to describe a social phenomenon where individuals or groups are publicly shamed, ostracized, or boycotted for behavior or speech that is deemed offensive, inappropriate, or problematic. This can sometimes lead to social or professional consequences for the person being "canceled." The rise of social media like the platform X-formerly known as Twitter has made it easier for individuals to engage in cancel culture, as it allows for the rapid spread of information and opinions, which can also sometimes lead to misunderstandings or misinterpretations. This has led to the perception that cancel culture is more prevalent among younger generations, who are more likely to use social media and the internet. As a result, public figures and ordinary individuals alike can be quickly and widely criticized, "lynched," or "canceled" for their actions or statements. While cancel culture is often associated with younger generations, particularly Generation Z, it is not unique to any specific generation and can be found across different age groups and demographics.

The ethics of cancel culture are complex and often debated. Some argue that cancel culture is a necessary tool for holding individuals and institutions accountable for their actions and words, particularly when they perpetuate harm or discrimination against marginalized groups. They argue that cancel culture can be a form of collective action and social justice, and that it can help to create a more inclusive and equitable society. Others argue that cancel culture can be harmful and counterproductive, particularly when it leads to the silencing of dissenting voices or the suppression of free speech as individuals may be afraid to express their opinions or engage in controversial discussions for fear of being "canceled" or facing social or professional consequences. They argue that cancel culture can create a climate of fear and self-censorship, and that it can be used as a form of bullying, lynching, or harassment. They argue that cancel culture can create a toxic and hostile online environment, where individuals are afraid to speak out or express their views for fear of being targeted or harassed. The ethics of cancel culture are often debated in the context of broader ethical principles, such as:

> Freedom of Speech: The right to express oneself freely without fear of censorship or retaliation.
> Justice: The fair and equitable treatment of all individuals, regardless of their background or beliefs.
> Empathy and Compassion: The importance of understanding and empathizing with the experiences and perspectives of others, particularly those who have been marginalized or oppressed.
> Accountability: The recognition of one's own responsibility in addressing and rectifying harm or wrongdoing, and the willingness to hold oneself and others accountable for their actions and words.
> Restorative Justice: The belief in the possibility of repairing harm and restoring relationships through dialogue, understanding, and reconciliation.

The ethics of cancel culture are complex and multifaceted, and they often depend on the specific context and circumstances of each case. It's important to consider these broader ethical principles when evaluating the ethics of cancel culture, and to strive for a balanced and nuanced understanding of the issues involved.

Woke Culture Ethics

"Woke ethics" is a term that refers to the ethical principles and values associated with the "woke" movement. The term "woke" originated in African American Vernacular English (AAVE) and has been adopted more broadly to refer to a social and political movement that seeks to raise awareness about social justice issues, including racial, gender, and economic inequality. It often emphasizes the importance of being sensitive to the experiences and perspectives of marginalized groups.

Woke ethics, therefore, are the ethical principles and values that guide the woke movement. These may include:

Intersectionality: The idea that various forms of oppression (such as racism, sexism, ableism, etc.) intersect and overlap, creating unique experiences of discrimination and disadvantage for individuals who belong to multiple marginalized groups.

Social Justice: The belief in the fair and equitable distribution of resources, opportunities, and rights across society, with a focus on addressing systemic inequalities and promoting the well-being of marginalized communities.

Empathy and Compassion: The importance of understanding and empathizing with the experiences and perspectives of others, particularly those who have been marginalized or oppressed.

Allyship: The practice of actively supporting and advocating for marginalized groups, even if one does not belong to those groups themselves.

Critical Thinking: The ability to critically analyze and question societal norms, structures, and power dynamics, with a focus on challenging and dismantling systems of oppression.

Accountability: The recognition of one's own privilege and responsibility in addressing and dismantling systems of oppression, and the willingness to hold oneself and others accountable for their actions and words.

Critics of woke culture often argue that it can lead to a culture of "false sensitivity" or "exaggerated sensitivity," where individuals claim to be sensitive to social justice issues but are actually more focused on their own image and reputation. They argue that this can lead to a lack of sincerity and authenticity, as individuals may be more concerned with appearing "woke" than with actually addressing social justice issues. Critics also argue that woke culture can lead to a culture of "cancel culture," where individuals are publicly shamed or ostracized for behavior or speech that is deemed offensive or problematic. They argue that this can create a climate of fear and self-censorship, and that it can be used as a form of bullying or harassment.

It's important to note that not all individuals who identify with woke culture engage in false sensitivity or cancel culture. Many individuals and groups within the woke movement are sincere in their commitment to social justice and equality, and they strive to create a more inclusive and equitable society. However, it is also important to recognize that there can be instances where individuals or groups within the woke movement may engage in behavior that is not in line with these values. It's also important to note that the term "woke ethics" is not universally accepted or used by all individuals or groups within the woke movement. Additionally, the woke movement itself is not a monolithic entity, and different individuals and groups may have different interpretations of what it means to be "woke" and what ethical principles should guide the movement.

Cringe Culture

Cringe culture is a term used to describe a social phenomenon where individuals or behaviors are publicly ridiculed or mocked for being perceived as awkward, embarrassing, or uncool. This can include anything from awkward social interactions to unpopular opinions or interests. Cringe culture has become more prominent with the rise of social media and the internet, where individuals can share and comment on content that they find cringe-worthy. It often involves the use of memes, jokes, or other forms of humor to mock or ridicule the person or behavior in question.

Critics of cringe culture argue that it can be harmful and counterproductive, particularly when it leads to the bullying or harassment of individuals who are perceived as cringe-worthy. They argue that cringe culture can create a toxic and hostile environment, where individuals are afraid to express themselves or share their interests for fear of being ridiculed or mocked. The writer, Shridhar (2019) calls cringe culture, "a cheap attempt at humor".

Others argue that cringe culture can be a form of social bonding or humor, and that it can help to create a sense of community among individuals who share similar tastes or interests. They argue that cringe culture can be a way of expressing frustration or dissatisfaction with certain behaviors or trends, and that it can be a way of challenging social norms and expectations.

The story of cringe is more like the story of a Russian doll (Kalia, 2022). In the 16th century "cringe" meant "to bend or crouch with servility or fear". By the 19th century, the meaning had cemented itself; and it meant to "recoil in embarrassment, shame, or fear". In 20th century, cringe culture was about empathy, a way of defiance, and secondhand embarrassment for others, and it had a compassionate origin; today, in 21st century "cringe" has lost its compassionate element and become a way of mockery which turn to become a serious infraction with contempt (Tiffany, 2022). Cringe culture is now evolved into "insulting people for harmless activity" and become a subculture claiming moral high ground over others (Tiffany, 2022).

Here are some ethical questions and considerations related to cringe culture:

Respect for Others: Is it ethical to publicly ridicule or mock someone for their behavior or interests, even if they are perceived as awkward or uncool? Is it respectful to make fun of someone for being themselves or expressing their interests?

Empathy and Compassion: How does cringe culture impact the mental health and well-being of individuals who are targeted for being perceived as cringe-worthy? Is it ethical to contribute to cringe culture that can be toxic and hostile?

Freedom of Expression: Is it ethical to mock or ridicule someone for expressing themselves or sharing their interests, even if those interests are not popular or mainstream? How does cringe culture impact the ability of individuals to freely express themselves online?

Social Responsibility: What is the responsibility of individuals and communities in creating and perpetuating cringe culture? How can we promote a more inclusive and respectful environment?

Power Dynamics: How does cringe culture intersect with issues of power and privilege? Are certain individuals or groups more likely to be targeted for being perceived as cringe-worthy? How does this impact their ability to be part of a society?

Cultural Sensitivity: How does cringe culture intersect with issues of cultural sensitivity and diversity? Are certain behaviors or interests more likely to be targeted for being perceived as cringe-worthy? How does this impact individuals from different cultural backgrounds?

Ultimately, the ethics of cringe culture are complex and multifaceted, and they depend on the specific context and circumstances of each case. It's important to consider these broader ethical principles when evaluating the ethics of cringe culture, and to strive for a balanced and nuanced understanding of the issues involved.

Morality of Humblebragging (False Humility/False Modesty)

Humblebragging is an increasingly ubiquitous form of boasting or self-promotion strategy that is disguised as modesty or self-deprecation. It is a bragging masked by a complaint (Sezer et al., 2018). It typically involves making a statement that seems to be humble or self-critical on the surface but is actually intended to draw attention to one's accomplishments or positive attributes. For example, someone might say, "I'm so ashamed of my privilege -I can't believe I have the luxury of taking a vacation while so many people are struggling", which appears to be acknowledging their privilege but is actually a way of bragging about their ability to afford a vacation. In these cases, the individual may be using the language of social justice and privilege to deflect attention away from their own privilege and accomplishments, while still drawing attention to them. This can be seen as a form of performative allyship, where someone claims to be an ally to marginalized groups but is actually more focused on their own image and reputation. Humblebragging can be seen as a form of social manipulation or a way of trying to appear modest while still drawing attention to one's achievements. It can also be seen as a way of trying to gain sympathy or approval from others by downplaying one's own accomplishments.

Humblebragging is mostly associated with younger generation professionals who are more likely to use storytelling as a way of self-marketing and to seek attention. Storytelling is an important part of our quest for personal and professional success. But the question is "How can one construct a personal narrative without committing the sin of pride or exaggerating one's own merits?" If one accepts that authenticity is essential to reinforcing leadership and respect from others, how does one forge the best impression of oneself with sincerity and objectivity (Iniguez, 2024)? Social networks provide us with many examples of humblebragging every day. Consider the messages from your colleagues that begin with the expression "humbled by", "thrilled at", "honored by" followed by the announcement of a new position, or some achievement that is little more than vulgar ostentation? False modesty consists of pretending to be humble for having had a success, but it is really a form of arrogance (Iniguez, 2024).

False modesty is often a self-presentation strategy displayed in job interviews and professional settings. Recruiters typically ask candidates to name their weaknesses and most candidates respond with clichés typical of false modesty (humblebragging) (Iniguez, 2024). For example, explaining that their weakness is excessive perfectionism, or that their problem is giving too much importance to taking on all the challenges that come their way, or that they cannot avoid completing tasks, to the detriment of their private life. The problem indeed resides in the question itself, since most of us, when looking for a job, are hardly likely to list our actual defects and say we tend to get angry under stress, we are not a team player, or that we feel sleepy after lunch (Iniguez, 2024).

The ethics of humblebragging culture are complex and often debated. On the other hand, some argue that humblebragging can be a harmless form of self-expression and can be used as a way of acknowledging one's accomplishments while still being modest. They argue that it is not always possible to accurately convey one's feelings or experiences in a way that is completely free from bias or self-promotion, and that humblebragging can be a way of navigating this complexity. Critics of humblebragging argue that it is insincere and manipulative. They argue that it can be harmful to genuine self-esteem and confidence, as it encourages individuals to downplay their own achievements and abilities.

It's important to note that not all instances of self-deprecation or modesty are examples of humblebragging. There are many instances where individuals genuinely feel modest or self-critical about their accomplishments, and there is nothing wrong with expressing these feelings. However, it's also important to be aware of the potential for humblebragging and to be mindful of how our words and actions may be perceived by others.

Ultimately, the ethics of humblebragging culture are subjective and depend on the specific context and circumstances of each case. It's important to consider these broader ethical principles when evaluating the ethics of humblebragging culture, and to strive for a balanced and nuanced understanding of the issues involved.

References

Cialdini, R. B. (2006). *Influence: The psychology of persuasion*. Harper Business.

Cohen, A. (2013). *Babylonian Talmud*. Cambridge University Press

Confucius. (1979). *The Analects*. Penguin Classics

Eaton, C. L.G. (2008). *The book of hadith: Sayings of the Prophet Muhammad from the Mishkat Al Masabih*. Book Foundation.

Feng, H. (2015). Understanding cultural variations in giving advice among Americans and Chinese. *Communication Research, 42*(8), 1143–1167. https://Doi.org/10.1177/0093650213486668

Feng, B., & Magen, E. (2016). Relationship closeness predicts unsolicited advice giving in supportive interactions. *Journal of Social and Personal Relationships, 33*(6), 751–767. https://doi.org/10.1177/0265407515592262

Han, K. H. (2016). The feeling of "Face" in Confucian society: From a perspective of psychosocial equilibrium. *Frontier Psychology 7*(1055), 1–9. https://doi.org/10.3389/fpsyg.2016.01055.

Holy Bible New International Version. (2011). *Biblica Inc.* https://www.biblegateway.com/passage/?search=John+8%3A7&version=NIV

Hou, M. (2022). The re-schematization of face in Chinese overseas students' intercultural experience. *International Journal of Language and Culture, 9*(1), 27–47. https://doi.org/10.1075/ijolc.20020.hou

Hwang, K. K., & Han, K. H. (2010). Face and morality in Confucian society. In M. H. Bond (Ed.), *Oxford Handbook of Chinese Psychology* (pp. 479–498). Oxford University Press.

Iniguez, S. (2024). *Real pride, grace, and the rise of humblebragging*. Linkedin. https://www.linkedin.com/pulse/real-pride-grace-rise-humblebragging-santiago-iniguez-5iqif/?trk=article-ssr-frontend-pulse_more-articles_related-content-card

Kalia, S. (2022, May 20). *A cultural history of 'cringe,' and how the internet made everything awkward.* The SWDL. https://www.theswaddle.com/a-cultural-history-of-cringe-and-how-the-internet-made-everything-awkward

Li, H. (2020). Towards an emic understanding of Mianzi giving in the Chinese context. *Journal of Politeness Research, 16*(2), 281–303. https://doi.org/10.1515/pr-2017-0052

Marx, K. (1976). *Introduction to a contribution to the critique of Hegel's philosophy of right* (A. M. Mckinnon, Trans.). Collected Works. (Original work published 1843)

Rockhill, W. W. (2000). *Udanavarga: A collection of verses from the Buddhist canon (trubner's oriental series).* Routledge.

Sezer, O., Gino, F., & Norton, M. I. (2018). Humblebragging: A distinct – and ineffective – self-presentation strategy. *Journal of Personality and Social Psychology, 114*(1), 52–74. https://doi.org/10.1037/pspi0000108

Shridhar, A. (2019, October 25). *Cringe culture is 'cringy'.* https://nique.net/opinions/2019/10/25/cringe-culture-is-cringy/

Tiffany, K. (2022). *How did we get so 'cringe'?* The Atlantic. https://www.theatlantic.com/technology/archive/2022/01/cringe-culture-everywhere/621272/

Vyāsa, V. (2020). *The Mahabharata – Book 5: Udyoga Parva (English Translation).* Independently Published.

Xiaoxi, G., & Stapa, M. B. (2022). Practices of Chinese businesspersons for saving addresser-oriented face in intercultural communication. *Eurasian Journal of Applied Linguistics, 8*(3), 260–269. http://dx.doi.org/10.32601/ejal.803021

Chapter 2 Some Valuable Insights From Behavioral Ethics

By combining insights from cognitive psychology and sociology, behavioral ethics attempts to explore how psychological, sociological factors and cognitive processes contribute to and influence ethical decision-making and behavior. Behavioral ethics investigates the gap between people's ethical intentions and their actual behaviors and how people develop strategies to bridge the gap between their intentions and actions in moral contexts (Prentice, 2014). By conducting experiments on moral development, cognitive processes, and moral reasoning, and exploring the role of situational factors, social dynamics, structures, emotions, and psychological factors that influence moral decision-making, behavioral ethics provide valuable insights to our understanding of how ethics function in human societies. This chapter starts with some insightful experiments and field research in the field of social psychology (Milgram Electric Shock Experiment and Leon Festinger's Cognitive Dissonance Theory), and then continues with some important concepts in behavioral ethics (such as bounded ethicality, altruistic cheating, and cognitive bias etc.) Here are some questions that arise at the intersection of cognitive psychology and behavioral ethics:

- How might people's perceptions of ethical stance vary based on personal experiences, cognitive level of development, personal experiences, preferences, emotions, cultural factors, ethical practices, beliefs, and norms that exist in different cultures and contexts.
- How do people reason through ethical dilemmas, process moral information, perceive and categorize situations as ethical dilemmas?
- How might cognitive biases or heuristics influence their moral judgments?
- How individuals make moral decisions and how their behavior deviates from or aligns with ethical norms?
- How come people behave unethically, even when they believe they are acting morally?
- What factors contribute to ethical blind spots?
- How individuals might fail to recognize ethical issues in certain situations
- How do social influences affect unethical behavior? Research can examine how social norms influence individuals to conform to unethical behavior in group settings.

- What role does moral reasoning play in behavior? Does moral reasoning translate into ethical behavior?
- Are people more likely to behave unethically when under cognitive load? Cognitive load, or mental strain, can affect decision-making. Research can examine how cognitive load impacts ethical decision-making and behavior.
- How does moral disengagement occur? Cognitive psychology can explore the cognitive mechanisms that allow individuals to justify or rationalize unethical actions, such as through moral disengagement.
- Can nudges promote ethical behavior? Behavioral ethics can study the effectiveness of cognitive nudges or interventions in encouraging ethical decision-making.
- How does empathy influence prosocial behavior? Cognitive psychology can examine the role of empathy in motivating individuals to engage in prosocial and ethical actions.
- What role do situational factors play in ethical behavior? Behavioral ethics can investigate how situational factors, such as time pressure or the presence of authority figures, impact ethical decision-making and behavior.
- Do individuals prioritize self-interest over ethical considerations? Research can explore the conflict between self-interest and ethical considerations and how cognitive processes influence this conflict.
- How do framing effects impact ethical judgments? Cognitive psychology can study how the framing of ethical dilemmas or decisions can influence individuals' judgments and subsequent behaviors.
- Does the mere presence of unethical options influence behavior? Behavioral ethics can examine how the availability of unethical options affects individuals' likelihood of engaging in unethical behavior.
- Can moral reminders enhance ethical behavior? Cognitive psychology can investigate whether subtle reminders of ethical values can positively influence individuals' behavior.

Cognitive Moral Development

Kohlberg (1969) proposed a theory of moral development based on cognitive reasoning. Kohlberg's Moral Judgment Interview typically involved presenting participants with moral dilemmas, such as the Heinz dilemma, where a man faces the dilemma of whether to steal the expensive drug to save his wife's life, knowing that stealing is typically considered morally wrong. Kohlberg (1969) was concerned with the reasoning behind the people's moral choices rather than the specific choices themselves. The dilemma is used to explore individuals' moral reasoning and to classify them into stages of moral development. He identified three distinct levels, each with two sub-stages (and each characterized by different ways of thinking about moral dilemmas) (Kohlberg, 1969). Here's a brief overview of the three levels and six stages in Kohlberg's model:

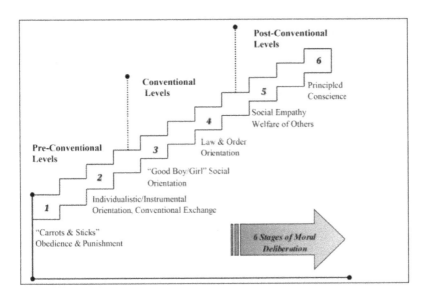

Figure 1. Kohlberg's Stages of Moral Development

Kohlberg's theory (1969) suggests that individuals progress through these stages as their moral reasoning becomes more sophisticated and complex. He also believed that individuals advance through these stages in a universal and sequential manner as they develop their capacity for moral reasoning from childhood to adulthood (Kohlberg, 1969). Each stage represents a different level of ethical development, with higher stages incorporating more abstract and principled reasoning. Individuals make ethical decisions based on their cognitive and moral development level, as outlined in Kohlberg's theory (1969). Kohlberg (1969) believed that moral reasoning becomes more advanced, complex and sophisticated as individuals progress through the stages.

Bounded Ethicality and Cognitive Biases

Our ability to make ethical choices has limits. We all commit cognitive errors (overconfidence bias, confirmation bias, stereotyping, anchoring effect, and over-generalization etc.) as when making ethical decisions (Prentice, 2004). Just like "bounded rationality" suggests that human decision-making is prone to satisfice, rather than optimize because of our limited cognitive abilities (Simon, 1990), the notion of "bounded ethicality" suggests that people are limited in their ability to make moral decisions due to some internal constraints and external pressures which lead them make ethically questionable choices (Kern & Chugh, 2009). Bounded rationality leads to bounded ethicality, and thus everyone is ethically bounded. Chugh et al. (2005) suggest that our moral decision-making process is biased by our own view of ourselves as moral persons and our tendency to commit errors of cognitive biases.

We mostly think of ourselves as rational thinkers (Simon et al., 1992), like J.A.R.V.I.S. – the artificial intelligence created by Tony Stark – from The Avengers. But even the smartest and most educated people can fall victim to cognitive biases and external constraints that limit their ability to make ethical decisions. Organizational or social pressures or our internal biases, may subconsciously make it hard to do the right thing (Hoyk & Hersey, 2008). For example, the police officers who believe stereotypes that link young black men to crime more than the white man, may be prone to process clues in a one-sided way when investigating a crime with a black suspect. Likewise, they may also commit the error of *confirmation bias*, and tend to interpret new information or evidence in a way that supports their prior beliefs, expectations, or hypotheses. People easily welcome new information that is consistent with their beliefs but are skeptical of information that contradicts their pre-existing beliefs. As Kahneman (2011) warns, even scientists who believe in a certain theory may tend to ignore data that does not match with the theory, concluding that the data is faulty but not the theory. So, all cognitive bias can easily cause us to reach inaccurate –and even unethical– conclusions. It's essential for us to recognize our brain is vulnerable to cognitive bias, and actively guard against them. But despite our efforts, we are not entirely immune to cognitive errors. Studies indicate that educating our minds about cognitive biases and external pressures that limit our ethical decision-making may help us improve our skills to become more effective ethical decision-makers (Chugh & Kern, 2016).

The Fundamental Attribution Errors

The fundamental attribution error is the tendency for people to overestimate personal characteristics and underestimate situational factors when evaluating the behavior of others. People tend to attribute the behavior of others to their personalities and ignore the possible influence that situational factors may have on that behavior. Due to a fundamental attribution error, we tend to assume that others do bad things because they are bad people, ignoring situational factors that may come into play. For example, when someone does something bad, we tend to blame that person's personality more than the situation; yet when we do something bad, we tend to blame the situational factors rather than blaming ourselves and shut our eyes to the fact that our actions may indeed reflect our own character. Imagine that someone cuts you off while you are driving, what would your first thought be? "What a jerk!"? or "Poor man, he must be in rush"? Most probably, instead of thinking the possibility that the driver is in rush to the hospital for an emergency, you would curse the man and reprimand his rudeness. On the flip side, when we do the same, we tend to convince ourselves that others should be tolerant to our behavior taking the possibility of emergency into account. So, the fundamental attribution error tells us why we tend to judge others harshly while letting ourselves off the hook by justifying our own unethical behaviors with creative excuses (Biasucci & Prentice, 2018).

Conformity Bias

Conformity bias refers to the tendency for individuals to adjust their behavior or beliefs to align with those of a group, even if it goes against their own beliefs or values (Crutchfield, 1955). In the context of ethics, conformity bias can lead individuals to prioritize fitting in with a group over making independent ethical judgments. This bias can be particularly strong in situations where there is social pressure to conform or where individuals perceive that others have more expertise or authority.

The power of conformity is extremely strong: psychological experiments such as the classic Line Study by Asch (1956) show that people will deny the evidence of their own eyes to fit in with a group of other people. People seem to be more comfortable and willing to take behavioral cues from other people and follow the herd, even regarding ethical matters and even change their own behaviors, beliefs, or attitudes to conform with others. We generally tend to follow the lead particularly in our ethical choices. Conformity bias can influence prosocial behavior in various contexts. When individuals observe others engaging in prosocial actions, such as donating to charity or participating in environmental conservation efforts, they may feel compelled to conform to those behaviors to maintain social harmony or to avoid standing out from the group. This phenomenon can lead to increased participation in prosocial activities, as individuals may be influenced by the actions of their peers. As behavioral economist Dan Ariely (2012) notes, the flip side is also true and "dishonesty is infectious and one bad apple can ruin the barrel". When we witness others achieve by cheating, it makes us more likely to act the same way -cheat and lie.

Dilemma Framing

Framing refers to the way information is presented or "framed," which can influence how individuals perceive and interpret a given situation or issue (Prentice, 2015). Different frames can highlight different aspects of the situation, leading to varying interpretations and reactions. In the context of ethical issues, framing can play a significant role in shaping people's moral judgments and decisions. By presenting information in a particular way, individuals or organizations can influence how others perceive the ethical implications of a situation, potentially leading to different responses or actions. It is widely accepted that moral judgments are generally made based on how people view the situation rather than the actual characteristics of the situation (Tenbrunsel & Messick, 1999; Trevino, 1986; Rhim et al., 2021). Thus, different individuals may perceive the same ethical situation differently based on how it is presented or framed to them. By exploring their framing, we can gain a better understanding of why they may interpret the situation in a particular way and how they are likely to respond to it. This understanding can be valuable for fostering empathy, resolving conflicts, and promoting ethical decision-making.

Mental framing plays a crucial role in ethical decision-making as individuals interpret and evaluate ethical issues based on the way they mentally structure and frame the situation. Thus, individuals need to be mindful of the frames through which they perceive situations (Tversky & Kahneman, 1981). The way a problem or ethical dilemma is presented can significantly influence how people perceive, analyze, and ultimately decide on the issue. How a person perceives the issue can affect her understanding of the facts and influence his/her judgement. For instance, corporate agents have ample room to justify compliance failures in the name of loyalty (Langevoort, 2018). Awareness in our own mental frames and actively incorporate ethical considerations in our decision-making processes can contribute to more responsible and morally sound choices in various aspects of life. Sometimes our mental framing may reduce or even disregard the ethical consideration in a situation. For example, as demonstrated in a famous study conducted by Gneezy and Rustichini (2000), when people tend to view a situation from an economic frame, they often tend to ignore the ethical aspects of the situation. In this study where an Israeli day care center introduced fine system for parents who pick up their children late, contrary to expectations, an increase was observed in the rate of parents picking up their children late rather than a decline. One of the strongest possible explanations offered by Gneezy and Rustichini (2000) was that before the introduction of fines, a social norm prevented parents from being late to pick up their children, but once the penalty was given, it changed the parents' frame of reference and, parents started to feel free to consume the extra care as a commodity with the payment of fine with no guilt or shame (Metcalf et al., 2020). Parents then transformed their frame of reference and rather than considering the ethical aspects of the issue, they started to this as a business deal. When individuals frame a situation solely in economic terms or other non-ethical perspectives, they may neglect or downplay the ethical dimensions of their choices. By critically evaluating how they mentally frame ethical dilemmas, people can enhance their ethical decision-making. Being aware of their mental framing and including ethical considerations in their frame of reference consciously helps people make more principled and morally responsible choices.

Diffusion of Responsibility

Diffusion of responsibility is a phenomenon that takes place when people in a group setting feel less inclined to assume responsibility and intervene when witnessing emergencies because they believe that others in the group may take charge and take an action (Kassin et al., 2012). Diffusion of responsibility is closely associated with the bystander effect, which is the observation that persons are less likely to take action in an emergency situation when others are present (Freeman et al., 1975). In ethical situations, the bystander effect can lead to a lack of intervention when unethical behavior is observed, as everyone assumes that someone else will address the issue (Darley & Latané, 1968). Generally, the presence of bystanders discourages people from stepping forward to assist. Individuals in a group may feel a decreased sense of personal accountability for taking action because they believe that others will or should assume the responsibility (Gallo, 2015). Pluralistic ignorance may occur when individuals look to others for cues on how to behave, and if everyone is hesitant to act, each person may assume that if others are not intervening, there must be a valid reason for inaction. Or if individuals believe that others are not acting, they may interpret the situation as less urgent or may not feel the need to intervene. This can lead to collective inaction and inhibit intervention in emergency situations. Remember the incident of Kitty Genovese murder where she was brutally attacked and murdered, and no one helped. The incident gained notoriety not only for the heinous crime but also for the fact that it occurred in the presence of numerous witnesses, yet no one intervened or called for help promptly. Factors such as fear, uncertainty, and diffusion of responsibility may have contributed to a state of psychological paralysis, where individuals hesitate to take action (Gallo, 2015). The presence of multiple witnesses contributed to a diffusion of responsibility, where each onlooker may have assumed that someone else would take action or call for help.

Diffusion of responsibility is also closely related to social loafing, which is the observation that when in groups, individuals may perceive that their contributions are less noticeable or critical. So, social loafing can contribute to the dilution of ethical responsibility when in a group. As a result, people might be less inclined to actively engage in ethical decision-making or more likely to intervene in potentially unethical actions, relying on the assumption that others will handle ethical considerations, and compensate for their inaction. Individuals in a group may experience diffusion of responsibility, thinking that their actions won't be as closely scrutinized or attributed to them personally (Karau & Williams, 1995). Individuals with a strong sense of personal ethics and moral development may be less prone to social loafing in ethical situations. Encouraging and developing individual ethical awareness can help counteract the negative effects of social loafing.

Altruistic Cheating

Altruistic cheating is a concept that describes instances where individuals engage in cheating behavior not for personal gain but for the perceived benefit of others (Ariely, 2012). It is a form of self-deception. This phenomenon highlights how people may rationalize wrongdoing when they believe it serves a greater good or benefits someone else, especially when those individuals are close to them, such as family members or friends. Because most people wish to think of themselves as good people, many would try their best to reconcile their actions with their self-image as good people and would employ a variety of reasons to justify their wrongdoing through their creativity, and it is much easier to do so when their wrongdoings benefits others (Gino et al., 2013; Shalvi et al., 2011).

As Langevoort (2018, p. 265) warns, "one of the most potent incentives to cheat is in the service of others"- "altrustic" cheating. Recognizing the potential for altruistic cheating is important in educational and workplace environments. Institutions need to foster ethical cultures that discourage rationalizations for dishonest behavior, even when framed as helping others. Understanding the psychological and ethical dynamics of altruistic cheating can help guide efforts to promote ethical behavior and integrity in various settings. It underscores the importance of addressing not only personal motives for cheating but also the moral justifications that individuals may use to rationalize their actions.

Ethical Fading and Moral Myopia

Ethical fading describes the tendency of individuals to omit the ethical aspects of a decision or choice when they focus intensely on other non-ethical dimensions of it and occurs when we subconsciously disguise ethical aspects of a decision and avoid ethical issues from coming into clear focus (Tenbrunsel & Messick, 2004). This allows us to behave unethically and still maintain the belief that we are good and moral people. Ethical fading is closely related to moral myopia which refers to a cognitive bias where individuals fail to recognize or adequately consider ethical issues, making them less visible or salient in their decision-making process (Drumwright & Murphy, 2013). When individuals concentrate predominantly on non-ethical aspects of a decision, such as financial gains, personal success, or achieving a competitive advantage, the moral implications of a decision or a choice fade into the background.

High-pressure situations, intense competition, or a strong emphasis on success can contribute to ethical fading, as individuals may prioritize achieving goals over ethical considerations. Humans demonstrate bounded rationality when they are under significant stress – that is, once in overload, our minds default to what they can process and push out everything else. This means often ethical considerations fade. Environments that prioritize performance metrics without adequate consideration of ethical implications may foster this phenomenon. When ethical considerations become less prominent in decision-making, individuals may experience a diminished sensitivity to the moral implications of their choices. Ethical fading increases the likelihood of individuals making decisions that may be ethically questionable or even unethical because they are not actively considering the moral dimensions of their choices. Individuals are all inclined to see what they are actively searching for. If they are primarily focused on non-ethical aspects, they may overlook or dismiss ethical issues involved in the decision-making process.

Ethical fading reminds us that we, as humans, are at risk of being too ready to make wrong and immoral decisions when under pressure. Making decisions without taking ethics into account can have very serious consequences. Understanding and addressing ethical fading is crucial for fostering a more ethical decision-making environment. Organizations and individuals should strive to maintain a balance between achieving goals and upholding ethical principles. Recognizing the presence of ethical fading is crucial for counteracting its effects. By actively promoting ethical awareness and accountability, it becomes possible to reduce the likelihood of ethical fading and its potential negative consequences on decision-making outcomes. Encouraging a culture of ethical awareness, providing ethical training, and incorporating ethical considerations into decision-making frameworks can help mitigate ethical fading.

Incrementalism

Incrementalism is "the slippery slope" that causes people's decisions and actions to evolve from small, seemingly insignificant wrongdoings into more significant ethical violations (Biasucci & Prentice, 2018). It often causes people to slide unintentionally from small wrongdoings to bigger ones. This concept is particularly relevant in discussions about the progression of unethical actions over time. Incrementalism involves a gradual progression from small, insignificant wrongs to more significant ethical wrongs (Gino & Bazerman, 2009). This process often occurs as individuals engage in seemingly minor transgressions that escalate over time. For example, small manipulations of financial figures can evolve into more substantial fraudulent activities if not addressed early.

The human brain is not skilled at perceiving slow and minor changes. Moreover, continued exposure to ethically dubious and flawed behaviors or immoral and possibly illegal acts can desensitize individuals, making such activities seem normal. Over time, people may never even notice that they are engaging in immoral and possibly illegal acts. The gradual nature of the process makes it difficult for individuals to perceive a clear boundary being crossed. Tenbrunsel and Messick (2004) argues that self-deception, aided by euphemisms, allows individuals to disguise and overlook their own wrongdoing and may blind them to the ethical aspects of a situation. For example, euphemistic language such as "We didn't bribe... but greased the wheels" help people playdown their own wrongdoing and minimize the guilt when violating ethical standards.

The psychological mechanism behind incrementalism is the tendency of individuals minimize guilt by restructuring reality in order to make their own actions look less harmful than they actually are and distancing themselves from the ethical components of their actions. By actively considering ethical concerns in decision-making and avoiding the rationalization of unethical actions, individuals can work to prevent the slide into incremental unethical behavior. Understanding the dynamics of incrementalism and its connection to unethical conduct is essential for individuals and organizations seeking to maintain ethical standards. Awareness, vigilance, and a commitment to ethical decision-making can help mitigate the risks related to the slippery slope of incrementalism (Gottlieb & Younggren, 2009).

Groupthink and Groupshift

Groupthink is a concept that was first introduced by psychologist Janis (1982). Groupthink is a phenomenon in which the desire for harmony or conformity in a group leads to dysfunctional decision-making (Janis, 1982). Group members may suppress dissenting viewpoints or avoid critical evaluation of alternatives in order to maintain cohesion within the group. This can result in flawed or irrational decisions, as important information or perspectives may be overlooked. Groupshift, on the other hand, refers to the phenomenon where group decisions tend to be more extreme than the initial inclinations of individual group members (Friedkin & Johnsen, 2011). It is also known as "choice shift" or "group polarization". This shift can occur in various directions based on the nature of the initial opinions, leading to decisions that are more extreme or riskier than those individual members might have made on their own. It is important to note that groupthink and groupshift are related concepts in the context of group decision-making, but they differ in their characteristics. Groupthink involves a desire for consensus and suppression of dissent over independent judgment while groupshift focuses on the tendency of the group to shift toward more extreme positions. Both phenomena highlight the complexities and potential pitfalls of decision-making within group settings which may lead to unethical behavior.

Individuals generally have difficulty in thinking and acting independently when in groups. Group members may prefer to remain silent or conform in order to avoid punishment or social exclusion or their desire to preserve group loyalty prevails over all other considerations. This can create an illusion of unanimity within the group, masking the existence of dissenting opinions and may result in the endorsement of unethical decisions or actions.

Groupshift, on the other hand, may lead to decisions that are more extreme or riskier than those individual members might have made on their own. Groupshift can lead to the adoption of extreme decisions that are far more extreme than any single member initially supported. Group discussions tend to intensify or exaggerate the initial views held by individual members. This amplification occurs as group members influence each other during the discussion. The group's social dynamics, shared values, and the persuasive influence of dominant members can all contribute to the direction and magnitude of groupshift. Groupshift can occur in various directions depending on the nature of the initial opinions. If the group leans toward a more cautious stance, the shift may result in an even more conservative decision. Conversely, if the initial inclination is risk-taking, the shift may lead to a more extreme choice. Groupshift may contribute to a lack of ethical accountability within the group. As decisions become more extreme, the group members may collectively minimize the ethical implications of their actions and tune out any ethical violations.

Unfortunately, if groupshift takes hold, group members may not even question ethically questionable decisions. The desire for group cohesion or the amplification of individual views may override individuals' ethical considerations and can lead the group to endorse or support actions that might be considered ethically dubious. Understanding groupshift is valuable in various contexts, such as organizational decision-making, policy formation, and social group dynamics. Awareness of this phenomenon can help individuals and groups critically assess the effect of group discussions on decision outcomes and find ways to mitigate the risks associated with extreme shifts in collective positions.

In-Group/Out-Group

In-group/out-group bias, also known as in-group favoritism, is a cognitive bias where individuals favor members of their own group (the in-group) over those who are not members of their group (the out-group) (Biasucci & Prentice, 2018). People tend to exhibit positive bias and show favoritism toward individuals who belong to their in-group. This bias can manifest in various ways, including empathy, cooperation, and a general inclination to view in-group members more positively. Conversely, individuals may display negative bias toward out-group members. However, our tendency to judge and treat in-group people more favorably than out-group people has some ethical implications. This in-group/out-group bias can lead to discriminatory attitudes, stereotyping, and, in extreme cases, harmful behaviors towards those perceived as different. The in-group/out-group phenomenon often operates at an unconscious level, influencing attitudes and behaviors without individuals being fully aware of the biases shaping their responses. The tendency to prioritize the well-being of the in-group over the out-group can lead to unjust and discriminatory actions. In-group and out-group distinctions can significantly influence moral judgments. Individuals may be more forgiving or dismissive of ethical lapses or misbehavior by in-group members, while being more critical and harsher in judging similar actions by out-group members. Studies have shown that when in-group/out-group distinctions replace conscious and thoughtful reflection, individuals may be more prone to harmful behaviors and unethical conduct.

Fostering awareness of in-group/out-group biases is crucial for mitigating the potential for unethical behavior. Encouraging empathy, promoting diversity and inclusion, and challenging stereotypes are important steps toward minimizing the negative consequences of this phenomenon. Conscious and thoughtful reflection is essential for individuals to recognize and challenge automatic in-group/out-group distinctions. Cognitive reflection allows for a more nuanced understanding of individual differences and can counteract knee-jerk reactions based solely on group membership. Understanding the In-group/Out-group phenomenon is essential for promoting ethical behavior, fostering inclusivity, and building more just and equitable societies. By recognizing and challenging these biases, individuals can contribute to creating environments that value diversity and treat all individuals with fairness and empathy.

Loss Aversion

Loss aversion is a cognitive bias where people tend to prefer avoiding losses over acquiring equivalent gains (Biasucci & Prentice, 2018; Prentice, 2014). In other words, the pain of losing something is psychologically greater than the pleasure of gaining the same thing (Schindler & Pfattheicher, 2017). This preference suggests that individuals have a stronger emotional reaction to the prospect of losing something than to the possibility of gaining something of equal value (Kahneman & Tversky, 1979). This psychological phenomenon can have profound effects on decision-making, risk-taking, and ethical behavior in various contexts, including economics, finance, and everyday life. For example, in financial markets, investors may hold onto losing investments longer than they should because they are averse to realizing the loss by selling. Similarly, in negotiations, people may be more willing to take risks to avoid potential losses than to pursue potential gains.

Loss aversion seemed to play a significant role in the General Motors (GM) scandal when the company failed to recall cars with faulty ignition switches and denied that there was a problem to avoid the financial losses and reputational damage associated with a massive recall (Biasucci & Prentice, 2018). Ironically, their reluctance to recall faulty cars led to more significant and enduring costs (e.g., legal consequences, and loss of trust) for GM in the long run. Natural aversion to loss and the desire to keep what one already has can be overwhelming and may lead individuals to make unethical choices, such as covering up mistakes or engaging in deceptive practices, to avoid the perceived losses. This behavior may be driven by a fear of negative consequences, both personal and organizational. Yet, ironically, those unethical choices might be more costly and substantial for us in the long run, just like the case of GM scandal.

Studies have shown that people may be more inclined to lie or cheat to avoid losses, than to achieve gains. For example, a person making an innocent mistake may prefer to lie intentionally to cover it up to avoid injury to her/his reputation. Recognizing the influence of loss aversion is crucial for individuals and organizations seeking to make ethical decisions. Creating a culture that values transparency, accountability, and learning from mistakes can help mitigate the impact of loss aversion on decision-making. Addressing loss aversion in ethical decision-making involves promoting a mindset that values long-term consequences over short-term losses. Emphasizing the importance of ethical conduct, encouraging truthfulness, and establishing systems that reward transparency can contribute to more principled and responsible decision-making in various contexts.

Moral Dissonance

Moral dissonance, also known as cognitive dissonance in the context of morality, refers to the psychological discomfort or tension that arises when individuals hold conflicting beliefs, attitudes, or values related to ethical principles or moral decisions. It occurs when a person's actions or behaviors are inconsistent with their moral beliefs or when they encounter conflicting moral judgments. Biasucci and Prentice (2018) argue that most people like to think of themselves as moral people, but they also often lie and cheat in ways they would not want others to know about. The conflict between how they like to see themselves and their true selves creates a moral dissonance and, in their attempt, to resolve this discomfort people may choose to stop their unethical actions and live up to their own (good) self-image or try to rationalize their immoral acts and justify their ethically dubious behaviors. Ideally, people will go for the first choice, but more often, people settle the conflict by finding ways to think of themselves as good people while keep on engaging in immoral acts.

Leon Festinger's Cognitive Dissonance Theory (1957) is a psychological theory that explores how individuals strive for consistency in their beliefs and attitudes and explains how individuals may distort their beliefs or adjust their attitudes to reduce the discomfort of holding conflicting ideas to restore a sense of cognitive harmony. Festinger developed this theory in the 1950s, in a field study where he studied a UFO cult led by Dorothy Martin (known pseudonymously as Marian Keech). In 1954, Festinger and his colleagues Riecken, and Schachter infiltrated

the cult led by Martin, who claimed to have received messages from extraterres-
trial beings predicting an imminent apocalypse (Festinger et al., 1956). The cult
believed that a catastrophic flood would destroy the Earth, but a selected few
would be saved by aliens. Festinger and his colleagues (1956) were interested in
studying how members of the cult would react when the prophesied events did
not come true. When the predicted apocalypse failed to happen, Festinger and
his colleagues (1956) observed that the discrepancy between their strong convictions and the lack of a catastrophic event led the followers to reinterpret the situation. However, rather than abandoning their beliefs, many cult members who
experienced cognitive dissonance tried to resolve the dissonance, by becoming
more fervent in their beliefs and sought ways to justify their continued commitment to the cult. Because admitting that they were fooled was not easy to digest,
they instead preferred to believe that their leader was even more sacred than they
have originally thought, or she have claimed, and they believed that flood did not
occur for the sake of their cult leaders (check the Turkish saying, "The sheikh
doesn't fly, but his followers make him fly"). This study provides a classic example of cognitive dissonance in action and explains how our brains are wired to
protect ourselves from hurtful truths by avoiding or ignoring unpleasant truths
and embracing pleasant lies.

Obedience to Authority

"Obedience to authority" is a psychological phenomenon wherein individuals
are inclined to comply with the orders or instructions of an authority figure, even
if it involves actions that go against their personal moral or ethical principles.
This concept gained significant attention through electric-shock experiments
conducted by Milgram (1963, 1965) where participants were asked to administer what they believed were increasingly severe electric shocks to another person
under the direction of an authority figure. The study raised ethical concerns and
stimulated discussions about obedience and authority. It remains a landmark
study in the field, illustrating the complex ways individuals can rationalize their
actions within a social context. The experiment showed that blind obedience
to authority can lead people to engage in actions that they might find morally
objectionable under normal circumstances.

   Stanley Milgram's Electric Shock Experiment provides a classic example of
blind obedience to authority in action and explains how individuals can rationalize and justify their behavior by attributing responsibility to authority figures.
The experiment was designed to investigate the extent to which people would
obey authority, even if it meant causing harm to others. In the study, participants

were instructed to administer electric shocks to a learner (an actor) whenever they answered questions incorrectly. The shocks were not real, but the participants believed they were inflicting genuine pain. The authority figure in the experiment was the experimenter, who urged the participants to continue the shocks despite the apparent distress of the learner. The findings of the Milgram experiment highlighted how ordinary individuals could engage in morally questionable behavior when directed by an authority figure. Several mechanisms of rationalization and justification were observed in participants' behavior:

> *Bureaucratic Language.* The authority figure, played by the experimenter, used formal and bureaucratic language to issue commands (Milgram, 1974). This impersonal language may have reduced the personal responsibility felt by participants.
>
> *Gradual Escalation.* The shocks were administered in incremental steps, allowing participants to become gradually accustomed to the increasing severity. This incremental progression may have contributed to the participants' ability to rationalize their actions.
>
> *Blurring Responsibility.* Participants may have felt that they were merely following orders, thus shifting responsibility from themselves to the authority figure. This diffusion of responsibility is a psychological phenomenon observed in various situations where individuals are part of a larger system. When we don't feel responsible for a situation, we feel less guilty.
>
> *Expertise of the Authority Figure.* The experimenter was presented as an authority figure with expertise, which likely influenced participants to defer to his judgment. Trust in the expertise of the authority figure played a role in the participants' willingness to follow orders. Psychological research has shown that people often defer to authority figures and are more likely to comply with their requests or commands, especially when they perceive those authorities to be legitimate or credible. Sometimes even implicit pressure from the authority figures can be sufficient to induce people to make unethical choices. Furthermore, most people even tend to anticipate the desires or expectations of superiors and act to fulfill them.
>
> *Social Conformity.* The experiment revealed the power of social conformity, as participants observed others (confederates) complying with the authority figure's commands. This social influence contributed to the rationalization of their own actions.

Milgram's Electric Shock Experiment has also been studied and discussed in various cultural contexts, including Western and Eastern cultures. While it's essential to recognize that individual responses can vary widely within any culture,

there are some general cultural considerations to keep in mind when exploring
how people from different cultures might interpret and respond to the dynamics
of authority and obedience depicted in the experiment.

First, Western cultures, particularly those influenced by individualism, often
emphasize personal autonomy and the questioning of authority. People in
Western cultures might be more inclined to resist authority or question its legitimacy. Eastern cultures, on the other hand, influenced by collectivism, may place
a higher value on conformity and respect for authority. Individuals in these cultures might be more inclined to comply with authority figures. Secondly, Western
societies might view unquestioning obedience with skepticism, and individuals
may assume a stronger sense of responsibility for their actions. The emphasis on
individual rights and freedoms may lead to a greater resistance to blindly following authority. Third, Eastern cultures might place a higher value on obedience
as a way of achieving social order and cohesion. The concept of filial piety, for
example, might encourage individuals to comply with authority figures, especially in hierarchical structures. Fourth, in some Western cultures, individuals
might experience shame or guilt for engaging in morally questionable behavior,
whereas in Eastern Culture, social shame or the fear of losing face might be more
important and influential to motivate people to comply with authority figures
to avoid bringing shame to themselves or their families. Fifth, direct communication and explicit expressions of dissent might be more common in Western
cultures and individuals may be more vocal in expressing disagreement with
authority, whereas indirect communication and non-verbal cues might be more
prevalent in Eastern cultures. Disagreement might be expressed more subtly, and
individuals may be less likely to openly challenge authority.

It's crucial to note that these are broad generalizations, and individual differences within cultures are significant. Cultural values and norms can vary widely
even within Western and Eastern contexts. Additionally, societal attitudes may
evolve over time, and cultural perspectives are subject to change. When inter-
preting Milgram's findings in different cultural settings, researchers must consider these nuances to avoid oversimplification and cultural stereotyping.

Another good example exploring "obedience to authority", the limits of obedience, and the ethical implications of blindly following commands is the film
"A Few Good Men"[1]. The story revolves around themes related to military discipline, the chain of command, and the obedience of soldiers to their superiors.

---

1   A Few Good Men is a 1992 American drama that was written by Sorkin, directed by
    Rob Reiner, and produced by Reiner, David Brown and Andrew Scheinman.

The movie is about a court-martial trial where two U.S. Marines are charged with murder, wherein the defense argues that the Marines cannot be charged with the crime of murder because they were merely following orders from higher-ranking officers. The movie raises some important questions by highlighting the tension between military discipline and following orders. Generally, willingness to follow instructions might be regarded as a good thing, but the film "A Few Good Men" reveals that blind obedience to those in charge can have unfortunate consequences particularly when leaders lack ethical conviction themselves and shows that it's important for individuals to critically evaluate their actions, even when following authority, and to consider the ethical implications of their choices.

To sum up, individuals may experience moral dissonance, feeling torn between their personal moral values and the desire to please their superiors or avoid negative consequences. While there may be pressure to conform to superiors' wishes, individuals ultimately bear moral responsibility for their actions. They must consider the potential consequences of their decisions not only for themselves but also for others affected by their choices. Ethical decision-making in hierarchical environments requires individuals to navigate competing priorities and weigh the potential outcomes of different courses of action. This may involve assessing the ethical implications of following orders, speaking up against perceived wrongdoing, or seeking guidance from trusted colleagues or external sources. Ultimately, individuals must strive to uphold their moral integrity and act in accordance with their values, even in the face of authority pressure. This may require courage, resilience, and a willingness to challenge norms or speak truth to power when necessary. By taking ownership of their decisions and actions, individuals can contribute to a culture of ethical leadership and accountability within organizations.

Banality of Evil

Let's start with a puzzling and intriguing question: "Can a person do evil deeds but is not actually an evil?" This is a difficult question to give a straight-forward answer for. This is the very question the philosopher Arendt dealt with when she reported on the war crimes trial of the Nazi operative Adolph Eichmann who is in charge of the transportation of Jews to concentration camps. Arendt (1963/ 2006) concluded that Eichmann was an ordinary bureaucrat, who was "neither perverted nor sadistic monster" who performed evil deeds without evil intentions. He acted no other motive than to advance in his career in the Nazi bureaucracy. In Arendt's telling, although Eichmann's deeds were monstrous, Eichmann was terrifyingly normal, shallow, and clueless man with no obvious intention of being evil. According to Arendt (1963/2006), Eichmann, he merely lacked the ability to think from the standpoint of somebody else and lacking this ability, he was merely a "joiner" who drifted into the Nazi Party.

"Banality of evil" is, therefore, the thesis of Arendt claiming that most evil is committed by people who never make up their minds to be evil or good (Arendt, 1963/2006). She argues that many evils are not necessarily done by sociopaths but ordinary people. So, she basically stands up for it by "de-demonizing" it. In most cases, evil is the result of incompetence, ignorance, or negligence instead of a demonic motive. So, both "holocaust" and "failure to respond swiftly and effectively to the pandemic" can be considered evil in the same way without demonizing both. Arendt's argument challenges traditional notions of evil as something inherently malicious or consciously perpetrated. Instead, she suggests that evil can manifest through mundane, thoughtless actions carried out by individuals who may not necessarily possess overtly malevolent intentions. Eichmann, in her view, was not driven by a personal desire to inflict harm but rather by a blind adherence to bureaucratic procedures and a lack of moral reflection on the consequences of his actions. This notion of "banal evil" raises important questions about the nature of responsibility, accountability, and the human's bounded ethicality. It forces us to confront the unsettling possibility that individuals can contribute to great atrocities through a combination of conformity, indifference, and a failure to critically examine their own behavior.

Arendt's exploration of the concept of the "banality of evil" through her analysis of Adolf Eichmann's case is indeed thought-provoking and has sparked extensive debate and reflection. Arendt's interpretation of Eichmann's actions and her concept of the banality of evil have been subject to criticism and controversy. Some argue that it underplays the moral agency of individuals like Eichmann and absolves them of culpability by attributing their actions to mere thoughtlessness or conformity to authority. Others contend that it overlooks the systemic and ideological forces that facilitated the Holocaust, as well as the potential for individuals to resist or challenge immoral directives. Ultimately, Arendt's exploration challenges us to grapple with complex moral questions and encourages a deeper understanding of the human capacity for both good and evil. It underscores the importance of critical reflection, ethical awareness, and the need to cultivate a sense of responsibility for our actions and their consequences.

References

Arendt, H. (2006). *Eichmann in Jerusalem: A report on the banality of evil.* Penguin Classics. (Original work published 1963)

Ariely, D. (2012). *The (honest) truth about dishonesty: How we lie to everyone - Especially ourselves.* Harper.

Asch, S. E. (1956). Studies of independence and conformity: I A minority of one against a unanimous majority. *Psychological Monographs: General and Applied, 70*(9), 1–70.

Biasucci, C., & Prentice, R. (2018). Teaching notes. *Ethics Unwrapped.* https://ethicsunwrapped.utexas.edu

Chugh, D., & Kern, M. C. (2016). A dynamic and cyclical model of bounded ethicality. *Research in Organizational Behavior, 36*(2016), 85–100. http://dx.doi.org/10.1016/j.riob.2016.07.002

Chugh, D., Bazerman, M. H., & Banaji, M. R. (2005). Bounded ethicality as a psychological barrier to recognizing conflicts of interest. In D. A. Moore, D. M. Cain, G. Loewenstein, & M. H. Bazerman (Eds.), *Conflicts of interest: Challenges and solutions in business, law, medicine, and public policy* (pp. 74–95). Cambridge University Press.

Crutchfield, R. (1955). Conformity and character. *American Psychologist, 10,* 191–198.

Darley, J. M., & Latané, B. (1968). Bystander intervention in emergencies: Diffusion of responsibility. *Journal of personality and social psychology, 8*(4), 377–383. https://doi.org/10.1037/h0025589

Drumwright, M. E., & Murphy, P. E. (2013). How advertising practitioners view ethics: Moral muteness, moral myopia, and moral imagination. *Journal of Advertising, 33*(2), 7–24. https://doi.org/10.1080/00913367.2004.10639158

Festinger, L. (1957). *A theory of cognitive dissonance.* Peterson

Festinger, L., Riecken, H. W., & Schachter, S. (1956). *When prophecy fails.* University of Minnesota Press. http://dx.doi.org/10.1037/10030-000

Freeman, S., Walker, M. R., Borden, R., & Latané, B. (1975). Diffusion of responsibility and restaurant tipping: Cheaper by the bunch. *Personality and Social Psychology Bulletin, 1*(4), 584–587. https://doi.org/10.1177/014616727500100407

Friedkin, N. E., & Johnsen, E. C. (2011). *Social influence network theory: A sociological examination of small group dynamics* Cambridge University Press. https://doi.org/10.1017/CBO9780511976735

Gallo, M. M. (2015). *No one helped: Kitty Genovese, New York City, and the myth of urban apathy.* Cornell University Press.

Gino, F., & Bazerman, M. H. (2009). When misconduct goes unnoticed: The acceptability of gradual erosion. *Journal of Experimental Social Psychology,* 45(4), 708–719.

Gino, F., Ayal, S., & Ariely, D. (2013). Self-serving altruism? The lure of unethical actions that benefit others. *Journal of economic behavior & organization, 93,* https://doi.org/10.1016/j.jebo.2013.04.005

Gneezy, U., & Rustichini, A. (2000). A fine is a price. *Journal of Legal Studies,* 29(1), 1–17. https://ssrn.com/abstract=180117

Gottlieb, M. C., & Younggren, J. N. (2009). Is there a slippery slope? Considerations regarding multiple relationships and risk management. *Professional Psychology: Research and Practice, 40*(6), 564–571. https://doi.org/10.1037/a0017231

Hoyk, R., & Hersey, P. (2008). *The ethical executive: Becoming aware of the root causes of unethical behavior: 45 psychological traps that everyone of us falls prey to.* Stanford University Press.

Janis, I. L. (1982). *Groupthink.* Houghton Mifflin.

Kahneman, D. (2011). *Thinking, fast and slow.* Farrar, Straus & Giroux.

Kahneman, D., & Tversky, A. (1979). Prospect theory: An analysis of decision under risk. *Econometrica, 47*(2), 263–291.

Karau, S. J., & Williams, K. D. (1995). Social loafing: Research findings, implications, and future directions. *Current Directions in Psychological Science, 4*(5), 134–140. https://doi.org/10.1111/14678721.ep10772570

Kassin, S., Fein, S., Markus, H. R., & Burke, T. M. (2012). *Social psychology.* Nelson College Indigenous.

Kern, M. C., & Chugh, D. (2009). Bounded ethicality: The perils of loss framing. *Psychological Science, 20*(3), 378–384. https://doi.org/10.1111/j.1467-9280.2009.02296.x

Kohlberg, L. (1969). Stage and sequence: The cognitive-development approach to socialization. In D. A. Goslin (Ed.), *Handbook of socialization theory and research* (pp. 347–480). Rand McNally.

Langevoort, D. C. (2018). *Research handbook on corporate crime and financial misdealing.* Edward Elgar Publishing. https://doi.org/10.4337/9781783474479.00020

Metcalf, C., Satterthwaite, E. A., Dillbary, J. S., & Stoddard, B. (2020). Is a fine still a price? Replication as robustness in empirical legal studies. *International Review of Law and Economics, 63,* 105906. https://doi.org/10.1016/j.irle.2020.105906

Milgram, S. (1963). Behavioral study of obedience. *The Journal of Abnormal and Social Psychology, 67*(4), 371–378. https://doi.org/10.1037/h0040525

Milgram, S. (1965). Some conditions of obedience and disobedience to authority. *Human Relations, 18*(1), 57–76. https://doi.org/10.1177/00187267650 1800105

Milgram, S. (1974). *Obedience to authority: An experimental view.* Harper and Row

Prentice, R. A. (2004). Teaching ethics, heuristics, and biases. *Journal of Business Ethics Education 1*(1), 57–74.

Prentice, R. A. (2014). Teaching behavioral ethics. *The Journal of Legal Studies Education 31*(2), 325–365. https://doi.org/10.1111/jlse.12018.

Prentice, R. A. (2015). Behavioral ethics: Can it help lawyers (and others) be their best selves? *Notre Dame Journal of Law, Ethics & Public Policy, 29*(1), 35–85.

Rhim, J., Lee, J. H., Chen, M., & Lim, A. (2021). A deeper look at autonomous vehicle ethics: An integrative ethical decision-making framework to explain moral pluralism. *Frontiers in Robotics and AI, 8,* 632394. https://doi.org/10.3389/frobt.2021.632394

Schindler, S., & Pfattheicher, S. (2017). The frame of the game: Loss-framing increases dishonest behavior. *Journal of Experimental Social Psychology, 69,* 172–177. https://doi.org/10.1016/j.jesp. 2016.09.009

Shalvi, S., Dana, J., Handgraaf, M. J., & Dreu, C. K. (2011). Justified ethicality: Observing desired counterfactuals modifies ethical perceptions and behavior. *Organizational Behavior and Human Decision Processes, 115*(2), 181–190. https://doi.org/10.1016/j.obhdp. 2011.02.001

Simon, H. A. (1990). Bounded Rationality. In J. Eatwell, M. Milgate, & P. Newman (Eds.), *Utility and probability* (pp. 15–18). Palgrave Macmillan. https://doi.org/10.1007/978-1-349-20568-4_5

Simon, H. A., Massimo, E., Riccardo, V., & Robin, M. (1992). *Economics, bounded rationality, and the cognitive revolution.* Edward Elgar Publishing.

Tenbrunsel, A. E., & Messick, D. M. (2004). Ethical fading: The role of self-deception in unethical behavior. *Social Justice Research, 17*(2), 223–236. https://doi.org/10.1023/B:SORE.0000027411.35832.53

Trevino, L. K. (1986). Ethical decision making in organizations: A person-situation interactionist model. *The Academy of Management Review, 11*(3), 601–617. https://doi.org/10.2307/258313

Tversky A., Kahneman D. (1981). The framing of decisions and the psychology of choice. *Science, 211*(4481), 453–458. https://www.jstor.org/stable/1685855

Chapter 3 Ethical Decision-Making Models

By adding the tools of psychology and behavioral ethics to those of philosophy, we may better understand the factors that contribute to our moral reasoning process and develop strategies to bridge the gap between intention and action in moral contexts (Prentice, 2015). Researchers from multiple disciplines have suggested a number of theories to explain our ethical decision-making process (Carlson et al., 2009). In this chapter, we are going to start with the rationalist approach to ethical decision-making and delve into dual process theory by incorporating intuitive approach into rational approach.

The rationalist approach is grounded in a cognitive perspective, emphasizing deliberate, intentional, and conscious thought processes. This approach assumes a moral absolutism, asserting that there is only one right in ethical dilemmas and this right can be discovered through rational analysis. The rationalist approach is characterized by its emphasis on reason, logic, and objective criteria in determining the morally right course of action.

Rest's Four Component Model

One widely recognized ethical decision-making framework that has inspired many others in the literature across many disciplines is Rest's four-component model (1986). The model provides a systematic framework for understanding how individuals navigate ethical dilemmas (Figure 2.). Initial phase begins with *Moral Awareness.* This is the phase where a person acknowledges that there is a moral conflict. It requires individuals to perceive that a situation involves moral considerations, signaling the need for ethical decision-making. Once individuals are aware of the moral issue, the next step is *engaging in reasoning.* During this phase, individuals assess the available options, weigh the ethical implications, and prioritize their ethical principles (Trevino, 1986). Then the third step follows, and the person establishes his/her *Moral Intent.* In this phase, people judge which course of action best suits their ethical ideologies and choose his course of action. Rest (1986) suggests that individuals draw on their cognitive moral development, as defined by Kohlberg's stages, to guide their moral intentions. The final step is *Engage in Moral Behavior.* It involves translating moral intentions into actions. Individuals make decisions and take actions based on their prioritized moral values. Engaging in moral behavior is the practical application of the ethical principles and values determined during the earlier stages. These four phases emphasize the importance of individual reasoning, moral awareness, and the translation of moral intentions into actions.

Figure 2. Rest's Four Component Model Adapted from Rest (1986)

Rest's model aligns with the broader understanding that ethical decision-making involves a thoughtful and intentional process rather than impulsive or arbitrary choices (Zollo et al., 2018). While Rest's model is influential, it's still worth noting that there are other ethical decision-making frameworks, each with its unique perspective and emphasis.

Ferrell and Gresham's Ethical Contingency Framework

Contingency framework proposed by Ferrell and Gresham (1985) recognizes that ethical behavior is influenced by various factors, and it accounts for the complexity of decision-making in real-world situations. The visual representation of the model (Figure 3) illustrates the dynamic interplays between individual factors, significant others, opportunity factors, and social and cultural environmental factors: Here are key elements of the contingency framework:

Individual Factors: It acknowledges that an individual's moral reasoning is shaped by several individual factors, including knowledge, values, attitudes, and intentions and play a crucial role in determining ethical behavior.

Significant Others: Ethical decision-making is not solely an individual process; it is also influenced by significant others. The framework considers factors such as differential association (interactions with others), role set configuration (social roles and expectations), and the impact of significant individuals on an individual's ethical choices.

Opportunity Factors: Opportunities also play a crucial role in shaping ethical decisions. The framework includes considerations such as professional codes, corporate policies, and the presence of rewards or punishments. These external structures provide the context within which individuals make ethical choices.

Social and Cultural Environmental Factors: The model acknowledges the importance of environmental factors and incorporates the social and cultural contexts that influence people's ethical intentions. This recognizes that ethical decision-making is not isolated but shaped by the broader societal and cultural milieu.

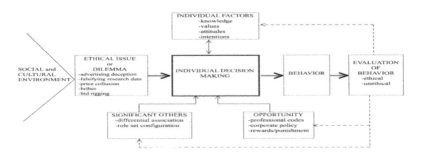

Figure 3. Ferrell and Greeham's Contingency Framework (1985, p. 89)

The contingency framework's strength lies in its recognition of the interconnected and multifaceted nature of ethical decision-making. By incorporating personal, interpersonal, and contextual elements, it provides a more comprehensive understanding of how individuals navigate ethical challenges.

Trevino's Person-Situation Interactionist Model

Trevino's Person-Situation Interactionist model (1986) integrates elements from Kohlberg's cognitive moral development stages while also incorporating individual and situational moderators. The visual representation of the model illustrates the dynamic interrelationships between moral judgment, individual moderators, and situational moderators (Figure 4). Let's explore the key components of Trevino's model:

Cognitive Moral Development: The model acknowledges the importance of Kohlberg's (1969) cognitive moral development stages as a predictor of moral or immoral action.

Individual Characteristics: Trevino's model introduces the concept of moral judgment, which is moderated by individual characteristics (Small & Lew, 2021). These moderators include:

Ego Strength: Indicates a person's capacity to cope with ethical dilemmas and challenges without resorting to unethical behavior.

Field of Dependence: Describes the extent to which an individual relies on the opinions and expectations of others in making moral judgments.

Locus of Control: Indicates whether individuals believe they have control over events affecting them (internal locus) or whether external factors control their outcomes (external locus).

Situational Factors: The model also recognizes the role of situational elements in moderating moral judgment. These situational moderators include:

Immediate Job Context: The specific features and demands of the job environment that influence ethical decision-making.

Organizational Culture: The moral values, norms, and ethical climate within the system that shape individuals' ethical choices.

Characteristics of the Work: Features inherent in the nature of the work that affect moral reasoning.

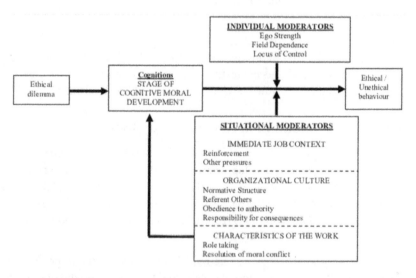

Figure 4. Trevino's Interactionist Model of Decision Making (1986, p. 603)

Trevino's Person-Situation Interactionist model contributes to the understanding that ethical behavior is contingent on both personal attributes and contextual factors by emphasizing the interaction between individual and situational factors. By incorporating individual and situational moderators, the model recognizes the complexity and variability in how individuals respond to ethical challenges based on their cognitive moral development and the characteristics of the situations they encounter. The Person-Situation Interaction model suggests that ethical behavior is not solely determined by personal characteristics or environmental factors but results from the interplay between the two.

Hunt and Vitell's Marketing Ethics Framework

Hunt and Vitell (1986) provide another perspective on moral reasoning, emphasizing the impact of specific moral doctrines on people's ethical judgements in Marketing Ethics. The visual representation of the model (Figure 4) provides a flowchart or diagram depicting the stages and interplay between moral doctrines and cognitive decision-making processes. Let's explore the key components of their model:

Moral Doctrines: The Hunt and Vitell model highlights the significance of moral doctrines, specifically deontological and teleological principles. Deontological ethics focuses on adherence to rules and duties, while teleological ethics emphasizes the consequences or outcomes of actions. Individuals may employ one or both of these moral doctrines to guide their ethical decision-making.

Perceived Ethical Problem Stages: The model suggests that individuals go through various stages when faced with a perceived ethical problem. These stages likely involve recognizing the ethical dimensions of a situation, considering potential consequences, and deliberating on the ethical principles that should guide their decision.

Micro Aspects of Cognitive Decision-Making: Emphasizing micro aspects, the model delves into the individual's cognitive decision-making process. It focuses on the intricate mental processes involved in evaluating ethical consequences, emphasizing the importance of personal cognitive factors in shaping ethical judgments.

Application of Moral Doctrines: Individuals, in this model, are expected to apply either deontological or teleological moral doctrines (or a combination of both) as they navigate through the stages of ethical problem-solving. The choice of moral doctrine can significantly influence the ultimate ethical decision.

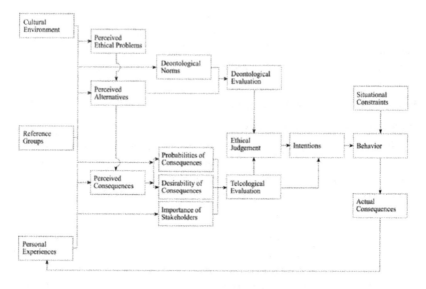

Figure 5. Hunt and Vitell's Marketing Ethics Framework (Marks & Mayo, 1991, p. 722)

This micro-level emphasis aligns with the idea that ethical decision-making is not only influenced by external factors but also deeply rooted in an individual's cognitive processes, beliefs, and moral frameworks. By highlighting the role of moral doctrines and the internal cognitive stages, this model contributes to a more detailed understanding of how individuals approach ethical decision-making. It complements broader frameworks by focusing on the nuanced thought processes individuals engage in when confronted with ethical dilemmas.

Jones' Issue-Contingent Model

Jones' issue-contingent model adds another layer to the understanding of ethical decision-making by incorporating the concept of moral intensity. The visual representation of the model illustrates the interplay between the four moral reasoning phases, environmental and individual factors, and the concept of moral intensity (Figure 6.). Let's explore the key components of Jones' model:

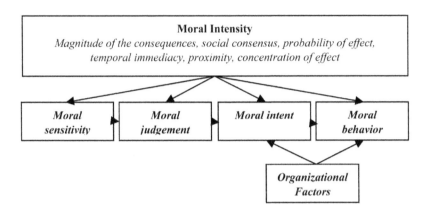

Figure 6. Jones' Issue-Contingent Model Adapted from Jones (1991)

Four Moral Reasoning Phases: Similar to other ethical decision-making models, Jones' model (1991) includes the four moral reasoning phases: moral awareness, moral judgment, moral intent, and ethical behavior. These phases represent the sequential steps individuals go through when navigating through an ethical dilemma.

Environmental Factors: The model recognizes the influence of environmental factors on ethical decision-making. Environmental factors may include aspects of the external context, such as organizational culture, industry norms, and societal expectations. These factors contribute to shaping the ethical dimensions of a particular situation.

Individual Factors: Personal characteristics, values, principles and beliefs, are acknowledged as factors contributing to the variation in ethical decision-making.

Moral Intensity: Perceived moral intensity, as proposed by Jones (1991), refers to the extent to which an issue is perceived as morally significant or as having important moral implications. This dimension recognizes that not all ethical dilemmas are perceived with the same level of moral urgency. Jones (1991) identified six components that contribute to the perceived moral intensity of an issue:

Magnitude of Consequences: The perceived significance of the outcomes or consequences associated with a particular decision or action. The larger the impact, the larger the magnitude of moral intensity.

Social Consensus: The extent to which members of a society or a relevant social group agree on regarding the morality of a particular behavior. The higher consensus, the higher perceived moral intensity.

Probability of Effect: The extent to which the consequences of a decision or action are likely to occur. If the potential effects are deemed more probable, the perceived moral intensity is higher.

Temporal Immediacy: The time delay between the action and its consequences. Issues with immediate consequences are often perceived as having higher moral intensity.

Proximity: The psychological or emotional closeness of an individual to the consequences of a decision. If the consequences feel closer or more personally relevant, the moral intensity is higher.

Concentration of Effect: The extent to which the consequences are concentrated on a few individuals versus dispersed among many. In general, the higher the concentrated effect, the higher the perceived moral intensity.

Jones' emphasis on moral intensity adds a contextual dimension to ethical decision-making, recognizing that the perceived ethical significance of a situation can vary. The combination and interaction of these components determine how an individual perceives the moral intensity of a particular issue. Issues with higher moral intensity are more likely to be recognized as ethical problems. This model aligns with the broader recognition in the literature that ethical decision-making is contingent upon various factors, both internal and external. It enriches the understanding of how individuals navigate ethical challenges in diverse contexts.

Zollo's Dual-Process Model

The dual-process theory is a theory that attempts to offer a comprehensive understanding of ethical decision-making by incorporating both rationalist and intuitive approaches (Zollo, 2020). The dual-process theory draws attention to the role of moral intuition as the first stage in ethical decision-making (Rhim et al., 2021) and asserts that it is an automatic response followed by rational moral reasoning (Sonenshein, 2007). Haidt (2001), one of the most well-known social intuitionist theorists, adopts the dual-process theory and suggests that when the decision makers face with a moral dilemma, they make moral judgments based on intuitions, followed by the post hoc rationalization. Zollo (2020), on the other hand, proposes that moral reasoning is comprised of two information processing systems (System 1 and System 2) (see Figure 7). The intuitive moral reasoning process involves the interplay of moral intuition, emotion, and reflection. While System 1 represents the intuitive, effortless, fast, reflexive, and unconscious cognitive process that is conducive to basic emotions such as happiness, fear, surprise, discomfort, and pain. Moral intuition refers to the automatic, immediate, and often subconscious judgments or responses individuals make when faced with moral dilemmas. It involves a quick and intuitive assessment of the rightness or wrongness of a situation. This intuition is driven by internalized moral values and norms that individuals have developed through socialization and personal experiences.

The next phase, System 2, represents the controlled, reflective, deliberate, rational, and analytical cognitive process which is conducive to more complex emotions such as loathing, sorrow, relief, contempt, guilt, empathy, and shame) (Dane & Pratt, 2007). Those emotions can influence how individuals perceive and respond to moral situations. Emotions often accompany moral intuitions, shaping the affective dimension of moral reasoning. For example, feeling empathy for someone in distress may trigger a moral intuition to help. Reflection follows the initial intuitive and emotional response. After automatic judgments and emotional reactions, individuals engage in reflective processes where they consciously consider and evaluate their moral intuitions. This involves a more deliberate and cognitive examination of the ethical dilemma, potential consequences, and the alignment with personal values. Reflection allows individuals to consider alternative perspectives, weigh the moral principles involved, and assess the implications of their actions on others. The interaction between moral intuition, emotion, and reflection is dynamic and context dependent. In some situations, individuals may rely more on intuition and emotions, while in others, they may engage in deeper reflection before making moral decisions.

Figure 7. Dual-Process Model Adapted from Zollo (2020)

The consensus among moral intuitionists is that conscious reasoning serves as a post hoc mechanism for justifying moral judgments. Intuitive processes generate initial moral intuitions, and conscious reasoning follows to rationalize and provide justification for those intuitions (Rhim et al., 2021). Understanding the intricate relationship between moral intuition, emotion, and reflection provides insights into the complexity of human moral reasoning and decision-making, acknowledging both automatic and deliberate cognitive processes involved in ethical judgments.

References

Carlson, D. S., Kacmar, K. M., & Wadsworth, L. L. (2009). The Impact of Moral Intensity Dimensions on Ethical Decision-making: Assessing the Relevance of Orientation. *Journal of Managerial Issues, 21*(4), 534–551. http://www.jstor.org/stable/40604668

Dane, E., & Pratt, M. G. (2007). Exploring intuition and its role in managerial decision making. *Academy of Management Review, 32*(1), 33–54. https://doi.org/10.5465/amr.2007.23463682

Ferrell, O. C., & Gresham, L. G. (1985). A contingency framework for understanding ethical decision making in marketing. *Journal of Marketing, 49*(3), 87–96. https://doi.org/10.2307/1251618

Haidt, J. (2001). The emotional dog and its rational tail: A social intuitionist approach to moral judgment. *Psychological Review, 108*(4), 814–834. https://doi.org/10.1037/0033-295x.108.4.814

Hunt, S. D., & Vitell, S. (1986). A general theory of marketing ethics. *Journal of Macromarketing, 6*(1), 5–16. http://dx.doi.org/10.1177/027614678600600103

Jones, T. M. (1991). Ethical decision making by individuals in organizations: An issue-contingent model. *The Academy of Management Review, 16*(2), 366–395. https://doi.org/10.2307/258867

Kohlberg, L. (1969). Stage and sequence: .e cognitive- development approach to socialization. In D. A. Goslin (Ed.), *Handbook of socialization theory and research* (pp. 347–480). Rand McNally.

Marks, L. J., & Mayo, M. A. (1991). An empirical test of a model of consumer ethical dilemmas. *Advances in Consumer Research, 18*(1),720–728. https://eds.p.ebscohost.com/eds/pdfviewer/pdfviewer?vid=0&sid=b8859561-1547-4e5b-b497-40c38b389b77%40redis

Prentice, R. A. (2015). Behavioral ethics: Can it help lawyers (and others) be their best selves? *Notre Dame Journal of Law, Ethics & Public Policy, 29*(1), 35–85.

Rest, J. R. (1986). *Moral development: Advances in research and theory.* Prager.

Rhim, J., Lee, J. H., Chen, M., & Lim, A. (2021). A deeper look at autonomous vehicle ethics: An integrative ethical decision-making framework to explain moral pluralism. *Frontiers in Robotics and AI, 8*(632394). https://doi.org/10.3389/frobt.2021.632394

Small, C., & Lew, C. (2021). Mindfulness, moral reasoning and responsibility: towards virtue in ethical decision-making. *Journal of Business Ethics, 169*, 103–117 https://doi.org/10.1007/s10551-019-04272-y

Sonenshein, S. (2007). The role of construction, intuition, and justification in responding to ethical issues at work: The sensemaking-intuition model. *The Academy of Management Review, 32*(4), 1022–1040. https://doi.org/10.5465/amr.2007.26585677

Trevino, L. K. (1986). Ethical decision making in organizations: A person-situation interactionist model. *The Academy of Management Review, 11*(3), 601–617. https://doi.org/10.2307/258313

Zollo, L., Yoon, S., Rialti, R. and Ciappei, C. (2018). *Ethical consumption and consumers' decision making: the role of moral intuition, Management Decision, 56*(3), 692–710. https://doi.org/10.1108/MD-10-2016-0745

Zollo, L. (2020). The consumers' emotional dog learns to persuade its rational tail: Toward a social intuitionist framework of ethical consumption. *Journal of Business Ethics, 168*, 1–19. https://doi.org/10.1007/s10551-019-04420-4

Part II Normative (Prescriptive) Ethics

Do not think that moral confusion is new. No matter how much we wish otherwise, simple straight-forward answers to ethical problems are not possible. For instance, if a person stands up against evil for an innocent just because he wants to avoid hell and guarantee heaven, can we call him virtuous?

Every dilemma can be explored using more than one approach. Of course, depending on the road taken, the end results may vary greatly. We are exposed to a variety of moral codes through the mass media and struggle amidst conflicting moral values. Even those who seek help from a single text – a clear-cut, no-nonsense guide for answers -find themselves perplexed in the middle of vast ambiguity. Let's consider the Golden Rule -the moral principle of all Abrahamic religions and a precept in the Gospel of Matthew (7:12) which calls upon people to treat others the way they would like to be treated.

Even though most of us are familiar with the Golden Rule, our interpretation of it may vary depending on the emphasis we place on the motivation that lies behind following the Golden Rule. Although the Golden Rule is a principle that is often associated with deontological ethics, it can also be interpreted from a teleological perspective depending on how it is applied. From a deontological standpoint, the Golden Rule is seen as a guiding moral principle that instructs individuals to treat others as they themselves would like to be treated. This principle emphasizes the inherent duty to treat others with respect and kindness, regardless of the potential consequences or outcomes. In this sense, it aligns with deontological ethics, which is focused on following moral rules and principles regardless of the outcomes.

From a teleological perspective, on the other hand, the Golden Rule is viewed in terms of its potential outcomes. Treating others well and following the Golden Rule might be seen as a way to create positive social interactions and a harmonious society. This aligns with the teleological idea of evaluating actions based on their consequences and whether they lead to desirable outcomes. To sum up, whereas some may prefer to follow the Golden Rule because they consider that it is their duty and an obligation to treat others well (from a deontological standpoint), others may regard it merely as a rule of reciprocity and follow the golden rule thinking its potential positive outcomes (from a teleological standpoint).

It is crystal clear that there are disagreements about what precisely gives an action, rule, or disposition its ethical force. Here is where the normative ethics come into play. Normative ethics is concerned about the practical means of determining a moral course of action. It is the study of ethical behavior and the branch of philosophical ethics that investigates the questions that arise regarding "how should we act, in a moral sense?", "What should the laws and norms be?", "What is right and wrong?", "Which actions are in fact right or wrong?", "Which things are in fact good or bad?", and "What does it takes in fact to be a good or bad person?". These are the questions studied primarily by philosophy and theology.

In normative ethics, there are two main competing views on "what we should do" or "how we should act": Character-focused theories (Ethics of character/ Virtue ethics) and Action-focused theories (Ethics of right action). Character-focused theories start with the question "How should I be?" and the answer determines "What should I do?". Action-focused theories start with the question "What should I do" and the answer determines "How should I be"? On the other hand, action-focused theories prioritize the evaluation of specific actions rather than the character of the individual. Deontological ethics, for instance, focuses on duties and rules, stating that certain actions are inherently right or wrong regardless of their consequences. Consequentialist theories, like utilitarianism, judge the morality of actions based on their outcomes, aiming to maximize overall happiness or utility. In these theories, the question "What should I do?" is paramount, and the moral character of the agent may not necessarily be central to determining the right course of action. Both approaches have their strengths and weaknesses, and different philosophers may advocate for one over the other based on various considerations such as practicality, coherence, and their understanding of human nature, yet they are also very much interrelated. In Part II, we are going to analyze normative ethics theories under three chapters: Virtue Morality, Deontological Morality and Teleological Morality.

In the chapter, **Virtue Morality,** we will attempt analyze character-based theories which define "the good" in terms of certain dispositions of the character/ or virtues of moral agents.

In the chapter, **Deontological Morality,** we will attempt analyze action-based deontological morality which attempts to define "the right action" in terms of duty or set of duties (*deons*) or some intrinsic drive, motivation, intent of actions/or agents.

In the chapter, **Teleological Morality,** we will attempt analyze action-based teleological morality which attempt to define "the good" in terms of the consequences of our actions and suggest determining the right action in terms of some particular end (*teleos*)

Important Note (criteria for evaluating ethical theories). This part aims to provide a general understanding of normative ethics theory and urges the readers to evaluate each theory based on the following criteria:

Logical Coherence Test: Assess the clarity and internal consistency of the ethical theory's fundamental concepts and principles. Evaluate whether the theory provides a systematic and coherent framework for ethical decision-making.

Consistency Test: Examine the ethical theory for any internal contradictions or conflicts among its principles. Ensure that the theory's tenets do not contradict each other or lead to paradoxical conclusions.

Applicability Test: Evaluate the ethical theory's ability to provide guidance in a wide range of situations. Assess whether the theory can address specific moral dilemmas and offer practical solutions.

Comprehensive Scope Test: Examine the breadth of ethical theory in addressing various aspects of moral life. Ensure that the theory is not overly narrow or limited in its coverage of ethical issues.

Compatibility Test: Compare the ethical theory with your own moral convictions and assess its compatibility. Determine whether the theory aligns with your deeply held beliefs and values.

Impartiality Test: Assess whether the ethical theory can be applied without bias or prejudice. Examine the theory's defense for reliance on accurate and unbiased information.

Practical Application Test: Evaluate how practical and applicable the ethical theory is in real-world scenarios. Assess whether the theory provides actionable guidance for individuals and institutions.

Cultural Sensitivity Test: Examine the ethical theory's adaptability to different cultural contexts. Ensure that the theory does not impose a culturally specific perspective that may be incompatible with diverse moral traditions.

Evolutionary Consistency Test: Assess whether the ethical theory can accommodate evolving societal norms and values. Determine if the theory can adapt to changes in moral perspectives over time.

Moral Intuition Test: Consider whether the ethical theory aligns with common moral intuitions. Evaluate the theory's capacity to resonate with widely shared moral sensibilities.

Here is another set of criteria outlined in Singer's D.A.R.M framework. Singer (1993) provides a set of criteria for evaluating ethical theories: The acronym D.A.R.M stands for Derivation, Application, Realism, and Motivation. Here's a brief explanation of each component:

Derivation: These address how the value or norm (the idea of goodness) is derived within ethical theory. Assess the clarity and coherence of the theory's foundational principles. Examine whether the theory can clearly articulate the basis for its ethical norms.

Application: Focuses on how easy it is to apply the ethical norm to real-world situations. Evaluate the practicality and effectiveness of ethical theory in providing guidance for moral decision-making in various contexts.

Realism: Examines the theory's view of human nature and its realism in understanding how people actually behave. Assess whether the theory's assumptions about human nature align with empirical observations and whether it provides a realistic understanding of human behavior.

Motivation: Explores how the theory answers the question, "Why should I be moral?" This considers the motivational aspect of ethical behavior. Evaluate whether ethical theory offers compelling reasons or motivations for individuals to adhere to its norms and principles.

Applying the D.A.R.M framework to any ethical theory involves a thorough examination of these four dimensions. By doing so, you can gain insights into the theory's foundational principles, practical utility, alignment with realistic observations of human behavior, and its ability to provide motivations for ethical conduct.

For example, if you were to apply the D.A.R.M framework to a specific ethical theory like utilitarianism:

Derivation: Utilitarianism derives ethical norms from the principle of maximizing overall happiness or well-being.

Application: The theory is relatively straightforward in its application, as it prescribes actions that lead to the greatest overall happiness.

Realism: The theory may be criticized for having an idealized view of human nature, assuming rationality and calculative decision-making.

Motivation: Utilitarianism provides a clear motivation for moral behavior by emphasizing the pursuit of the greatest overall happiness as a compelling reason to act ethically.

By subjecting an ethical theory to these tests, one can gain a comprehensive understanding of its strengths and weaknesses in terms of coherence, consistency, applicability, compatibility, and impartiality. Keep in mind that ethical theories may not score perfectly on all criteria, and a balanced assessment should consider the overall merit of the theory.

The Trolley Problem (Would You Sacrifice One Person to Save Five?)

The trolley problem is a well-known thought experiment in ethics and moral philosophy that explores the moral implications of making choices in situations involving harm and the greater good. It has been widely discussed in philosophy, psychology, and other disciplines to explore human moral judgments and the factors that influence decision-making in ethical dilemmas. The trolley problem serves as a valuable tool for ethical discussions and highlights the complexity of moral reasoning. It is generally employed to elicit moral intuitions and responses, allowing for the examination of ethical theories such as consequentialism, deontology, and virtue ethics. The scenario is designed to investigate normative ethical principles and theories by presenting a choice between two or more conflicting moral values. In the context of the trolley problem, individuals are asked to make a moral choice in a hypothetical situation involving a moral dilemma. The scenario is often presented as follows:

Imagine a runaway trolley heading towards five people who are tied up to a track and unable to move. You are standing next to a lever that can switch the trolley to another track. However, there is one person tied up on the second track. You have a choice: do nothing, and the trolley continues on its current path, killing five people, or pull the lever, diverting the trolley onto the second track, but causing the death of one person. The dilemma raises questions about moral decision-making, the consequences of actions, and the concept of utilitarianism. Several variations of the trolley problem exist, each introducing different elements to test moral intuitions and reasoning. Some variations introduce the element of personal involvement, such as physically pushing a person off a bridge to stop the trolley, sacrificing one to save many, to question about the moral significance of actively causing harm versus allowing harm to occur passively.

Act Utilitarian: An act utilitarian would likely choose to divert the trolley onto the track with one person because it maximizes overall happiness or pleasure by saving five lives at the expense of one.

Rule Utilitarian: A rule utilitarian would likely follow a rule that, when consistently applied, leads to the greatest overall happiness or pleasure. In this case, the rule might be to always divert the trolley onto the track with fewer people, as it maximizes overall happiness or pleasure by saving more lives.

Rule Deontologist: A rule deontologist would likely follow a moral rule or principle, such as the principle of respect for individual rights or the principle of non-maleficence. In this case, the rule might be to always respect the rights of individuals and not intentionally cause harm to others, even if it means saving more lives.

Act Deontologist: An act deontologist would likely choose not to divert the trolley onto the track with one person because it violates.

The trolley problem often pits consequentialist reasoning (maximizing overall well-being or minimizing harm) against deontological principles (adhering to moral rules or duties). However, character traits involved in each choice may also be of importance (virtue ethics). For instance, courage in pulling the lever or respecting the principle of not causing harm in refraining from action. Some individuals may prioritize saving more lives (consequentialism) over adhering to a principle of not causing harm directly and may be inclined to pull the lever or redirect the trolley to minimize harm and save more lives. In others, on the other hand, the moral rule of not intentionally harming others may take precedence (deontology) and they may resist actively causing harm even if the consequence is saving more lives. their moral beliefs or values, even if it means saving more lives. The most plausible and realistic solution to the trolley problem is subjective and depends on the individual's ethical framework. However, from a utilitarian perspective, the solution that saves the most lives is generally considered the most ethical. In this case, both act utilitarianism and rule utilitarianism would likely lead to the same solution of diverting the trolley onto the track with one person.

To sum up, responses to the trolley problem vary among individuals, and philosophers use it to explore the role of intuitions in moral decision-making. Some people may find certain actions morally permissible in the pursuit of a greater good, while others may prioritize following moral rules.

Chapter 4 Virtue (Aretaic) Theory

*"What kind of a person do you want to be and what
kind of a life do you want to pursue in life? Will you then
choose, act, and vote accordingly?"*

Aretaic ethics is a moral approach that places virtues and character development at the center of ethical evaluation. Virtue ethics can be investigated under
three categories: Eudaimonism, agent-based theories, and the ethics of care.
Eudaimonism which was proposed predominately by Ancient Greek emphasizes personal excellence and flourishing as the ultimate goals of moral action
where excellence and flourishing are seen as performing one's function dis-
tinctively well. An agent-based theory, on the other hand, emphasizes that virtues are admirable characteristics that people can figure out by their instincts.
Agent-based virtue ethics places a primary focus on the development of virtuous
character traits in individuals, while eudaimonistic virtue ethics emphasizes the
connection between virtues and the overall flourishing or well-being of individuals. These approaches can complement each other, as virtues are both qualities
of character and contributors to a good life. The ethics of care argues that focusing on justice and autonomy as primary virtues is too biased and masculine; suggests that more feminine virtues, such as caring and nurturing. While Nietzsche
and Wolf are not typically associated with virtue ethics in the traditional sense,
some elements of their philosophies can be interpreted in relation to virtues and
character development (Thus, we have discussed their interpretation of morality
as bonuses at the end of this chapter). Cynicism and Stoicism are both philosophical schools of thought that have unique interpretation of virtue, but they
differ in their approaches to ethics and how individuals should navigate the challenges of life.

Aretaic ethics place great importance on virtues that enable individuals to
lead morally admirable lives. Rather than asking, "What should I do now?", a virtue ethicist would ask "What kind of person I would like to be"? (Abend, 2014).
Thus, the central tenet of virtue ethics is not on consequences, duties, or social
contracts but on being a moral person. Shortly, unlike deontological and utilitarian theories which are "action/or rule-oriented", virtue ethics is "agent-oriented".

Aretaic ethics is often associated with moral excellence in the concept of
"eudaimonia," which can be translated as "flourishing" or "living well" (Jacob,
2023). Virtues can include qualities like courage, perseverance, honesty, compassion, humility, and wisdom. Aristotle (350 B.C.E/2012) argued that in order to be

a moral person, one first had to acquire the right virtues (excellences) and should be inclined to do the right thing (Skorupski, 2010). It has an agent-centered approach. Instead of focusing on external actions, aretaic ethics considers the moral character of the individual performing those actions. It emphasizes personal growth, self-improvement, and the development of virtuous habits. Aretaic ethics often looks to moral exemplars or role models who embody virtuous qualities. According to aretaic ethics, studying these individuals can provide guidance for ethical behavior. Virtue ethics criticize the rigidity of rule-based ethics (deontology) and the narrow focus on outcomes in consequence-based ethics (consequentialism). Instead, it encourages a more holistic and nuanced understanding of ethics. Virtue ethics is arguably the oldest ethical philosophy in the world, with origins in Ancient Greece.

To illustrate what virtue ethics advocates, White (2008) refers to the movie "The Dark Knight" where Batman gets the chance to take life of the Joker to emphasize the difference between consequentialist, non-consequentialist and virtue ethics. He suggests that utilitarians would prefer to kill the Joker, because by killing him, Batman would be able to save many more lives (White, 2008). Non-consequentialists would oppose the murder of the Joker simply because it is not right to take one's life. A virtue ethicist, on the other hand, would underline the character of the person and ask this question: "Is Batman a kind of person who kill the lives of his enemies?" and the answer would go like this: "No, Batman is never a man who would take the life of his enemies" (White, 2008). Thus, White (2008) concludes that virtue ethics simply helps us understand and live a life of virtuous movie character in life.

Although Confucius, Socrates, Plato, and Aristotle who are most associated with virtue ethics laid the groundwork for the approach in ancient philosophy, contemporary philosophers like Alasdair MacIntyre and Rosalind Hursthouse have developed and refined virtue ethics in modern times. Even though these notable virtue theorists, among themselves, disagree about what it is to flourish, and therefore about which character traits are the virtues, Stocker (2007) argues that they would agree on three propositions: (1) genuine virtue should reveal itself just like a second nature, such that patterns of choice are not random but natural and predictable by others. And this can only be achieved through education. And this (i.e., predictability) is indeed what differs a virtuous person from an average person, (2) Genuine virtue should always be in the interest of one's own self and (3) Genuine virtue should always be a source of gratification.

Questions to Ask (from a Virtue Ethics Standpoint)

When facing moral dilemmas from a virtue ethics standpoint, you might ask yourself a series of questions that encourage reflection on your character, values, and the cultivation of virtues. Here are some important questions you might consider:

- *What virtues are relevant to this situation?* Identify the virtues that are relevant to the specific moral dilemma. Consider virtues such as honesty, compassion, courage, justice, and others that may apply.
- *How would a virtuous person approach this dilemma?* Envision the actions of a virtuous person facing a similar dilemma. Consider how someone with well-developed virtues would navigate the situation.
- *Am I acting in accordance with virtuous traits?* Reflect on your own character and virtues. Consider whether your proposed actions align with virtuous traits or if they may compromise your moral integrity.
- *What virtues are in tension, and how can they be balanced?* If there are conflicting virtues in the dilemma, explore ways to balance them. Consider how you might navigate the tension between virtues to achieve a morally sound resolution.
- *Is this action consistent with my core values?* Evaluate whether the proposed action aligns with your core values. Virtue ethics emphasizes the connection between virtues, values, and ethical decision-making.
- *How will my actions impact my character development?* Consider the long-term impact of your actions on your character development. Will the chosen course of action contribute to the cultivation of virtues or potentially hinder moral growth?
- *What example am I setting for others?* Reflect on the example you are setting for others, especially if your actions are visible or influential. Consider how your choices might influence the moral development of those around you.
- *How can I promote virtuous behavior in others?* Explore ways to encourage virtuous behavior in others. Consider how your actions can contribute to a virtuous community and inspire others to cultivate virtues.
- *What does integrity require in this situation?* Consider the concept of integrity and what it requires in the given situation. Virtue ethics places importance on acting with integrity and maintaining moral coherence.
- *Am I balancing self-interest with the common good?* Consider how your actions impact not only yourself but also others and the broader community.

- *What role do relationships play in this dilemma?* Consider the impact of your actions on relationships. Virtue ethics recognizes the importance of virtuous interactions in building positive relationships.
- *Have I sought wise counsel or different perspectives?* Seek guidance and different perspectives. Virtue ethics values wisdom and prudence, and consulting others can contribute to a more thoughtful decision.
- *How will this decision contribute to human flourishing?* Evaluate how your decision aligns with the promotion of human flourishing or eudaimonia. Consider whether your actions contribute to the overall well-being and fulfillment of the individuals involved.
- *Have I reflected on similar dilemmas in the past?* Draw from past experiences and similar dilemmas. Reflect on lessons learned and how those experiences shaped your understanding of virtue.
- *What virtue can guide the resolution of this dilemma?* Identify a specific virtue that can guide the resolution of the dilemma. Consider how embodying that virtue can lead to a morally sound and virtuous course of action.

These questions are designed to prompt individuals to approach moral dilemmas through the lens of virtue ethics, encouraging thoughtful reflection on character, virtues, and the pursuit of a morally good life.

Eudaimonistic Virtue Ethics

Eudaimonistic virtue ethics -the most ancient branch of virtue ethics -is an ethical framework that centers on the concept of eudaimonia, which can be translated as "flourishing" or "living well". Scholars within this tradition emphasize the cultivation of virtues that contribute to human flourishing and the pursuit of a meaningful and fulfilling life. Eudaimonistic virtue theorists believe that living a virtuous life is integral to realizing human potential and achieving overall well-being. The virtues, according to this perspective, contribute to a meaningful and flourishing existence, and the pursuit of eudaimonia is closely tied to the cultivation of virtues.

In his work "Nicomachean Ethics" Aristotle (350 B.C.E/2012) argued that the highest good (eudaimonia) is achieved through the cultivation of virtues. He identifies moral virtues as the means to finding the right balance between deficiencies and excesses in one's actions (Aristotle, 350 B.C.E/2012). While Plato and Socrates are not typically categorized as virtue ethicists in the same way as Aristotle, the dialogues written by Plato, featuring Socrates as the main character, contain discussions on virtue and moral philosophy. Socrates' emphasis on self-examination, questioning, and the pursuit of wisdom can be seen as aligning with eudemonistic ideals of self-improvement, self-fulfillment, and excellence. In Plato's major work, "The Republic" the character of Socrates engages in a detailed exploration of justice, which involves discussions on the virtues of wisdom, courage, moderation, and justice itself (Plato, 2007). While Plato does not represent virtue ethics theory in the modern sense, he does consider the interplay of virtues and their role in an individual's character. In Plato's dialogues, virtue is often portrayed as a form of knowledge or wisdom. The Socratic method involves questioning others to help them recognize their lack of knowledge and encourage them to seek wisdom and virtue. While Plato and Socrates are not commonly labeled as virtue ethicists, their contributions to the exploration of virtue ethics, and moral philosophy laid the groundwork for later developments in philosophical thought, including Aristotle's more systematic treatment of virtue ethics.

Aristotle (384–322 BC) is often considered as the father of aretaic ethics. Yet, his work has been subject to various interpretations and criticisms throughout history, and contemporary moral philosophy continues to explore and refine ethical theories in light of new perspectives and challenges. Alasdair MacIntyre, for example, is a contemporary ethicist who has made important contributions to eudaimonistic virtue ethics. In his influential book "After Virtue" MacIntyre (2007) argues for a return to Aristotelian ethics and emphasizes the importance of virtues in moral philosophy. He explores how virtues contribute to the development of moral character and a flourishing human life (Smith & Kouchaki, 2021). Martha Nussbaum, on the other hand, is another philosopher who has integrated eudaimonistic elements into her capability approach. In works like "The Fragility of Goodness" and "Upheavals of Thought," Nussbaum (1986, 2003) explores how virtues and capabilities contribute to human flourishing and a life of eudaimonia. Julia Annas is another philosopher who has written extensively on virtue ethics, from eudaimonistic perspective. In works like "The Morality of Happiness" and "Intelligent Virtue", Annas (1995, 2011) explores the connection between virtue and eudaimonia, emphasizing the importance of practical wisdom and moral character in achieving a flourishing life. In the following sections, even though Socrates and Plato are not considered strictly as virtue ethicists, we will first explore their ideas on virtue as they are the inspiration of Aristotle's Nicomachean Ethics which is the foundational text in the field of eudaimonistic virtue ethics, and then explore Stoic School of Thought in connection to eudaimonistic virtue ethics.

Socrates' Ethics

"No one can knowingly or rationally do evil"
Socrates, Brainy Quotes

Although Socrates did not leave written works, his philosophy greatly influenced later thinkers like Plato and Aristotle. Socrates was a teacher and mentor to Plato, who went on to become one of the most important philosophers in Western philosophy. Plato, in turn, was a teacher to Aristotle, who is widely considered to be one of the most influential philosophers in history. Plato was an Idealist (Platonic Idealism) believing in eternal values whereas Aristotle was more of a realist believing in the need for judgment in particular situations. Aristotle was the first scientist in a true sense. He studied this world, while Plato studied the other world. The whole western civilization is influenced directly and indirectly by these three great minds. Their philosophies complement each other. Plato went on to become the guiding spirit of western idealism and religion while Aristotle was a man of science and common sense. Almost all the philosophers after these two are found to be siding with either of them -idealism vs empiricism, religion vs science, mysticism vs common sense. However, I find Socrates to be the wisest of the three, because he has given us something that will be as valid in ten thousand years as it is today. Whereas many scientists are attached to the paradigm they've spent decades exploring, such that a new paradigm will probably be met with some unease and contempt, Socrates urges us to lose attachment to particulars, and embrace the whole and argues that doing otherwise only serves to breed dogma not to the truth, as people become attached to their thoughts. I find Aristotle to be the second wisest of the three because of his Golden Mean maxim -stating that one should always find the balance between two extremes and act on it. Socrates is famously known for his maxim that "I know that I know nothing". This maxim highlights his belief in the value of humility and continuous learning (Dutra, 2022). Socrates used the dialectical method as a midwife to arrive at universal definitions, truth, and virtue (Dutra, 2022). To him, "the unexamined life was not worth living!" (Brickhouse & Smith, 1996) and "the best way to examine that life was through reasoning" with the method of dialectical inquiry (Beck, 2006). Socrates tried to teach the young Athenians who idolized the older Socrates how to live a virtuous life by taking no assumption for granted and by questioning everything (Dobrin, 2002). Yet, his approach to moral education was so unsettling, he was condemned to death by the Athenian court for having such unconventional conversations with his fellow Athenians and corrupting them with his wayward teachings (Dobrin, 2002).

Everything has a function, thinks Socrates, ranging from racehorses to cutting knives. A good horse, a good knife or a good farmland are those that have the specific set of traits (i.e., speed, sharpness, and fertility) that enables them to fulfill their function as horses, knives, or farmlands (Dutra, 2022). What determines their virtuousness is indeed the presence or absence of these characteristics. Everything is built or created for a purpose (Dutra, 2022). So, everything is virtuous as long as they can perform their function properly, do what they are supposed to do with excellence (i.e., with the fullest expression of their potential). This means that a knife is good as long as it cuts well, a horse is good as long as it runs fast, a farmland is good as long as it is fertile. We can also speak of the virtues of the plan or the brand that we prefer. The most important thing to note here is that this thought pattern might be applied to anything, including to people and the specific set of characteristics that determine the virtue of a thing is, of course, the nature of that thing (Dutra, 2022). It implies that we can pursue a virtuous life only when we know our function/role in that life, and that's why Socrates's philosophy emphasized the pursuit of knowledge.

Plato's Ethic

> *"Good people do not need laws to tell them to act*
> *responsibly, while bad people will find a way around*
> *the laws"*
> *Plato, Brainy Quotes*

Plato grew into a family of high social class and political influence in that; he would have taken a noble role in Athenian politics. Nevertheless, he did not wish to live a political life because he witnessed injustices committed by rulers, who were, indeed, his relatives and friends. Plato witnessed the unfortunate execution of Socrates and his fellow philosophers and thus preferred to receive severe penalties than to be in service of promoting injustice and evil by participating in politics. Plato noticed how the new regimes instituted other injustices by avenging perceived enemies from previous regimes and concluded that people will only achieve a just society "if a king becomes philosopher or philosopher becomes a king" (Plato, c. 375 BC/2007).

Plato's ethics differ considerably from Socrates'. As opposed to Socrates who argues that *"no one can knowingly do evil"*, according to Plato, *"Good people do not need laws to tell them to act responsibly, while bad people will find a way around the laws"* (Brainy Quotes, n.d.). Plato (c. 375 BC/2007) holds that there is a power problem in politics because politicians misuse power to achieve their desired ends no matter whether the means is just or unjust. Therefore, he urges people to *measure the man by what he does with power*. In order to unravel the problem of power associated with politics he suggests to ask some challenging and mind-provoking questions: "*Are you willing to live under the rule of fools or a man less capable than yourself?*", "*Do you think that you can lead a virtuous life if you let people who are not in love but not worthy of power to rule you?*" and "*Will you be able to forgive yourself when you are doomed to live under the rule of fools just because you do not take an interest in the affairs of your government?*" According to Plato, "*the worst of all deceptions is self-deception*", and the only way to lead a virtuous life is to control access of people to power. According to Plato (c. 375 BC/2007), access to power must be confined to those *who are not in love with it*, because *those who seek power are not worthy of that power*. He furthers his argument by claiming that "*the best suited to rule are least likely to want to rule.*" Because anyone who is genuinely interested in the good would have no interest in ruling the pitiful lives trapped inside the cave. On the contrary, merely those who are less suited to rule would be willing to rule with the aim of acquiring power and material wealth. According to Plato (c. 375 BC/2007), philosopher-kings should be the rulers, as only they are qualified to rule, have the capacity to discern what is expedient for humanity, and have the knowledge of the ideal polis. Therefore, he concludes that the best way to avoid abuses of political powers is by electing philosophers as rulers because they have the wisdom to discern justice from injustice, and thus prevent the occurrence of political injustices. Although philosophical rulers do not abuse their political powers, it is essential that a government should have a constitution that guides rulers and prevents them from committing injustice associated with excessive political powers. Absence of the constitution provides immense freedom to rulers to make subjective decisions that suit their own interests, even though they are disadvantageous to people. Philosophers are wise, knowledgeable, and virtuous, which are the best attributes that rulers require in preventing the occurrence of injustice due to ignorance and immorality.

Aristotle's "Nicomachean Ethics"

Aristotle's "Nicomachean Ethics" is a foundational text in the field of eudaimonism. Eudaimonism asserts the highest good and ultimate goal of human life is eudaimonia, which is often translated as "flourishing" or "living well", where excellence and flourishing are meant performing one's unique and distinctive function well (Lalor, 2020). Aristotle also believed that human beings are rational animals, and a man is a political, or social animal. Therefore, he argued that life outside the community is only possible for a god or an animal. Aristotle's virtue ethics is a philosophical theory that focuses on the development of moral character and underlines the cultivation of virtues as the key to leading a flourishing and fulfilling life. Aristotle endorsed that a virtuous person is the one who has ideal character traits (Sachs, n.d.). According to Aristotle, although virtues derive from natural internal tendencies, they are not entirely innate but rather learned through practice and habituation, therefore they need to be nurtured continually. He also argued that we nurture our moral virtues primarily through habit and practice rather than through reasoning and instruction. Once we acquire the virtues and once they are established over time, they become stable and predictable. Therefore, he suggested that eudaimonia should be achieved through continual cultivation and exercise of virtues. The virtue approach suggests that by cultivating virtuous habits, people can increase their chances of choosing the right course of action when challenged by an ethical dilemma. According to Aristotle, the virtuous person not only knows what the morally right thing to do is, but s/he is also prone to do so (Gottlieb, 2009).

Aristotle distinguished between the forms of virtues: moral virtues and intellectual virtues (Deslauriers, 2002). *Moral virtues* pertain to a person's character and include qualities such as decency, modesty, temperance, bravery, generosity, integrity, and courtesy and lie in the realm of the irrational but conscious part of the soul. They are developed through repeated actions that are chosen deliberately with the aim of achieving the good. Over time, these actions become ingrained habits, shaping one's character and disposition towards virtuous behavior. *Intellectual virtues,* on the other hand, involve the development of one's intellect and include qualities such as wisdom, knowledge, and understanding. *Intellectual virtues,* on the other hand, belong to the rational self. They include five elements, (1) artistry or craftsmanship (Greek: techne); (2) Prudence or practical wisdom (phronesis); (3) intuition or understanding (nous); (4) Scientific knowledge (episteme) and (5) Philosophic wisdom (sophia). Intellectual virtue, including both theoretical and practical wisdom, goes beyond mere knowledge. While knowledge is certainly a crucial component, true intellectual virtue also involves the ability to apply that knowledge effectively in practical situations, discerning what is morally right and choosing the appropriate course of action.

Aristotle introduces us with a very important tool and a notion -*Golden Mean*- to understand what characteristics should indeed be considered as virtues and needs to be nurtured. In Aristotle's Nicomachean Ethics, the virtues can be achieved only with the *Golden Mean*, which is *a moderate* position between two extremes of excess and deficiency. (see Figure 1) For example, consider the virtue of courage. Courage is the mean between the extremes of cowardice (deficiency) and recklessness (excess). A courageous person is neither too timid nor too rash but finds the appropriate balance in facing danger. Or consider the virtue of "pride" which is flanked by two vices: "empty vanity" and "undue humility", just like "honesty" is the golden mean between "brutal bluntness" and "deceitful flattery". Aristotle would advise being honest to people because being honest is the "golden mean" where one is generally truthful, and never fails to say what needs to be said but knows when to be "tactful" and "diplomatic", and when to tell "white lies". Being witty is also one of Aristotle's virtues, for instance. It is the 'Golden Mean' between two vices: "boorishness" and "buffoonery". Aristotle would also advise to be witty (pleasant and funny in conversations with ease and a good sense of humor, but neither a vulgar (taking jokes too far in excess or, the polar opposite), nor a buffoon (awkward or boring who takes offence at everything and fouls everybody's mood). The goal, therefore, is to achieve the mean rather than apply excess or lack of a character trait. The same rule applies for too much idealism and too little idealism, or too much individualism and too much collectivism. Too much idealism means lack of understanding of how practical world works and bad policy decisions. Too less idealism and too much realism, on the other hand, may lead to loss of virtue and the narrow parochial selfish interest at expense of others. Similarly, too much individualism may lead to the loss of social identity, identity crisis and longing for belongingness, whereas too much collectivism may lead to self-alienation, loss of individual identity and sacrificed self-interests.

Table 1. Aristotle's Golden Mean

Domain	Deficiency (vice)	Mean (virtue)	Excess (vice)
Fear & Prudence	Cowardice	Courage	Recklessness
Telling the truth	Flattery	Honesty	Brutal bluntness
Kindness; Confidence	Arrogance	Confidence/Modesty	Self-deprecation
Conversation	Buffoonery	Wittiness	Boorishness
Honor	Undue humility	Pride	Empty vanity
Fidelity	Infidelity	Loyalty	Doormat
Pleasures & Pains	Asceticism	Temperance	Self-indulgence
Money & Prudence	Stinginess	Generosity	Extravagancy
Sensitivity	Indifference	Sensitivity	Drama Queen
Trust & Skepticism	Gullibility	Open mindedness	Prejudice

So according to Aristotle, being virtuous requires a very delicate balance without breeching into extremes. Thus, we need to be confident but not cocky; brave but never reckless; generous but never extravagant; loyal but not a doormat; flexible but not spineless; honest but not obnoxiously blunt; and witty but never vulgar or buffoon.

To sum up, Aristotle emphasizes the importance of virtuous character and personal development as the foundation of ethical living. Furthermore, according to Aristotle, virtues are developed through a process of moral education and practice. Virtuous actions are not the result of following strict rules or adhering to moral guidelines but are instead the outcome of cultivating virtuous habits. Virtue is therefore seen as a state of character that is acquired through consistent practice and the development of good habits.

Stoic Ethics

Stoicism is explicitly eudaimonistic, with the ultimate goal being the attainment of eudaimonia through a virtuous life. Stoic school of thought places a strong emphasis on individual virtue and the development of a virtuous character. Stoic ethics is characterized by an emphasis on virtue and moral character. Stoicism emphasizes virtue as the core of ethical living and identifies four cardinal virtues: wisdom (practical wisdom or good judgment), courage, justice, and temperance. These virtues guide moral reasoning and contribute to the development of a well-lived life. Virtue, in the Stoic sense, involves acceptance of fate, cultivation of resilience and maintaining moral character in the face of adversity and challenges. Stoicism encourages individuals to accept the natural course of events and focus on what is within their control.

Stoicism incorporates the concept of natural law, suggesting that there are fundamental principles governing the universe that can be apprehended by reason. Living in accordance with these natural laws is considered virtuous. Stoicism teaches the importance of accepting events and circumstances beyond one's control. The Stoic maxim "Amor Fati," meaning "love of fate," reflects the idea that individuals should embrace and accept their fate, recognizing it as part of the natural order. Reason plays a central role in Stoicism, guiding individuals to align their actions with virtue and live in accordance with rational principles. The Stoic sage is characterized by an inner peace that comes from aligning one's actions with virtue. Stoicism holds the view that the ideal life must be in harmony with nature, and people should be indifferent to external events. In common language, although stoic describes any person who seems calm and almost without any emotion (blank) and accepting of whatever is happening, as a philosophical doctrine, it describes a person aiming at achieving inner tranquility by living in accordance with reason and virtue.

Agent-Based Virtue Ethics

Agent-based virtue ethics is a branch of virtue ethics that focuses on the character of the moral agent and emphasizes the development of virtuous traits. Agent-based virtue ethics centers on the cultivation of virtuous traits in individuals. Virtues, such as honesty, courage, compassion, and integrity, are seen as central to leading a morally good life. In agent-based virtue ethics, the character traits of the moral agent is considered fundamental to moral judgment. The theory underscores the importance of personal development and the intentional cultivation of virtues over time. Moral education, reflection, and practice are seen as essential for becoming a virtuous person. Practical wisdom, or phronesis, is a key concept in agent-based virtue ethics. It involves the ability to discern the relevant moral considerations and the potential consequences of various courses of action and to apply virtues appropriately. Practical wisdom is cultivated through experience and moral reflection. Agent-based virtue ethics recognizes the importance of context in moral decision-making. Virtuous actions are not determined by rigid rules but are contextually sensitive, taking into account the specific circumstances and relationships involved. The approach is holistic, considering various aspects of a person's life and character. Virtue is not compartmentalized but is viewed as part of an integrated and flourishing life. Philosophers associated with agent-based virtue theories include Rosalind Hursthouse, Michael Slote, and Martha Nussbaum. Hursthouse, for instance, emphasizes the role of virtues in guiding action and highlights the importance of overall flourishing. Agent-based virtue ethics provides a nuanced and person-centered approach to moral philosophy, emphasizing the development of moral character as a key aspect of ethical living. In the following sections, we will first explore Cynic School of Thought in connection to agent-based ethics, and then proceed to Master-Slave Morality to understand how Nietzsche's ideas align with and differ from eudaimonistic virtue ethics, and finally explore how Susan Wolf's critique of moral saintliness aligns with agent-based virtue ethics,

Cynic School of Thought

The Cynics were an ancient philosophical school of thought founded by Antisthenes, a disciple of Socrates, and later developed by Diogenes of Sinope. The Cynics were known for their ascetic lifestyle, rejection of social conventions, and emphasis on virtue as the highest good. While the Cynics did promote certain virtues, their approach to virtue was distinctive and often unconventional. Cynics often embrace a minimalist lifestyle, and practice extreme simplicity and asceticism, rejecting material possessions and societal norms. They believed that a virtuous life required living in accordance with nature and free from the distractions of wealth and luxury.

Diogenes of Sinope is one of the most well-known figures of the Cynic school, believed in living in accordance with nature and sought to simplify his life to the bare essentials. His choice to reside in a large ceramic jar, often referred to as a barrel or tub, was a symbolic rejection of material comforts and a demonstration of his commitment to an ascetic lifestyle. His famous declaration that he only needed a place to sleep and food to sustain himself epitomizes Cynic philosophy. The story of Diogenes telling Alexander the Great to "get out of my sunlight" is another well-known anecdote. When Alexander visited Diogenes and asked if there was anything he could do for him, Diogenes, who was basking in the sunlight, replied with this famous phrase. The response is often interpreted as a rejection of worldly power and a reaffirmation of Diogenes' commitment to a simple, independent, and self-sufficient life. The quote "In a rich man's house, there is no place to spit but his face" (Diogenes, *Brainy Quotes)* is another provocative expression of Diogenes' contempt for wealth, luxury, and social hierarchies which captures the essence of his philosophy and his willingness to challenge societal norms through bold and unconventional means. Diogenes, for instance, is also said to have walked through the streets in daylight with a lamp, claiming to be looking for an honest man. Diogenes' unconventional and often humorous behavior, as well as his pithy sayings, made him a memorable and influential figure in the history of philosophy. His life and teachings continue to be studied and admired for their emphasis on living authentically and in harmony with nature.

Cynics advocate living in accordance with one's own principles rather than conforming to societal expectations and they often question the motivations behind moral codes, viewing them as arbitrary or hypocritical. Cynicism involves a critical perspective on social institutions, including ethical or moral institutions (Institutional Skepticism). Cynics may be distrustful of authority and question the legitimacy of established ethical structures. Cynics rejected societal conventions and norms, often engaging in provocative behavior to challenge established practices. Diogenes for example, argued that as a guiding principle, "if an act is not considered shameful when performed in private, then that same act when performed in public should not made shameful" (Piering, n.d.).

Cynics valued philosophical integrity and believed in practicing what they preached. They were critical of those who claimed to be virtuous but did not live in accordance with their professed values. While the Cynics did promote virtues such as self-sufficiency, simplicity, and philosophical integrity, their approach was characterized by a radical rejection of conventional morality and a focus on living a life in line with nature.

Master-Slave Morality

Friedrich Wilhelm Nietzsche (1844–1900) was a German philosopher who is considered to be one of the most influential, misunderstood, and controversial thinkers of all time. His work has been widely read, but also widely misunderstood. Nietzsche's philosophy is too deep and can be difficult to unravel. Nietzsche's works, including "Thus Spoke Zarathustra (1883)" and "Beyond Good and Evil (1886)" offer a nuanced and often provocative exploration of morality. Nietzsche can be considered as a "virtue ethicist," like Aristotle, though his virtues are obviously very different. Nietzsche's philosophy is not typically categorized within the framework of traditional virtue ethics. While he does discuss concepts related to morality, virtues, and values, his perspective on these matters differs significantly from classical virtue ethics. Nietzsche (1886/1997) challenges traditional moral systems and questions the notion of universal virtues. He criticized what he saw as the repressive effects of conventional morality and championed individualism, personal growth, and creativity. He often critiqued moral systems as being expressions of power dynamics and believed that individuals should critically evaluate and create their own values rather than adhering to fixed virtues. Nietzsche (1883/1961) introduced concepts like "will to power" and "Übermensch" (or "superman") as alternatives to traditional moral values. Nietzsche's concept of the "will to power" suggests that individuals and societies strive for dominance and influence, leading to the creation and imposition of moral systems that serve particular interests. He viewed moral values as products of historical and psychological processes rather than inherent truths.

In this book, -Beyond Good and Evil (1886)- Nietzsche challenged traditional notions of morality by contrasting master morality to slave morality (see Figure 2) and explored the nature of good and evil. Nietzsche's ideas are complex, multifaceted, and challenging. He presented a critique of moral values and questioned the foundations of conventional ethical systems. Nietzsche presented a sharp critique of traditional morality, particularly Christian morality, in his works. He introduced the concept of "slave morality" in contrast to what he termed "master morality," suggesting that Christian virtues emerged as a reaction of the weak and oppressed against the strong and dominant Nietzsche

(1886/1997). In Nietzsche's analysis, slave morality, which he associated with Christianity, valorizes qualities such as humility, meekness, and compassion. These virtues, according to Nietzsche, arise from a position of weakness and subjugation, where the oppressed reinterpret their suffering as virtuous and condemn the qualities associated with power and dominance. Nietzsche critiqued "slave morality," because he saw this kind of morality as a product of the laziness and resentfulness of insignificant people (i.e., herd people). Nietzsche (1886/1997) regarded the ideas and beliefs of slave morality as a revolt originated among the weak of society.

He thought "slave morality" as an attempt of resentful, timid, and lazy people who avoids taking the responsibility of their own life unrightfully imposing the values of pity, tolerance, modesty, compassion, sympathy, and humility on society for their own benefit Nietzsche (1886/1997). He suggested that slaves resent people who are able take responsibility of their own lives and create values and called all who are morally creative "evil". He (1886/1997) argued that in slave morality, "good" equates with the values of mercy, compassion, humbleness, pity, tolerance, modesty, patience, compassion, sympathy, and humility because these values highly benefit those who are lazy (Nietzsche, 1886/1997). He defined slave values as herd values that help lazy and insignificant people avoid taking responsibility in life. He contrasted "slave-morality" with what he saw as a more life-affirming "master morality". Nietzsche (1886/1997) argued that a "good" man evokes fear in others because, he acts passionately and independently and never hesitates taking risks, and by doing so he challenges others and evokes fear in others; to him, a "bad" man, on the contrary, is pitiful and insignificant because he is not capable of making any difference in life. He equated values of master morality with the expressions of strength, power, and nobility.

Table 2. Comparison of Nietzsche's Master and Slave Moralities Adapted from Taumaturgo (2017)

Master Morality	Slave Morality
Focused on significant those who are powerful, or above the herd	Focused on insignificant those who are weak, oppressed, exploited or suffering
Concerned with ethical codes that emphasize excellence, virtue, strength, merit, and toughness	Concerned with ethical codes that emphasize humility, modesty, empathy, mercy, equality, justice, and fairness
Legitimizes power imbalances	Works to de-legitimize power differentials
Orients towards hierarchical or authoritarian political systems	Orients towards socialist or communal political systems

Thanks to religion, Nietzsche (1886/1997) thought that there had been a "slave revolt in morals" -a terrible event which turned human values upside down. He argued that slave morality does not exert strength but questions the values of the masters and seeks to enslave them too. He also rejected the idea of the majority finding the common good, because to him, "what is common is of little value". He called slave morality "living a lie" and argued that those slavish values seek to topple the rightful rule of the strong. Nietzsche's work "Beyond Good and Evil" challenges conventional notions of good and evil, suggesting that these concepts are not fixed but have been used as tools of power, manipulation, and control. He encourages individuals to question and critically examine the origins and implications of moral values and clearly preferred the moral morality over slave morality in order to avoid "total degeneration of humanity" and hoped for an end to established religious values, with a return to the heroism of the classical world (Nietzsche, 1886/1997). Nietzsche criticizes certain aspects of virtue ethics, especially the emphasis on meekness, humility, and self-denial found in Judeo-Christian virtues. He challenges the traditional virtues and notions of good and evil, proposing a reevaluation of values based on individual strength, creativity, and power.

Nietzsche (1883/1967) also envisioned individuals who overcome conventional morality and societal constraints and embrace their individuality and creative potential (Übermensch). Nietzsche valued art and creativity as means for individuals to express themselves authentically and to transcend societal limitations. Nietzsche (1883/1967) also suggested the notion of the "eternal recurrence," where individuals imagine living their lives repeatedly for all eternity. With this thought experiment he encouraged people to live their lives in a way that they would be willing to repeat indefinitely. Overall, Nietzsche is known for his critique of traditional morality and values, which he believed were based on Christian ethics and the suppression of individual potential. Nietzsche (1883/1967) introduced the concept of the "will to power," emphasizing individual creativity, self-overcoming, and the pursuit of personal greatness. Nietzsche rejected the idea of fixed, universal virtues and moral rules, and instead focused on the complexities of human nature, societal influences, and individual expression.

Nietzsche attacks the "suffers-with" attitude and the altruistic doctorine which calls for "self-destruction" for the "sake of others" and does not value the self except as a way of helping others (Swanton, 2015). He rejects traditional altruistic morality because he thinks it prevents those capable of living the highest kind of life from doing so. One of his main criticisms of altruism is that it takes away from the individual. He believes that individuals should be encouraged to focus on their own growth and fulfillment, rather than the growth of others. He also believes that altruism can lead to weakness and a lack of self-confidence. Consequentialism for Nietzsche, on the other hand, is the shallowest of all the major types of moral theory, simply because it considers that the appropriate standards for evaluating moral behavior should be their consequences, but not the psychological states of individuals. His ideas on morality and values are more complex and divergent, emphasizing individualism, critique of traditional values, and the pursuit of personal greatness rather than adhering to a set of prescribed virtues. While Nietzsche's philosophy challenges conventional notions of morality and societal norms, his work does not provide a clear blueprint for how society should be structured or how individuals should live. Interpretations of his philosophy vary, and his ideas continue to provoke discussion and debate among scholars and thinkers. Nietzsche's philosophy often centers on the affirmation of life (amor fati) and the pursuit of one's own will to power. Rather than focusing on a specific set of virtues, Nietzsche encourages individuals to embrace life's challenges and express their unique qualities. While he critiques traditional virtues and moralities, he doesn't propose a fixed set of virtues as guiding principles. Nietzsche's emphasis is on individual strength, creativity, and the continual process of overcoming and becoming.

Sanction of the Victim

> *"Evil requires the sanction of the victim."*
> Ayn Rand, Brainy Quotes

Rand's ethical theory is often the most misunderstood and misrepresented theory in ethics. People think that she advocated the strong exploiting the weak, and people treating one another like garbage, or at best as a means to their own ends. Rand (1964) refuted this concept of selfishness in the first pages of her book "The Virtue of Selfishness". Rand did not reject benevolent virtues like charity and kindness. What she in fact did was to put these virtues on a more solid foundation. Rand (1964) urged people to understand what happens when society urges us to be unselfish, to sacrifice our own needs and desires for the "good of others" and realize and understand this "good of others" from the perspective of those others. From their perspective, it is their own selfish interests. She argued that it is good to be kind to one another, because kindness is based on selfishness (Rand, 1964). Not only your own selfishness, but the understanding that other people are selfish as well. To fully understand how to help others, how to be kind to them, you should be able to see them as others' selves and understand their own selfish interests. And so, charity and kindness require the understanding that other people are individuals with their own self-interests. She argued that every moral philosophy that pretends to be altruistic and other-centered indeed disguises and hides their true premise of self-interest under a false altruistic motive. For instance, religious morality threatens you with eternal torment, or requires you to serve the interests of a god. So, the god is being selfish. Any more secular moral philosophy that advocates self-sacrifice with the hidden assumption that the others that you sacrifice have their own selfish values or are of selfish value to you. Let us consider the notion of "altruism". Altruism in its original meaning and Rand's, is the moral virtue of sacrificing oneself for the service of others. Rand hated altruism because it lies behind the worst types of crimes such as fascism and war with the assumption that it is persons' duty to serve your nation, and to kill or die by doing. She objects to communism on similar grounds because she does not believe in the duty to serve to a party or the proletariat masses at the expense of yourself and instead of yourself. She basically argued that there is a tacit assumption in altruism claiming that self-interest is important unless it is your own self-interest and asks this question: Why should I think that somebody else's self-interest has more of an importance and more moral worth than my own? She argued that some individuals are better off when others are willing to sacrifice for them, and they are better off when they can exploit those people's sacrifices by denying the virtue of self-interest as righteous and rightful one.

Rand (1957) rejects altruism and advocates for individualism and rational egoism, in favor of reason, self-interest, rationality, and emphasizes the importance of the pursuit of one's own well-being as the basis for ethical decisions. So, it favors the evaluation of actions and choices based on their alignment with the rational pursuit of a person's own well-being. In order to understand Rand's ethical egoism, one must first choose to live, then understand that any moral values are selfish values to someone. So according to Rand's basic arithmetic, every morality is built on someone's or some Gods' self-interest (1957). So, the only moral thing to do would be to choose your own self-interest and be your own God. She explained that "Sanction of the victim" refers to a victim of evil actively participating in his own victimization *by supporting her own destroyers* (Rand, 1957). The principle of "sanction of the victim" means that in practice you should not give evil any fuel, any power, any means of continuing whatsoever. Evil requires good for potency, but good does not require evil. To sum up, when properly understood, Rand rejected the sacrificial ethics and argued that selfishness is a proper virtue to pursue as it prevents one to fall victim to evil by giving them the "sanction of victim". In Rand's view, selfishness does not mean exploitation or disregard for others, but rather the recognition of one's own worth and the commitment to achieving one's values through productive and voluntary interactions with others. In Rand's view, selfishness does not mean exploitation or disregard for others, but rather the recognition of one's own worth and the commitment to achieving one's values through productive and voluntary interactions with others.

Moral Saint Theory

While Wolf is not primarily known as a virtue theorist, her exploration of the concept of the moral saint has had a significant impact on ethical discussions, highlighting the complexities and potential drawbacks of an idealized moral life. Here is an interesting question to ask from Wolf's perspective: how are we to decide when and how much to be moral? Susan Wolf (1952–...) in her influential essay titled "Moral Saints" critiques the traditional virtue ethics framework that idealizes the morally perfect or saintly person. According to Wolf (1982), there are two kinds of moral saints: The rational saints and loving saints. Rational saints are the perfect Kantians who are committed to executing their moral duties. The loving saints, on the other hand, are the perfect Utilitarians who dedicate their entire lives to enhance everyone's wellbeing. The moral saint, according to Wolf (1982), is an individual who devotes their entire life to moral virtue, exhibiting exemplary moral character to the highest degree. Wolf (1982) raises several concerns about the implications and limitations of such a moral ideal. Firstly, Wolf argues that the moral saint, while morally virtuous, may lack well-roundedness and engagement in non-moral aspects of life (1982), because if the moral saints consume all their time to helping others, then they will have no time or energy to themselves (meaning that he is not necessarily reading any novel, playing piano, or tennis...The exclusive focus on moral virtue may lead to a diminished richness in experiences and pursuits such as enjoying a movie). Second, moral saints tend to prioritize certain virtues at the expense of others, potentially leading to a lack of diversity in virtues. Wolf (1982) suggests that a morally good life should include a balance of virtues, and the moral saint may neglect important non-moral virtues. Though we would certainly admire moral saints for their moral and unconditional commitments, very few of us would choose to be friends with them or live in a world full of them. Third, moral saints may face challenges in relating to others who do not share the same level of moral commitment. This difficulty in forming meaningful connections could be a consequence of the moral saint's singular focus on moral virtue. For example: a moral saint cannot develop a sense of humor, an interest in anything or a cynical or sarcastic wit. According to Wolf (1982) it appears that there is a limit to how much morality we can tolerate, and moral saints are indeed not that desirable in life. The paradox arises from the tension between the demands of moral perfection and the complexities of human existence. Wolf suggests that while moral excellence is important, it should not be the sole criterion for evaluating a person's life. Instead, she argues for a more nuanced understanding of moral goodness that allows for a broader range of values and pursuits beyond strict moral obligations. Thus, Wolf's paradox of Moral Saint theory urges us to question and reevaluate our moral theories to ensure they provide a comprehensive account of human flourishing. This involves not only considering what is moral but also recognizing the importance of non-moral aspects of life, such as personal interests, relationships, and individual fulfillment.

The Ethics of Care

Care ethics represents a departure from traditional ethical theories, such as those based on Kantian deontology or utilitarianism, which often prioritize abstract principles or the maximization of utility over interpersonal relationships and caring behaviors. The ethics of care argues that duties, rights, obligations, and the stereotypical justice view of morality is just one way of thinking about ethics and it is a male-centered view. Gilligan (1982) argued that female-centered emotions such as cooperation, empathy, and compassion matter too. The care perspective suggests that individuals have a natural capacity for caring and should prioritize the interests and well-being of those who are close to them, such as family members, friends, or community members. This contrasts with the impartiality often emphasized in traditional ethical theories, which may prioritize the interests of strangers or abstract moral principles. Care ethics emphasizes the interconnectedness of individuals and the importance of recognizing and responding to the needs of others. It suggests that by cultivating our capacity for care and empathy, we can create more just and compassionate societies where the well-being of all individuals is valued and prioritized.

Virtue theorists within the ethics of care tradition focus on cultivating and embodying virtues such as empathy and understanding of interconnectedness that enhance caring relationships. Lawrence Kohlberg and Carol Gilligan are both known for their contributions to the field of moral development. However, they approached the study of morality from different perspectives. Gilligan's ethics of care addresses how individuals approach moral dilemmas and make decisions based on caring relationships and responsibilities. Gilligan (1982) proposed that there are different but equally valid perspectives on morality. She argued that women, in particular, tend to emphasize care and relationships in their moral reasoning, as opposed to the more justice-oriented approach often emphasized by Kohlberg. Gilligan's ethics of care highlights the importance of empathy, compassion, and consideration of the needs and perspectives of others. She challenged the notion that justice-based moral reasoning is the only valid approach and advocated for a broader understanding of ethical decision-making.

Virtue theorists within the ethics of care emphasize virtues such as empathy, compassion, attentiveness, solidarity, caring about one another and responsiveness. Gilligan (1982) argued that this approach to ethics has been marginalized in the history of moral philosophy, largely because it reflects values and experiences traditionally associated with women, who historically occupied positions of limited power and influence. Apart from Carol Gilligan, there are some other notable figures associated with virtue ethics within the ethics of care. Eva Feder Kittay, for example, is a philosopher who has contributed to the ethics of care, particularly in the context of disability studies. She emphasizes the importance of care in relationships, particularly in the care of individuals with disabilities, and discusses the virtues necessary for providing ethical care (2011). Virginia Held is another one who has written extensively on care ethics and explored the relational aspects of moral life and the virtues required for responsible caregiving (Held, 2006). Some contemporary feminists have critiqued ethics of care theory for potentially fortifying conventional gender stereotypes, particularly the idea of the "good woman" who is nurturing, self-sacrificing, and primarily concerned with the welfare of others. Critics argue that by focusing on caring and nurturing qualities as central to ethical reasoning, care ethics may inadvertently perpetuate the idea that women are inherently predisposed to such roles, reinforcing traditional gender roles and expectations.

Criticisms of Virtue Ethics

Virtue ethics, while having notable strengths, is not without its critics. Various philosophical perspectives and ethical theories offer critiques of virtue ethics. Here are some common objections to virtue ethics:

1. *Lack of clear guidance:* Critics argue that the emphasis on character traits and virtues may not offer concrete solutions for determining right or wrong actions in particular situations. Furthermore, a virtue may not always lead to happiness (e.g., self-sacrifice).
2. *Cultural relativism critique:* Critics argue that virtue ethics can be culturally relative, as different cultures may uphold different virtues. This raises questions about the universality of virtues and whether virtue ethics can provide objective moral standards.

3. *Subjectivity and open-endedness:* Virtue ethics is accused of being too subjective and open-ended. Critics contend that virtues may be interpreted differently by individuals, making the theory less objective and more reliant on
   personal perspectives.

4. *Role of rules and principles:* Critics from deontological or rule-based ethical
   perspectives argue that virtue ethics downplay the importance of rules and
   principles in ethical decision-making. They suggest that virtues alone may
   not be sufficient for resolving complex moral dilemmas.

5. *Conflict resolution challenges:* Virtue ethics may face challenges when virtues
   come into conflict. Critics argue that it may not provide adequate guidance
   on how to prioritize virtues when they compete with each other.

6. *Potential for elitism:* Some critics express concerns about virtue ethics potentially leading to elitism. They argue that certain virtues may be valued more
   highly in specific cultural or social contexts, creating hierarchies of virtue
   that could be exclusionary.

7. *Overemphasis on character:* Critics contend that virtue ethics places too much
   emphasis on character and not enough on actions. They argue that focusing
   on virtues alone may neglect the ethical evaluation of individual actions.

8. *Insufficient attention to consequences:* Critics from consequentialist perspectives argue that virtue ethics does not give sufficient consideration to the
   consequences of actions. They believe that an exclusive focus on virtues may
   lead to morally undesirable outcomes.

9. *Historical and cultural bias:* Some critics suggest that the virtues emphasized
   in virtue ethics may be historically or culturally biased. They argue that certain virtues may have been favored based on specific cultural or historical
   contexts. Individuals' ability to foster the right virtues can indeed be influenced by various factors beyond their control, including education, society,
   friends and family (Athanassoulis, n.d.).

10. *Practicality in moral education:* Critics question the practicality of virtue
    ethics in moral education. They argue that teaching virtues may be chal-
    lenging, and there may be difficulties in assessing and measuring virtue
    development.

11. *Incomplete as a comprehensive theory:* Critics argue that virtue ethics, on
    its own, may be incomplete as a comprehensive ethical theory. They con-
    tend that it might benefit from integration with other ethical frameworks to
    address various ethical aspects.

12. *Potential for inaction in moral dilemmas:* Some critics express concerns that
    virtue ethics may lead to inaction in moral dilemmas if individuals priori-
    tize character development over making difficult decisions.

13. Lack of emphasis on justice: Critics argue that the emphasis on virtues may lead to a neglect of justice concerns, particularly in situations where there are conflicts between virtues and justice considerations.

It's important to note that these criticisms do not negate the value of virtue ethics but rather highlight areas where the theory may face challenges or require careful consideration. Virtue ethics continues to be a subject of philosophical debate and discussion as scholars explore ways to refine and strengthen the theory.

References

Abend, G. (2014). *The moral background an inquiry into the history of business ethics.* Princeton University Press. https://doi.org/10.1515/9781400850341

Annas, J. (1995). *The Morality of happiness.* Oxford University Press.

Annas, J. (2011). *Intelligent virtue.* Oxford University Press.

Aristotle. (2012). *Aristotle's Nicomachean Ethics* (R. C. Bartlett, & S. D. Collins, Trans.). University of Chicago Press. (Original work published 350 B.C.E.)

Athanassoulis, N. (n.d.). *Virtue ethics.* The Internet Encyclopedia of Philosophy (IEP). Retrieved October 22, 2024, https://iep.utm.edu/virtue/

Beck, S. (2006). *Confucius and Socrates: Teaching wisdom.* World Peace Communications.

Brickhouse, T. C., & Smith, N. D. (1996). *Plato's Socrates.* Oxford University Press.

Deslauriers, M. (2002). How to distinguish Aristotle's virtues. *Phronesis, 47*(2), 101–126. http://www.jstor.org/stable/4182692

Diogene. (n.d.). BrainyQuote.com. Retrieved from https://www.brainyquote.com/authors/diogenes-quotes

Dobrin, A. (2002). *Ethics for everyone: How to increase your moral intelligence.* Trade Paper Press.

Dutra, J. (2022, June 12). *What did Socrates, Plato, and Aristotle think about wisdom?* The Collector. Retrieved October 18, 2024, from https://www.thecollector.com/socrates-plato-aristotle-wisdom/

Feder Kittay, E. (2011). The ethics of care, dependence, and disability. *Ratio Juris, 24*(1), 49–58. https://doi.org/10.1111/j.1467-9337.2010.00473.x

Gilligan, C. (1982). *In a different voice: Psychological theory and women's development.* Harvard University Press.

Gottlieb, P. (2009). *The virtue of Aristotle's ethics.* Cambridge University Press. https://doi.org/10.1017/CBO9780511581526

Held, V. (2006). *The ethics of care: Personal, political, and global.* Oxford University Press.

Jacobs, R. M. (2023). Ethics education in the professions: Those who have taught and what they have taught. In D. C. Poff & A. C. Michalos (Eds.), *Encyclopedia of business and professional ethics* (pp. 825–829). Springer. https://doi.org/10.1007/978-3-030-22767-8_1187

Lalor, C. (2020). *Responsible leadership: developing the concept of leader character from a virtue ethics perspective* (Order No. 30703993). Available from ProQuest Dissertations & Theses Global. (2901483411). https://www.proquest.com/dissertations-theses/responsible-leadership-developing-concept-leader/docview/2901483411/se-2

MacIntyre, A. (2007). *After virtue* (3rd ed.). University of Notre Dame Press. (Original work published 1881)

Nietzsche, F. (1961). *Thus spoke Zarathustra: A book for everyone and no one.* (R. J. Hollingdale, Trans.), Penguin Classics. (Original work published 1883)

Nietzsche, F. (1997). *Beyond good and evil* (H. Zimmern, Trans.), Courier Dover Publications. (Original work published 1886)

Nussbaum, M. C. (1986). *The fragility of goodness: Luck and ethics in Greek tragedy and philosophy.* Cambridge University Press

Nussbaum, M. C. (2003). *Upheavals of thought: The intelligence of emotions.* Cambridge University Press

Piering, J. (n.d.). *Diogenes of Sinope (c. 404–323 B.C.E.).* The Internet Encyclopedia of Philosophy (IEP). Retrieved October 22, 2024, https://iep.utm.edu/diogenes-of-sinope/

Plato (2007). *The Republic* (D. Lee, Trans.). Penguin Classics. (Original work published c. 375 BC)

Plato. (n.d.). *BrainyQuote.com.* Retrieved October 22, 2024, from https://www.brainyquote.com/authors/plato-quotes

Rand, A. (1957). *Atlas shrugged.* Generic.

Rand, A. (1964). *The virtue of selfishness.* Penguin.

Rand, A. (n.d.) *BrainyQuote.com.* Retrieved from https://www.brainyquote.com/authors/ayn-rand-quotes#:~:text=Evil%20requires%20the%20sanction%20of%20the%20victim.&text=Ask%20yourself%20whether%20the%20dream,now%20and%20on%20this%20earth.

Sachs, J. (n.d.). *Aristotle ethics.* The Internet Encyclopedia of Philosophy (IEP). Retrieved October 22, 2024, from https://iep.utm.edu/virtue/

Skorupski, J. (2010). *The Routledge companion to ethics.* Routledge.

Smith, I. H., & Kouchaki, M. (2021). Ethical learning: the workplace as a moral laboratory for character development. *Social Issues and Policy Review, 15*(1), 277–322. https://doi.org/10.1111/sipr.12073

Socrates. (n.d.). BrainyQuote.com. Retrieved October 22, 2024, from https://www.brainyquote.com/search_results.html?q=socrates

Stocker, M. (2007). Shame and guilt: Self-interest and morality. In P. Bloomfield (Online Ed.), *Morality and self-interest* (pp. 287–304). Oxford Academic. https://doi.org/10.1093/acprof:oso/9780195305845.003.0015

Swanton, C. (2015). *The virtue ethics of Hume and Nietzsche.* John Wiley & Sons.

Taumaturgo, A. (2017, February 27). *Morality and the magician.* THAVMA: Catholic Occultism and Magic in General. Retrieved September 22, 2024, https://thavmapub.com/2017/02/27/morality-and-the-magician/

White, M. D. (2008). Why doesn't Batman kill the Joker? In M. D. White, R. Arp, & W. Irwin (Eds.), *Batman and philosophy: The dark knight of the soul* (pp. 5–16). John Wiley & Sons.

Wolf, S. (1982). Moral saints. *The Journal of Philosophy, 79*(8), 419–439. https://doi.org/10.2307/2026228

Chapter 5 Deontology
(Non-Consequentialism)

"Is there a universal moral rule that I ought to follow?"

Deontology (deon, "obligation, duty") is an absolutist approach to ethics that determines goodness or rightness of an act based on rules, obligations, and duties that one must adhere to. Rules, obligations, and duties may come from God, or the rights of others which stem from the social contracts of rational agents. What matters is the intent and your motive and whether you follow the rules or fulfill your duties, but not what happens. The motto of the deontological morality is to comply with the rules, honor obligations and duties, and respect one's own and others' rights.

Generally, rights and duties can be considered as the two sides of the same coin. One person's rights impose a duty on others to honor those rights. This seems to be the case if we think about the demands of justice, giving each person what is their due. But one can also consider ethical "duties" that go beyond justice (Kantian Ethics). A right is something you have an option to do or not do as you choose. You have a right to speak out against some proposed law that you think should not be mandated, or you can ignore it. Legally, you may have a legal right to keep and bear arms, but that is not required. A duty, on the other hand, is something you are either morally, or legally obligated to do, that you have no legal or moral choice to avoid. In this regard, to respect the rights of others is a duty.

Rights are split up into positive and negative rights (Spinello, 2020). Negative rights are rights that impose a duty of non-interference on others and refer to freedom from intervention by others in the exercise of certain rights which are defined by the social norms stems from the certain circumstances. Such rights are the right to freedom of speech, right to liberty, right to private property, right to bodily autonomy and privacy. So, from a duty theory perspective, the duty associated with negative rights assumes that people or institutions have a duty to refrain from interfering with the exercise of these rights. Positive rights are on the other hand, rights that impose a duty of action on others. Such rights are the right to health care, right to education, the right to a minimum standard of living and other similar services and assistance from others. Positive rights typically require active efforts from individuals or institutions to fulfill the rights of others. From a duty theory perspective, the duty associated with positive rights is often framed as a duty to provide or assist.

In deontological ethical framework, there are two approaches to ethics: *A rights-based approach and a duty-based approach.* Both incorporate deontological elements, in their emphasis on inherent rights, duties, and principles that guide individual and collective behavior, regardless of the consequences -even if these elements may conflict with other considerations (i.e., self-interest). *Duty-based ethics* focuses on the inherent moral obligations or duties that individuals have towards others or towards society as a whole. This means that ethical decisions are made with a sense of duty or responsibility. On the other hand, ethics emphasizes the importance of respecting and upholding the rights of individuals, which are often seen as fundamental and inalienable. So, a rights-based approach prioritizes the goal of protecting and promoting the rights of individuals. While both frameworks aim to guide ethical decision-making, they differ in their emphasis on either duties or rights as the primary basis for ethical action.

Questions to Ask (from a Deontological Standpoint)

As a deontologist, your ethical perspective is grounded in the belief that actions are morally right or wrong based on their adherence to moral rules, duties, or principles. Here are some important questions you might ask yourself when approaching moral dilemmas from a deontological standpoint:

- *What are my moral duties in this situation?* Begin by identifying the specific moral duties or principles that might be relevant to the situation you're facing.
- *Is there a rule that applies directly to this situation?* Consider whether there are established moral rules or guidelines that address the type of action or scenario you're encountering.
- *Am I treating individuals as ends or means?* Reflect on whether your actions respect the intrinsic value and dignity of individuals, rather than using them as mere instruments to achieve a goal.
- *What are my intentions behind this action?* Examine your motivations and intentions to ensure that they align with moral principles, as deontology places strong emphasis on the motives behind actions.
- *Are there conflicting duties?* If you perceive conflicting duties or principles, evaluate which duties take precedence and why.
- *Does this action respect rights?* Consider whether your action respects the rights of individuals involved, and whether these rights outweigh other considerations.

- *Would I want this action to be a universal rule?* Apply the "categorical imperative" test – consider whether the action you're contemplating could be turned into a universal rule without contradiction.
- *Could this action lead to a contradiction?* Think about whether the action you're considering could lead to a logical contradiction if everyone were to act similarly in similar circumstances.
- *Am I willing to accept the consequences of this action becoming a universal law?* Reflect on whether you'd be comfortable living in a world where everyone acted according to the same principle you're considering.
- *Does this action treat people fairly and impartially?* Assess whether your action treats all individuals involved fairly and without favoritism.
- *Is there a non-moral reason that justifies this action?* Consider whether there are non-moral factors influencing your decision and evaluate whether they can be justified within a deontological framework
- *Does this action uphold my ethical principles even if it leads to unfavorable outcomes?* Reflect on whether you're willing to prioritize the adherence to your moral principles even if it results in undesirable consequences.

By asking these questions, you can navigate moral dilemmas and make ethical decisions in accordance with your deontological principles and commitments.

Rights-Based Ethics, Contractarianism, the Social Contract Theory

In moral philosophy, contractarian ethics are usually considered as a type of deontology, because it examines the rightness of a behavior based on its conformity to rules and duties arising from the rights of others (Solum, 2024). According to this approach, morality is based on the social contact between rational agents (e.g., government and its citizens). This approach suggests that ethical action is an action that would not infringe on the rightful actions of others. Right-based ethics stems from the tradition of Thomas Hobbes and John Locke whose account is rooted on mutual self-interest and contractarianism (Ashford & Mulgan, 2018).

Thomas Hobbes (1588–1689) is a natural law theorist and a classical contractarian who has a rights-based approach to morality, yet he is also considered as teleologist because his work is rooted in the pursuit of certain outcomes or goals (i.e., self-interest). Hobbes is best known for his work "Leviathan (1651)" in which he outlines his social contract theory and the concept of the state of nature. Hobbes' Social Contract theory starts with the concept of a "state of nature" where he describes a society without rules and laws as living in a "state of nature" (McCartney, & Parent, 2015). He, then, challenges us to imagine how life would be without a government or similar institution that can provide security, order and primary goods and protect people's rights to property (McCartney, & Parent, 2015). He proposed that such a primitive state would create a "dog eat dog" society without the comforts and necessities that we take for granted in a civilized society In Hobbes' state of nature, while people would be completely free to pursue their own interests and desires, each person would also have to take care of herself, prevent the constant threats of others and resolve any conflicts by their own means (Hobbes, 1651/2016). For Hobbes, this would create violence and inconvenience, because the lack of law would mean that everyone would be their own judge in their own case, and disagreements would be resolved by violence (McCartney, & Parent, 2015). Hobbes (1651/2016) argued that because people are naturally selfish, violent, and untrustworthy, in such a primitive state, life would be Darwinian, where the strongest live and the weak die. People would be totally egoistic, violent, and brutal. They would lie, steal, or kill whenever it is in their best interest. And so no one would be able to produce and live safely and happily under the constant threats of others. Hobbes argued that people would plunge into chaos, and the resulting social catastrophe would make the world an insecure and dreadful place to live for everyone. It would make every-one miserable and serve nobody's interests (McCartney & Parent, 2015). In such a state, people would act on their own accord, without any sense of responsibility and as a consequence, in Hobbes's words, life in such a state of nature would be "solitary, poor, nasty, brutish, and short" due to the absence of a social order to enforce cooperation and prevent conflict. His proposed solution to this dilemma is the establishment of a social contract and a sovereign authority to ensure peace and security. Hobbes (1651/2016) argued that based on enlightened self-interest, the only wise thing to do "in a state of nature" would be to agree on the rules of a contract or bargain. Following the golden rule pattern, wanting their own property to be respected, rational egoists would agree to respect the property of others; wanting their own lives to be respected, they would agree to respect the lives of others. Succinctly, he appeals to self-interest to garner the obedience of people to the social contract. He thinks that the "desire for prosperity" or the "fear of violent death" are valuable tools to convince self-interested people to keep their word and secure their obedience to laws and rules (Harvey, 1998). Enlightened egoists would be fond of a golden-rule society because a golden-rule society would serve better to their self-interest than a "dog eat dog" society without any rules. Morality (as summed up in the golden rule) is, then born, as a social contract in order to further the interests of rational egoists and avoid the constant threats of social chaos. Thus, Hobbes (1651/2016) explicitly recognizes that violence and insecurity which characterizes the state of nature creates the motivation for individuals to enter into a social contract (Solum, 2024) and explains the source of the power of the state; the reason we agree to follow authority from the perspective of social-contract theory. Hobbe argued that the primary goal of this social contract is to achieve a stable and orderly society that minimizes conflict and maximizes individual security.

John Locke (1632–1704)'s perspective is somewhat different from Hobbes's when it comes to rights and ethics. For Hobbes, the primary right is the right to self-preservation, and individuals give up certain rights to ensure their safety in a civil society. Hobbes' view is more about a contractarian obligation for the sake of self-preservation, rather than a natural rights perspective. Locke's contractarianism, on the other hand, stresses the importance of human dignity and the ability to choose freely how to live a life. Locke was a right ethicist and a classical contractarian who defended liberty rights and thus called libertarian. He believed that legitimate governments should be formed to secure the inherent rights of individuals and protect their interests. According to Locke, there are three cores of liberalism: (1) Moral core which secures the inherent rights of humans such as the right to live a dignified life (Locke, 1689/2018). (2) Economic core which protects the rights and freedoms of individuals to produce, to consume, to freely enter into contractual agreements, to own property, engage in market transactions and to dispose of their property and labor as they see fit; and lastly (3) Political core which ensures the right to vote, right to participate in governance, right to decide what kind of policies to support, and to be informed truthfully about matters affecting their choices (Locke, 1689/2018). Locke's philosophy of natural rights, including life, liberty, and property, is grounded in the idea that these rights are fundamental (not contingent on the outcomes they may produce) and intrinsic to human beings and should be respected and protected by society and limited government, regardless of the potential outcomes. Therefore, Locke's libertarian ethics which focuses on adhering to principles and duties that guide ethical behavior regardless of the potential consequences (Macpherson, 1980) aligns more with deontological ethics than Hobbes' interest-based contractarianism. Locke (1689/2018) often highlights individual autonomy and embrace the Kant's famous notion of "treating others as ends in themselves, rather than as means to an end". He believed that government's role is to protect these rights, and if it fails to do so, individuals have a duty to resist or overthrow that government (Locke, 1689/2018). According to his theory, social contract ensures others respect our choices as free and rational people as long as we respect others in the same way.

Thomas Hill Green (1836–1882), a British philosopher in the late 19th century and other philosophers who followed, on the other hand, argued that individuals have not only negative rights that protect them from interference but also positive rights to truly exercise their freedom, to live a meaningful, a dignified and fulfilling life and realize their potential (Nettleship, 2011). He rejected the notion that individual rights are solely about protecting individuals from interference and argued that society should actively promote the welfare and ensure the well-being of its members within the context of a just and equitable society (Nettleship, 2011). Green's ideas laid the foundation for modern discussions about positive rights and the role of government in securing those rights. This perspective emphasizes that society has a moral obligation to provide conditions that allow individuals to flourish and exercise their autonomy effectively.

John Rawls (1921–2002) is the most influential contemporary contractarian who emphasizes the importance of principles, rights, and duties as the foundation for ethical decision-making. Rawls (1999) introduces the concept of the "original position" and the "veil of ignorance," where individuals in a hypothetical society make decisions about principles of justice without knowing their own positions or characteristics in that society. This approach is meant to ensure fairness and impartiality, as *it ensures that* individuals are not biased by their own advantages or disadvantages. The principles of justice that emerge from this process are seen as binding and non-negotiable deontological moral rules. Rawls' theory is commonly referred to as "justice as fairness" and focuses on principles of distributive justice within a social contract framework. Rawls (1999) had us imagine a hypothetical choice situation and asks us to choose principles of justice behind a "veil of ignorance" that masks the identities and other attributes of people to ensure that the choice situation is fair, and no one is unfairly advantaged or disadvantaged because of these attributes. He describes this hypothetical choice situation as "the original position" and defends that only under a "veil of ignorance" we can produce a "fair" and "impartial" agreement (contract) to regulate the basic structure of a society as true equals not biased by their place in society (Rawls, 1999). To sum up, Rawls (1999) reinvented Social Contract Theory by devising a procedure to ensure equality and justice for all the parties participating in a social contract. This procedure aiming to eliminate issues regarding tacit consent and disputes over the contract consists of the following three steps. The first step involves determining your contingent characteristics -physical, psychological, intellectual, cultural, and social characteristics- which may give you an unfair advantage or disadvantage in life. The second step is to urge us to think of an unbiased "original position" (a condition of not yet knowing your own personal contingent characteristics). And finally, the last step urges us to consider what moral and legal rules we would agree to in a state of ignorance (Rawl's veil of ignorance), to protect your primary goods (e.g., access to health care and education); to secure your rights to liberty (e.g., freedom to pursue your own interests within acceptable limitations); and opportunity to possess secondary wants through your own efforts (e.g., wealth). Rawls (1999) argued that by following the above procedure, people would ultimately agree on the two "principles of justice" (famously known as *Rawls' Principles of Justice*) -Liberty principle and Fairness principle:

> *Liberty principle* (also known as fully adequate principle). This principle ensures that each person can claim and possess a "fully adequate" number of basic rights to liberty (such as right to freedom of speech, right to private property, right to bodily autonomy and privacy, right to free assembly, right to freedom of religion, right to be safe from harm and injury, etc.) as long as these claims do not breach the same rights of others (Rawls, 1999).
>
> *Fairness principle* (also known as the difference principle). This principle is about the fair equality of opportunities and consists of two sub-principles. According to this principle, first, any differences (social or economic) must be the result of positions that everyone has a fair and equal chance to attain (Equal opportunity principle), and second, any inequalities in the allocation of the "primary goods" must be the result of governments' affirmative action to favor the least-advantaged members of society (Quinn, 2008).

Duty-Based (Obligation-Based) Ethics and Contractualism

Contractualism has its roots in Rousseau, but it is most strongly associated with Kant. While Rousseau vs Hobbesian self-interest-based ethics (contractarianism) is based on the idea of a self-interested contract between rational egoists for the sake of individual self-interest; traditional morality-based ethics (contractualism) like Kantian contractualism is based on the duties and the idea of a morally constrained agreement among people who consider themselves and one another as free and equal human beings worthy of respect (Southwood, 2011). It is important to note that Rawls distinguishes between "contractualist" or "contractarian" theories (Stark, 2009). While "contractarianism" focuses on rights and self-interest based on the notion of law, "contractualism" focuses on duties and justifiability of an act on moral grounds (Stark, 2009). A contractarian justification for obedience to laws and rights of others is the best interest of everyone and motivation for contacts is merely strategic and instrumental because it enables individuals to get others to do what serves to their best interests (Stark,

2009). Whereas contractualist theories argue that each rational person would agree on the contracts because they are morally motivated by an intrinsic desire to justify themselves to others other and this desire does not stem from the pure self-interest but care for one another (Stark, 2009).

Jean-Jacques Rousseau (1712-1778) believed that individuals have a duty to uphold and follow the general will, and the social contract is the embodiment of individuals collective fundamental duty in order to achieve the common good and collective interests (1762/1913), This duty is an obligation to act in a way that contributes to the well-being and harmony of the community as a whole and is grounded in the moral principles of civic virtue (1762/1913). Instead of putting an emphasis on rights, he puts an emphasis on the duties incurred by the social contract. He emphasized the importance of social contracts where individuals participate in a community in order to adhere to the general will as a fundamental duty and the fact that individuals both gain rights and incur duties toward the community and its laws.

According to Rousseau (1762/1913), in an ideal society, no one is above the rules. He also advocates separation of powers as it prevents the government from enacting bad rules. His ideas on citizenship rights, and duties (i.e., taxing, soldiering) are intertwined with his vision of a just and harmonious society based on the common good. Rousseau's focus on the general will and the duty to the community aligns with deontological ethics, because it suggests that individuals have a duty to prioritize the well-being of the community (i.e., common good and the collective interests) over their individual interests. General will, according to Rousseau, is a moral duty that individuals should uphold irrespective of the potential outcomes -even if it might not always lead to personal advantage.

Immanuel Kant (1724-1804) is one of the most popular duty ethicists and a contractualists in the deontological moral philosophy who put the concept of categorical imperative at the heart of his philosophy. Categorical imperative is a rule of conduct which applies to all people unconditionally and absolutely, meaning that the validity or claim of it does not change depending on any person's desire, attributes, or interest. Kant expresses the motto of categorical imperative as acting in such a way that we would want others to act in a similar manner in similar circumstances towards everyone. Kant (1873/2010) advocated that if everyone were to follow the categorical imperative, then we could have a genuinely moral system, because then moral decisions would be made impartially and fairly as the exact same rules would be applicable universally to all individuals with no discrimination (Sullivan, 1994). It's an absolutist view upholding the idea that right is right and must always be done, regardless of the circumstances. It suggests that our actions are morally right only if we can apply them universally with no exceptions. The categorical imperative can tell us which actions are morally permissible and prohibited. Kant suggests using three maxims to test whether an act is right or violates the categorical imperative.

1. *Maxim of Universalizability/impartiality:* We should treat all people as free and equal to ourselves and be willing to have everyone act as we do. According to Kant, an action is morally permissible if its maxim could be willed as a universal law by everyone without contradiction (Sloan, 2018).
2. *Maxim of Human Dignity:* Respecting human dignity is the fundamental duty. For Kant, all duties derive from one fundamental duty which is "respect to human dignity" meaning that respecting people's autonomy and rights. According to Kant, humans are always ends in themselves, and not means to ends, thus, in Kant's view, unlike Machiavelli, "ends" do not justify the "means" (Sloan, 2018). Consequently, we always need to act in ways to treat humanity as ends in themselves, never as a means (Mizzoni, 2010).
3. *Maxim of Autonomy:* humans are rational, autonomous agents. So, act by your own rationality, do not let others interfere with your judgement.

Kant argued that moral principles should be grounded in the concept of duty or obligation. For Kant, morality is not about the outcome of an act or the pursuit of happiness, it is all about acting in accordance with universalizable principles that are based on rationality and the inherent worth of human beings. Kant argued that good outcomes may be produced by an accident from an action that intended to cause harm, and bad outcomes may result from an innocent act that was well-intended. He claims, a person who has goodwill is morally right when he "acts out of duty", because he considers he has a duty to do even though bad consequences come out of his act. So, Kant argued that the only thing that is truly and absolutely good is goodwill regardless of the consequences, and goodwill is only good when the person freely prefers to do something out of his/her "respect" for the rule or law (Sullivan, 1994). Thus, for Kant, the only factor which determines whether an act is morally right the intent of the person performing that act (Mizzoni, 2010). If the intent is not right, then the act is not right, even if some good outcomes come out of it. Whatever the moral law commands are, they must be executed regardless of the consequences.

In Kantian ethics, moral actions are guided by the categorical imperative, which are rooted in principles of autonomy, duty, and rationality. Kant valued motivation to fulfill the duty over the potential consequences of actions (Sullivan, 1994). Acting and living morally must be done because of a commitment to duties. Moral worth carries out a crucial role in Kantian duty-ethics. According to Kantian ethics, only actions done for the "duty's sake" have moral worth. An action has a moral worth if it is done out of respect for the duty, not out of "vain glory", not because one is so inclined to do so, or the "avoidance of punishment" (Sullivan, 1994). The prospect of rewards (such as heaven) or punishments (such as hell) typically does not play a direct role in Kant's ethical framework. Kant's emphasis is on acting out of respect for moral principles rather than acting to attain personal gain or avoid punishment (Sullivan, 1994). The idea of acting morally solely to avoid punishment or to gain rewards could potentially conflict with Kant's principles. Kant's philosophy prioritizes the motive behind an action, and he argues that actions motivated by self-interest or external rewards are not genuinely moral. For Kant moral actions should be guided by goodwill - the intention to act in accordance with duty and moral principles, irrespective of personal gain or consequences (Sullivan, 1994). In this sense, Kantian ethics encourages individuals to act in a way that respects the dignity and autonomy of themselves and others, rather than being driven by desires for reward or fear of punishment. The moral worth of an action is derived from its conformity to the moral law, as determined by reason (Kant, 1873/2010), rather than from external factors like potential rewards or punishments in an afterlife. Succinctly, the moral worth of an action cannot be determined by the 'act' itself but by the 'motive' (Kant, 1873/2010). Kant argued that to be morally praiseworthy one must carry out an action for the right reasons (Sullivan, 1994).

William David Ross (1877–1971) does not agree with Kant who centered his ethical theory around a single fundamental principle which he called the categorical imperative (Simpson, n.d.). As opposed to Kant's monistic deontology, Ross believed in a plurality of prima facie duties (Ross's deontological pluralism), and he contended that determining what is right and what is wrong is not an easy and straightforward job (Simpson, n.d.). According to Ross (1930/2002), in some situations we may experience a moral dilemma where we may have more than one duty and the requirements of one duty may violate the demands of another duty. In such a situation (i.e., when we are faced with a moral dilemma) our common sense may tell us that one duty (e.g., helping someone in emergent need) may be "more of a duty" than another duty (e.g., fulfilling a promise). Ross (1930/2002) argues that moral dilemmas need to be judged based on their specific conditions and deserve case-by-case attention. Thus, whenever we are confronted by a moral dilemma in which more than one prima facie duty applies, we must "study the situation as fully as we can until I determine the 'a duty proper'".

In order to solve moral dilemmas, Ross (1930/2002) introduces us to the concepts of "prima facie duties" and "absolute duty" by highlighting the distinction between these two concepts. Ross (1930/2002) conceptualizes a prima facie duty as a duty that is binding under normal circumstances but can be overridden by other, more pressing duties in certain situations. Ross (1930/2002) put forwards the idea that prima facie duties are general principles whose validity is self-evident and intuitive but also "conditional because virtue of fulfilling a certain duty might be more important than the virtue of fulfilling another depending on the circumstances. "Prima facie duties" are also called "conditional duties". Absolute duty (a duty proper or actual duty), on the other hand, refers to a specific moral obligation that applies to a particular situation. Unlike prima facie duties, which are general moral principles that guide ethical behavior across various contexts, absolute duties are context-specific and require careful evaluation on a case-by-case basis. Simply, it is our duty to find and determine what our absolute duty is in every single case. It must be noted that absolute duty can only be singled out when we take every single factor into account, "prima facie duties", on the other hand, are just the general duties people are supposed to fulfill in general without taking all considerations into account.

Ross argues that some prima facie duties arise from our own prior actions, such as the duty to fulfill our promises or duty to make up for our previous wrongful actions (Simpson, n.d.). Some others stem from the previous actions of others such as the duty to return the favors done by others (Simpson, n.d.). Other duties are the duty of nonmaleficence (duty to not to hurt others), the duty of beneficence, the duty of self-improvement and the duty of justice (duty to allocate benefits and burdens fairly, prevent any mismatch in this regard and correct it in case it happens) (Ross, 1930/2002).

Criticisms of Rights-Based and Duty-Based Ethics

1. *Minimalist Approach towards Morality.* One main criticism of the rights-based and duty-based approach is that it has a minimalist approach towards morality and gives us a very narrow conception of it (Kapoor, 2019). It provides a minimalist framework because it does not necessarily promote the values of a maximalist morality such as compassion, mercy, benevolence, solidarity, and community and assumes that individuals are obliged to behave morally only when there is a contract in place or when it is their duty to do so. So, when there is no explicit contract between the agents then it means that there is no moral obligation other than refraining yourself from causing harm to others and from infringing on the rights of others.

2. *Lack of Guidance in Dilemmas:* Rights-based ethics or duty-based ethics may not provide clear guidance on how to prioritize conflicting rights conflicting duties or resolve ethical dilemmas where duties and/or rights compete

with each other. Right-based ethics may often prioritize the protection and promotion of individual rights at the expense of larger groups or society as a whole without sufficient consideration of substantive rights or the underlying conditions necessary for individuals to truly exercise their rights. Likewise, duty-based ethics may struggle to provide clear guidance in morally ambiguous or gray areas.

3. *Absolutism and Exceptionless Rules:* Some critics argue against the absolutist nature of duty-based ethics, particularly when it involves exceptionless rules. They contend that there might be situations where exceptions are morally justified, and a more nuanced approach is needed.

4. *Rigidity and Inflexibility:* Critics caution that a strict adherence to duty-based ethics might lead to dogmatism, where individuals blindly follow rules without considering the context or the specific circumstances of a situation. One of the main criticisms is that duty-based ethics can be rigid and inflexible. Critics argue that adhering strictly to moral duties may lead to morally questionable outcomes in certain situations, where a more flexible approach might be more appropriate.

5. *Neglect of Consequences:* Critics often point out that a strict adherence to duty-based ethics or rights-based ethics may neglect the importance of potential consequences of actions in ethical decision-making. In situations where following a duty or respecting rights leads to harmful outcomes, critics contend that a consequentialist approach might be more appropriate.

6. *Vagueness and Ambiguity of Rights:* The definitions and boundaries of rights can sometimes be vague and open to interpretation. Critics argue that this ambiguity may make it difficult to apply rights-based ethics consistently.

7. *Emphasis on Motivation:* Kantian deontology places a significant emphasis on the motivation behind actions. Critics argue that this focus on motivation might be too demanding and that it may not be feasible or necessary to consistently act from a sense of duty in every situation.

8. *Practicality and Everyday Decision-Making:* Some critics contend that duty-based ethics may be impractical for everyday decision-making. The strict adherence to moral duties might not align with the complexities and nuances of real-life situations.

9. *Individualism vs. Communitarian Critique:* Some critics argue that rights-based ethics, especially in its individualistic forms, may not adequately address the importance of community and communal values. Communitarian perspectives emphasize the interdependence of individuals and the role of community in shaping ethical norms.

10. *Cultural Variability Critique*: Critics argue that duty-based ethics might not adequately account for cultural variations in moral values. Different cultures may have diverse perspectives on what constitutes moral duties, and a universal approach might not be applicable.

It's important to note that these criticisms do not negate the value of duty-based or right-based ethics, but rather highlight areas where the framework may face challenges or require careful consideration and refinement. Different ethical frameworks have their strengths and weaknesses, and ongoing philosophical debates explore how to navigate these complexities in ethical decision-making.

References

Ashford, E., & Mulgan, T. (2018). *Contractualism*. The Stanford Encyclopedia of Philosophy (E. N. Zalta, Ed.). Retrieved February 1, 2024, from https://plato.stanford.edu/archives/sum2018/entries/contractualism/

Harvey, M. T. (1998). *Hobbes's deontological science of morals* (Publication No. 9830720) [Doctoral dissertation, New York University]. ProQuest Dissertations & Theses Global. https://www.proquest.com/dissertations-theses/hobbess-deontological-science-morals/docview/304426969/se-2

Hobbes, T. (2016). *Leviathan*. CreateSpace Independent Publishing Platform. (Original work published 1651)

Kant, I. (2010). *Kant's theory of ethics: Or practical philosophy* (T. K. Abbott, Trans.). Kessinger Publishing. (Original work published 1873)

Kapoor, R. (2019). What is wrong with a rights-based approach to morality? *Journal of National Law University Delhi, 6*(1), 1–11. https://doi.org/10.1177/2277401719870004

Locke, J. (2018). *Two treaties of government*. Forgotten Books. (Original work published 1689)

Macpherson, C. B. (1980). *Second treatise of government*. Hackett Publishing.

McCartney, S., & Parent, R. (2015). *Ethics in law enforcement*. BCcampus. https://opentextbc.ca/ethicsinlawenforcement/chapter/social-contract-theory/

Mizzoni J. (2010). *Ethics: The basics*. Wiley-Blackwell.

Nettleship, R. L. (2011). *Works of Thomas Hill Green*. Cambridge University Press.

Quinn, M. J. (2008). *Ethic for the information age* (3rd ed.). Addison Wesley.

Rawls, J. (1999). *A theory of justice* (2nd Ed.). Belknap Press.

Ross (2002). *The right and the good* (P. Stratton-Lake, Ed.). Oxford University Press. (Original work published 1930)

Rousseau, J. J. (1913). *On the social contract* (G. D. H. Cole, Trans.). Chump Change. (Original work published 1762)

Simpson, D. L. (n.d.). *William David Ross (1877–1971)*. The Internet Encyclopedia of Philosophy (IEP). Retrieved March 8, 2024, https://iep.utm.edu/virtue/

Sloan, J. J. (2018). *Criminal justice ethics: A framework for analysis*. Oxford University Press.

Solum, L. B. (2024, January 14). *Contractarianism, contractualism, and social contract*. Legal Theory Lexicon. https://lsolum.typepad.com/legal_theory_lexicon/2006/09/contractarianis.html

Southwood, N. (2011). Introduction: Contractualism and the foundations of morality (Online ed.). Oxford Academic. https://doi.org/10.1093/acprof:oso/9780199539659.003.0001

Spinello, R. A. (2020). *Business ethics: Contemporary issues and cases*. Sage Publications

Stark, C. A. (2009). Contractarianism and cooperation. *Politics, Philosophy & Economics, 8*(1), 73–99. https://doi.org/10.1177/1470594X08098872

Sullivan, R. J. (1994). *An introduction to Kant's ethics*. Cambridge University Press.

Chapter 6 Teleology (Consequentialism)

"How am I supposed to choose the course of action more likely to result in the best outcome? Are there morally relevant differences between potential outcomes of my action?"

Teleological ethics (Consequentialism) suggests that the moral worth or rightness of an action is determined by the goodness, desirability, or utility of its outcomes (Chen, 2021). In other words, consequentialist theories focus on the ends or outcomes that result from an action rather than the intentions behind it or adherence to moral rules or principles (Bulley et al., 2022). The central idea is that actions are morally right if they produce good outcomes or consequences, such as happiness, pleasure, well-being, or the realization of certain values (Downie, 1987). Both ethical egoism and utilitarianism can be considered under teleological ethics. Consequentialist theories emphasize the idea that what matters most in ethics is the overall result that an action produces. This result can be positive (promoting well-being, happiness) or negative (causing harm, suffering). Consequentialism doesn't prescribe a specific moral principle, but it rather provides a general approach to evaluating actions based on their outcomes.

The most well-known form of teleology is utilitarianism, asserts that the morality of actions is assessed based on their capacity to produce maximum level of happiness or well-being for everyone affected by the action, often referred to as the "greatest good for the greatest number." The other form of consequentialism, on the other hand, is ethical egoism which advocates that we ought to do whatever most promotes our own individual good, regardless of how this affects others. The third form of consequentialism is ethical hedonism which declares that pleasure, or the absence of pain, is the most essential factor to determine the rightness or wrongness of a potential course of action. It is important to note that while utilitarianism is agent-neutral and it takes the interests of every stakeholder affected by the action into account, ethical egoism and ethical hedonism is merely concerned with the agent's (decision-maker's) interest or pleasure. Succinctly, while ethical egoism and egoistical hedonism focus on the individual itself, utilitarianism focuses on all the stakeholders involved in the dilemma. More specifically, utilitarianism focuses on the collective happiness; egoistical hedonism, on the other hand, focuses on individual happiness; and egoistical egoism focuses on the individual's self-interests and prioritizes self-serving acts (Sidgwick, 1894). While utilitarianism is concerned with what will make everyone better off, ethical egoism and egoistical egoism are not. In other words, the main difference between them lies over "whom happiness" is for. For utilitarians, it's for everyone affected by the act impartially. For ethical egoists, it's strictly for the person acting. The main similarity between them is their core moral value (i.e., self-interest and utility) and the second similarity is that they both uphold the idea that your own utility is valuable although in varying degrees (while it is an absolute value in ethical egoism and a relative one in the other) (Sidgwick, 1874/2010). This core is entirely different from pure altruism which states that only working for the benefit of others is morally worthwhile. Unlike utilitarianism, the term "ethical egoism" does not specify what the ultimate good is, it just holds that self-interest should be the central principle in determining morality of a potential course of action, but it does not clarify exactly what is it in our self-interest. Utilitarianism, on the other hand, holds that happiness, pleasure and well-being should be at the center of our search for ultimate good, making utilitarianism clearly hedonistic. While ethical egoism is solely concerned with the individual self-interest and agent-focused, utilitarianism differs from egoism claiming that your own interest is no more valuable than anyone else's. In other words, ethical egoism argues that only and only your own hedonistic utility (happiness, pleasure, good) matters ultimately, or at least matters more than any other's. For utilitarianism, on the other hand, everyone's utility matters equally.

So, all things being equal, a utilitarian moral system would say that you have an obligation to make a sacrifice to help someone so long as it helps them more than it hurts you. An example would be buying someone who is starving food rather than purchasing a luxury item for yourself. An egoist philosophy, on the other hand, would say that you have no obligation to anyone but yourself. So, you have no obligation to help others unless you derive more enjoyment from doing so than from helping yourself. Succinctly, ethical egoism is the principle that only your own interests are of moral worth. Utilitarianism on the other hand claims that the relative utility of any action must be judged carefully as everyone's utility has a moral worth.

Questions to Ask (from a Teleological Standpoint)

As a teleologist, your ethical perspective is centered around the idea that the morality of actions is determined by their outcomes or consequences. Here are some important questions you might ask yourself when approaching moral dilemmas from a teleological standpoint:

- *What are the potential outcomes of this action?* Begin by considering the various possible consequences that might result from the action you're contemplating.
- *Which outcome maximizes overall well-being or goodness?* Evaluate the outcomes to determine which one would lead to the greatest overall well-being, happiness, or goodness for the individuals affected.
- *Are there positive and negative consequences to consider?* Think about both positive and negative outcomes of your action and weigh their significance.
- *Who will be affected by this action?* Consider the individuals or groups who will be impacted by your decision and how the consequences might affect them.
- *Does this action promote the greatest good for the greatest number?* Apply the principle of utilitarianism, which suggests choosing actions that result in the greatest aggregate happiness or well-being.
- *Are there any unintended consequences to be aware of?* Reflect on whether there might be unforeseen or unintended consequences that could arise from your action.
- *Could this action lead to long-term benefits or harm?* Consider not only the immediate consequences but also the potential long-term effects of your action.
- *Does this action respect individual rights and autonomy?* Examine whether your action respects the rights and autonomy of individuals, as some teleological perspectives also consider individual rights.
- *Is it ethical to use people as a means to an end?* Reflect on whether your action treats individuals as mere instruments to achieve an outcome, and whether this is ethically justifiable.
- *Is there a morally relevant difference between available options?* Compare different courses of action and their outcomes to determine if one option stands out as morally superior.
- *Are there trade-offs between different values or goals?* Reflect on situations where different values or goals might come into conflict and evaluate which outcomes should be prioritized.

By asking these questions, you can navigate moral dilemmas and make ethical decisions in accordance with your teleological principles, focusing on achieving the best overall outcomes.

Egoistical Hedonism (for the Agent)

Hedonism is a type of consequentialism and mostly related to the ancient Greek philosopher Epicurus who advocates that every pain is bad and should be avoided, and every pleasure is good and should be preferred, so all our actions should aim to minimize pain and maximize pleasure (Broad, 2012). Hedonists believe that pleasure, or the absence of pain, is the focal point of ultimate good (Crisp, 2006).

Ethical hedonism has two main forms. Egotistical hedonism which suggests that one should merely watch out for pleasure of his or her own in determining the morality of the course chosen and altruistic hedonism which proposes that one should always consider not only the pleasure of his or her own but also the pleasure of *all* affected by the action when making choices (Zweig, 1971). Regardless of the type of hedonism, critics think that hedonism is flawed as a guide for morality because it does not take other values into consideration, such as justice in determining the course of a right action. Another critic for hedonism is that if we were to single-mindedly pursue happiness, we would never achieve it as it would vanish instantly from the sight (The Paradox of Hedonism) (Butler, 2009), because pleasure can be derived as a result of satisfying a desire for something else such as a desire for a sport, art, music, intellectual curiosity, achievement in politics or a job (Feinberg, 1999).

Ethical Egoism (for the Agent)

The theory of ethical egoism argues that morality should be guided entirely by self-interest. It also claims that it is always moral to act in ways to promote one's self-interest, and it is never moral to sacrifice one's own interests to meet those of others. In other words, ethical egoism states that the only morally correct act is the one that results in our own self-interest and that, not by acting in our own self-interest, is always immoral. According to ethical egoism, promoting one's own good should always be the overarching goal of a person and failing to do so should be considered immoral. To put it another way, it is never moral and always immoral not to pursue one's own interest. For example, according to Rand (1957), failing to pursue one's own good may lead to one's own self-destruction and serve the evil purposes of the evilest. So according to Rand, 1964, we ought to do whatever most promotes our own individual good, regardless of how this affects others and that doing so is morally the only right thing to do. Ethical egoism presumes that self-interest defines what is good or right. It is strictly opposed to altruism (beneficence to others), and universalism (the interests of all).

Although ethical egoism is often confused with psychological egoism or used interchangeably, they are fundamentally different. While ethical egoism seeks to prescribe what individuals ought to do, psychological egoism is just an empirical claim that describes and explains what individuals actually do (May, n.d.). Thus, psychological egoism is not a prescription about what ought to be but a theory about psychological facts. It refers to the idea that on a deep-down level, all our behavior is explainable by our desire to achieve what we believe is our greatest good (Baier, 1991). All human beings are naturally selfish, and this is our undeniable nature and simply who we truly are. Thus, psychological egoism suggests that individuals always act in their own self-interest, and it is just the inevitable end. It simply advocates that the pursuit of one's self-interest is the most natural and primitive motive of all humans, and therefore inevitable. They believe that since we are naturally built to pursue our own desires and our own self-interests, it is simply absurd and pointless to deny or fight against our true egoistic nature. Ethical egoists argue that even actions that appear altruistic could be interpreted as ultimately benefiting the individual in some way (Kao, 2017). It is common that we deceive ourselves into thinking that our motives are not selfish when in fact they are (Corcoran & Bennett, 2015). It's important to note that ethical egoism does not inherently reject altruistic actions. Rather, it suggests that actions are justified when they serve one's own self-interest, thus altruistic actions are justifiable as long as it is a calculated choice that aligns with one's own well-being, either in the short term or as part of a broader strategy for personal success.

Psychological egoism argues that the golden rule is not aligned with human nature and requires us to act against our true nature. So psychological egoism tells us that we are all guided entirely by self-interest, even if we appear to be acting with altruistic motives (Feinberg, 1999). Suppose you see a person drowning in a lake. According to psychological egoism, your immediate reaction might be to jump into the lake and save the person, but it also claims that this action is not motivated by altruism but by your own self-interest. Because witnessing someone drowning can make you feel overwhelmed by stress that you may feel compelled to jump into the lake to save the person so to relieve your own distress. In other words, you are acting in a way that makes you feel better, regardless of the benefit of the person in the water. In contrast, ethical egoism would argue that jumping into the river to save the drowning person is not only natural, but also morally right if it is going to benefit you by alleviating your discomfort even if it does not benefit the drowning person.

The primary tenet of ethical egoism is that "things that are good for you are good, period, purely and wholly". However, this is a bit extreme. It's sure to reduce altruistic actions which lead to a happy and cohesive society. At least to most people's personal sensibilities, this notion is distasteful. Furthermore, the pragmatic effect of adopting such a philosophy would be costly if enough other people within the society adopt the same philosophy. Maintaining the belief that it is right for each person to promote his or her own interests, even if this would bring about worse consequences for everyone including to one's own self is collectively self-defeating (Parfit, 1984).

Utilitarianism (for Everyone Affected)

Utilitarianism is a social welfare ethic which concerns maximizing pleasure for the greatest number of people (Hardin, 2001). Utilitarians believe that the moral worth of an action is determined solely by its ability to create the greatest net benefit (in terms of the amount of happiness or pleasure it creates) (Felzmann, 2017). Although it is most often confused with ethical egoism, unlike ethical egoists they do not agree to the claim that acts which benefit others at one's own expense are immoral, they just endorse acting in ways that one perceives to be in one's own self-interest.

John Stuart Mill, Jeremy Bentham and Peter Singer are three influential philosophers that are most closely associated with utilitarianism. Table 3 shows the main differences between their approaches to utilitarianism.

Table 3. Comparison of Main Versions of Utilitarianism

Act-utilitarianism (Bentham)	Rule-utilitarianism (Mill)	Preference-utilitarianism (Singer)
Focus on the morality of each individual action and the specific consequences of each individual act separately, rather than following general rules or principles.	Focus on the overall utility or happiness that would result from everyone following a particular rule in similar situations.	Focus on satisfying as many of the first preferences of people as possible to maximize happiness.
This calculation does not consider the long-term effects and has short-term orientation.	This calculation considers the long-term effects and general tendencies of adhering to the rules, rather than the specific consequences of each individual act.	Actions are considered morally right if they lead to the greatest overall fulfillment of individuals' preferences.

Act Utilitarianism

"It is vain to talk of the interest of the community, without understanding what the interest of the individual is."
Bentham, Brainy Quotes

Jeremy Bentham (1748–1832) is an English philosopher who laid the groundwork for the development of utilitarian ethical theories. Bentham (1781/1996) believed that people are naturally hedonistic; hence strive to maximize their self-interest and pleasure and avoid pain. Bentham's version of utilitarianism is often referred to as "act utilitarianism" or "quantitative utilitarianism". Act-utilitarianism is case-specific calculation which holds the primacy of case over general rules. Accordingly, if killing a person or cheating leads to better consequences, it may be better!

He advocated that the moral worth of actions could be measured based on the quantity of pleasure, happiness, or pain they produced, and the actions that lead to a greater overall balance of pleasure over pain (Hewitt, 2010) should be considered morally right, while those that result in more pain than pleasure should be deemed morally wrong. As a method for determining and quantifying the pleasure and pain, he also introduced us to the concept of "hedonistic/felicific calculus". This calculus consists of various factors like intensity, duration, certainty, propinquity, fecundity, purity, and extent.

1. *Intensity* is concerned with the level of pleasure or pain. Higher intensity contributes to a greater overall utility.
2. *Duration* is concerned with the length of time that the pleasure or pain is likely to last. The longer the pleasure and shorter the pain is better for the overall greater utility.
3. *Certainty* is concerned with the likelihood of pleasure or pain. When the pleasure is more likely and the pain is less likely, it is better for the overall greater utility.
4. *Propinquity* is concerned with the remoteness of pain or pleasure. Immediate pleasure or delayed pain is often considered more valuable for the overall greater utility than the delayed ones.
5. *Fecundity* is concerned with the likelihood that the action resulting in pleasure or pain will lead to more of the same kind in the future. Actions with high fecundity in pleasure and actions with low fecundity in pain are more likely to contribute to overall utility.
6. *Purity* is concerned with the likelihood that action resulting in pleasure or pain will not be followed by sensations of the opposite kind in the future.

Actions that bring about pleasure are better when purer, and actions that bring about pain are worse when purer for the overall utility.

7. *Extent* is concerned with the number of people affected. A greater number of people affected by pleasure is better, whereas a lesser number of people affected by pain is better for a higher overall utility.

Bentham suggested that individuals should consider each of these factors when evaluating the morality of an action (Troyer, 2003). According to Bentham, by assigning weights or values to each factor, individuals can theoretically calculate the overall pleasure and pain produced by an action and compare it to alternative actions (Troyer, 2003).

Bentham (1781/1996) argued that people in general have been inclined to behave well only when it is made plain to them that "there is something in it for them" and more interested in avoiding blame and punishment for the wrong action than pursuing right action for pleasure and self-interest (see loss aversion). According to Bentham (1781/1996), moral education should start with the assumption that humans are more interested in avoiding wrong actions than pursuing right actions and utilize what Bentham calls the "sanctions of pleasure and pain". As a social reformer, he concluded that if a crime is left unpunished it does not only cause harm to the victim, but everyone by endangering the stability of society. So just like Hobbes, he suggested severe punishments for the rule-breakers (legal penaties) and applied this principle to the laws concerning crime and punishment in England. It is also important to note that recent Hobbesians such as Brandt (1959) argues that apart from legal penalties society needs to make rule-breakers suffer with alienation and social disapproval; and rule-followers should be praised and made to feel good about themselves. These sanctions assure that it's in everyone's best interest to follow the rules and not to violate the golden rule.

Rule Utilitarianism

> *"War is an ugly thing, but not the ugliest of things: the decayed and degraded state of moral and patriotic feeling which thinks that nothing is worth a war, is much worse. "*
>
> Mill, Brainy Quotes

John Stuart Mill (1806–1873) is an 19th-century British philosopher, and social reformer who made considerable contributions into the fields of utilitarian ethics. Mill made modifications and refinements to address some of the criticisms and limitations associated with Bentham's approach. While Bentham focused on evaluating individual actions, Mill introduced the concept of "rule utilitarianism." Rule-utilitarianism holds the primacy of general rules over case-specific acts. According to this approach, instead of assessing each action's consequences, one should follow general rules of conduct that, if universally accepted, would produce the greatest overall happiness. Rule utilitarianism helps address the complexities of decision-making and avoids the constant calculation of consequences for each action (Baier, 1991). He believed that actions should be guided by general rules that, if followed consistently, would produce the greatest overall happiness for everyone. This approach focuses on the general consequences of adhering to certain rules rather than the specific consequences of each individual act.

Mill introduced us to the concept of "qualitative utilitarianism" addressing the concern with quality of pleasure, experience, or lifestyle (Troyer, 2003). He argued that not all pleasures are of equal value and that higher intellectual, moral, and cultural pleasures are more valuable than lower physical or sensory pleasures (Mill, 1864/2014). This nuanced view aimed to address criticisms of utilitarianism as overly focused on mere pleasure. Mill expanded upon Bentham's conception of pleasure by introducing the idea of "higher" and "lower" pleasures. This distinction between pleasures acknowledges that the quality of happiness matters. Intellectual and moral pursuits, even if they might involve less immediate pleasure, are more valuable in the long run (Troyer, 2003). He argued that not all pleasures are equal, and some pleasures are considered superior or more valuable than others (Mill, 1864/2014). He concluded that intellectual, moral, and cultural pleasures are of higher quality than mere physical or sensory pleasures. Therefore, according to Mill (1864/2014), a utilitarian should consider the quality of pleasure when evaluating actions.

Furthermore, on Liberty, Mill (1859/2014) linked moral individualism to requirements of education and enlightenment by introducing us the concept of "Enlightened Self-Interest" and explained that an enlightened person may forgo an immediate happiness to get a greater one later and or may prefer to make favors to others rather than to risk all s/he has. He also argued that it is the obligation of the state to enlighten society by education and transform essentially hedonistic individuals into a body of civic-minded individuals who would put the general good above their own pleasure (1859/2014). Mill also introduced the concept of individual rights and the importance of justice. He recognized that certain actions, even if they might increase overall happiness, should not be done if they violate the rights of individuals or principles of justice (Baier, 1991). Mill (1859/2014) advocated for personal liberty and individual rights and limited government intervention believing that people should be free to pursue their own happiness and lead their lives according to their own preferences, values, and interests so long as they do not harm others in the process. He discussed that individuals' freedom to pursue their own wishes is constrained by the requirement not to harm others in the process which often referred to as the "harm principle," which suggests that the only legitimate reason for interfering with someone's actions is to prevent harm to others (Mill, 1859/2014).

In summary, John Stuart Mill's utilitarianism expanded upon Jeremy Bentham's ideas by considering the quality of pleasure, introducing rule utilitarianism, acknowledging individual rights, and emphasizing the importance of personal freedom and the harm principle. Mill's version of utilitarianism strives to balance the pursuit of overall happiness with the recognition of individual rights and the complexities of focusing on the specific consequences of each individual act.

Preference Utilitarianism

> *"The notion of what makes a better person is secondary to the right thing to do."*
>
> Singer, Brainy Quotes

As articulated in his book "Practical Ethics", Singer (1979/2011) proposes that if we have the ability to prevent something bad from happening without sacrificing anything of comparable moral worth, then we have a moral obligation to do so. This principle implies a radical redistribution of resources, where individuals would need to sacrifice luxuries like second cars and homes to benefit those who are worst off. Thus, utility, not rights, is the deciding principle.

Singer (1979/2011) emphasized the importance of preventing harm and argued that the moral worth of an action should be evaluated based on its consequences for the preferences and interests of all sentient beings, including not only humans but also animals. His approach reflects a commitment to minimizing suffering and promoting the well-being of all sentient creatures. Singer (1979/2011) introduces two tiers of moral relevance based on individuals' capacity for desires and goals for the future and then introduces two standards of judgement for each tier. Tier 1 typically includes beings that are considered to have a higher level of moral consideration due to their capacity for desires, goals, and cognitive abilities. This often includes humans and higher-order primates. Tier 2 includes humans who cannot state preferences like infants or severely handicapped people and lower-order animals such as chickens and ducks. Singer (1979/2011) applies preference utilitarianism to Tier 1 beings and focuses on satisfying as many of the first preferences of people as possible in order to maximize happiness. Singer (1979/2011) applies hedonistic act utilitarianism to Tier 2 beings, considering whether they can suffer and extend the moral consideration to all sentient beings, including animals, based on their capacity to suffer. Singer (1979/2011) condemns practices such as meat consumption, the practice of keeping hens in battery cages, which involve confined and crowded conditions, animal testing in cosmetics, and farming of animals for their fur as morally wrong due to the suffering they cause. Singer (1979/2011) concludes that, based on utilitarian reasoning, individuals should become vegetarians because meat production causes significant suffering to animals, and alternative vegetarian meals are equally nourishing.

Singer (1979/2011) also challenged the notion that newborn infants inherently possess significant ethical significance or a right to life comparable to that of mature persons. He suggested that considering the fact that a fetus does not have the same claim to the right to live as a person, then a newborn baby should not have either, implying that a newborn baby might have a less value than that of certain non-human animals (Singer, 1979/2011). Where does this questioning take us? "Is an orphan less valuable than a valuable racing horse or a beloved pet loved and cared by their owners over the years?" Singer (1979/2011) controversially proposes that the moral value of a being should be based on its capacity for consciousness, self-awareness, and the ability to experience pleasure and pain, rather than simply on its membership in the human species. This reflects his belief that ethical considerations should be based on a nuanced understanding of the value of life rather than rigid, absolute principles. From Singer's preference utility standpoint, the worth of human life may vary based on factors such as the capacity for suffering and the potential for future happiness or well-being (Singer, 1979/2011).

In summary, Peter Singer's perspective challenges conventional ethical beliefs about the sanctity of human life by emphasizing the variability of its worth and advocating for a more nuanced approach to medical ethics, including considerations of euthanasia and the value of newborn infants. His utilitarian framework prioritizes minimizing suffering and maximizing overall well-being, even if it leads to controversial conclusions about the value of human life. Peter Singer's Preference Utilitarianism is a radical version of utilitarian morality which challenges the conventional notions of utilitarianism by questioning the very principle of traditional utilitarian morality: Are we supposed to prioritize the satisfaction of preferences even at significant personal cost? In contrast to more minimalist utilitarianism approach of Mill (1864/2014) who endorses setting the standard of morality so far as the nature allows, Singer (1979/2011) set the standard so high that merely the moral saint would be capable of such a huge sacrifice proposed by Singer's principle of maximizing preferences. Furthermore, I would prefer giving up my second home to my own child even if somebody else needs it more than my own child. While Singer's denial of the influence of kinship duties on our decision-making in favor of absolute utility and might be considered saintly, deep down unless you are not a moral saint, you would not want to live a life ruled by Singer's preference utilitarianism (Abboud & Mendz, 2018). As suggested by Wolf (1982) striving for such a moral perfection would be dreary and would lack depth, richness, and diversity.

Bonus 1: Machiavellianism

> *"It seems that Machiavelli was far less 'Machiavellian' than we might like to think. He is indeed the complete contrary of a Machiavellian since he describes the tricks of power and gives the whole show away."*
>
> Merleau-Ponty, Quotefancy

Niccolò Machiavelli (1469–1527) is most famously known for his work "The Prince" and often considered as a political realist rather than strictly fitting into categories like ethical egoism or utilitarianism. While his works, especially "The Prince," are influential in political philosophy, focusing primarily on the effective exercise of political power and its maintenance (stability), we can still explore how certain aspects of his thinking relate to the ethical frameworks of utilitarianism and ethical egoism.

First and foremost, both Machiavelli's political philosophy and ethics of utilitarianism and egoism have a consequentialist orientation and share some commonalities in their considerations of the relationship between means and ends. Machiavelli's emphasis on political success and the well-being of the ruler or the state aligns with the focus of ethical egoism. The primary concern is the flourishing and survival of the ruler or the political entity. Machiavelli's advice to rulers often reflects a recognition of the importance of self-interest. He advises leaders to prioritize the stability and success of their states, even if it means employing ruthless or morally questionable tactics (Machiavelli, 1532/2003). He is known for his pragmatic approach to politics and his famous expression "the ends justify the means". This suggests that in the pursuit and maintenance of political power, leaders should be willing to adopt any means necessary, regardless of their moral character, to achieve their objectives (Machiavelli, 1532/ 2003). Machiavelli's political realism provides a very down-to-earth approach to leaders and acknowledges that leaders may need to make morally questionable decisions or engage in actions that, under normal ethical considerations, might be condemned. The central focus is on the effective exercise and preservation of political power. His second most well-known advice to rulers, on the other hand, is that "since love and fear can hardly exist together, if we must choose between them, it is much safer to be feared than loved" because, according to Machiavelli (1532/2003), love is a bond that can be broken at every opportunity for one's advantage; but fear protects you by a dread of retaliation which never fails. Machiavelli's advice can also be seen as an attempt to maximize political utility -maintaining stability, power, and success for the ruler or the state. This parallels the utilitarian idea of maximizing overall happiness or well-being. In summary, while Machiavelli's advice for rulers may share some elements with ethical egoism and utilitarianism, his primary focus is on the pragmatic and effective exercise of political power.

Bonus 2: The Wealth of Nations

> *"Virtue is more to be feared than vice, because its excesses are not subject to the regulation of conscience."*
>
> Smith, BrainyQuote

Adam Smith is a Scottish philosopher and economist, whose contributions to economics and philosophy have had a profound and lasting impact. He is often associated with teleological ethics that shares some commonalities with both ethical egoism and utilitarianism. However, Smith is not easily classified as a strict ethical egoist or utilitarian because his works encompass a range of ideas that go beyond these classifications. Smith's ethical philosophy is nuanced and includes elements that align with both ethical egoism and utilitarianism, but it also extends beyond them. He can be considered as an ethical egoist in the sense that he recognizes the importance of individual self-interest and the pursuit of one's own well-being. He discussed the idea of moral sentiments and the role of empathy, sympathy, and generosity in ethical decision-making. Smith (1759/2010) argued that individuals have a natural tendency to care about the well-being of others, and moral actions are influenced by a desire for social approval. Citing his book "The Theory of Moral Sentiments" we can argue that Smith is an ethical egoist endorsing acting in ways that one perceives to be in one's own self-interest (Smith, 1759/2010).

However, Smith is most famously known for his work "The Wealth of Nations" - the "bible" of liberal economic theory- where he laid the foundation for classical economics and explored the concept of the "invisible hand" and "welfare Ethics". In this work, he argued that individuals pursuing their own self-interest in a free market context unintentionally contribute to the overall economic well-being of society (Smith, 1776/2018). He endorsed the idea that individuals, in pursuing their self-interest in a competitive market, unintentionally promote social and economic harmony (Smith, 1776/2018). The invisible hand suggests that the law of supply and demand -fundamental economic laws- provide self-regulation of the economy through the divine hand (Smith, 1776/2018). According to him, free competition and interplay of economic interests and forces would eventually and unintentionally lead to positive outcomes for all (Smith, 1776/2018). Smith was a proponent of free trade, laissez-faire economics, advocating for minimal government intervention in economic affairs.

His concepts of "invisible/divine hand" and "welfarism" can be seen as teleological because it focuses on the positive collective outcomes that result from individuals pursuing their own interests. Smith defends welfare ethics fairly well by citing both self-interest and the golden rule. He holds the idea that following the golden rule may promote our own good –and not just the good of the other person and considers promoting greater overall happiness as consonant with self-interest. Smith's welfarism is based on the premise that actions, policies, and/or rules should be judged in terms of the outcomes they produce. He believed that individuals, guided by self-interest and competition, could create a more prosperous and efficient economic system without the need for excessive government regulation. Smith (1776/2018) defended limited government intervention in economy and argued that in attempting to provide what it cannot, government may destroy its ability to provide what it can and as Novak once said, create hell – "which is what happens when you pursue heaven-on-earth" (cited in Fulmer, 2022). Thus, citing his most influential work "The Wealth of Nations", we can consider him as utilitarian rather than an ethical egoist.

Criticisms of Utilitarianism

1. *Overemphasis on Consequences:* Critics argue that utilitarianism places an excessive focus on the consequences of actions, potentially neglecting the moral significance of intentions, motives, or the inherent nature of the actions themselves.
2. *Quantification of Happiness:* The attempt to quantify happiness or pleasure and compare it across individuals or situations has been criticized as problematic. Critics argue that assigning numerical values to subjective

experiences is arbitrary and may not accurately capture the complexities of well-being.

3. *Treatment of Individuals as Means:* Utilitarianism's emphasis on maximizing overall happiness can lead to situations where the interests or well-being of individuals or minority groups are sacrificed for the greater good. Critics argue that this approach may violate principles of justice and individual rights.

4. *Lack of Rights Protections:* Utilitarianism has been criticized for not providing a strong foundation for protecting individual rights. Critics argue that a purely consequentialist approach might justify violating certain rights if it leads to a better overall outcome.

5. *Difficulty in Predicting Consequences:* Accurately predicting all the consequences of an action, especially in complex social situations, is challenging. Critics argue that the utilitarian approach requires foreseeing all possible outcomes, which may be practically impossible.

6. *Injustice and Unfairness:* Utilitarianism may justify actions that are perceived as unjust or unfair if they contribute to overall happiness. Critics argue that the theory may not adequately address concerns related to distributive justice and fairness.

7. *No Inherent Value in Certain Acts:* Some critics argue that utilitarianism may fail to recognize the inherent moral value or disvalue of certain actions. If the consequences are the only consideration, then actions such as lying or breaking promises might be justified if they produce greater overall happiness.

8. *Tyranny of the Majority:* Utilitarianism's focus on maximizing overall happiness might lead to a "tyranny of the majority," where the interests or well-being of minority groups are consistently overlooked or sacrificed for the greater happiness of the majority.

9. *Neglect of Individual Integrity:* Critics argue that utilitarianism might neglect the importance of individual integrity and moral character. The emphasis on outcomes could potentially justify actions that compromise personal values or moral principles.

10. *Challenges in Measuring Preferences:* Determining and aggregating individual preferences and values, especially in diverse and pluralistic societies, poses significant challenges. Critics argue that the utilitarian calculus may not accurately represent the diversity of individual perspectives.

11. *Trolley Problem Critiques:* Thought experiments like the trolley problem, often used to illustrate utilitarian reasoning, have faced criticism for

oversimplifying ethical decision-making and not capturing the complexities of real-world moral choices.

Despite these criticisms, it's important to note that utilitarianism has evolved over time, and contemporary scholars have proposed various modifications and hybrid approaches to address some of these concerns. The critiques contribute to ongoing debates about the strengths and limitations of utilitarian ethics.

References

Abboud, A. J. & Mendz, G. L. (2018). *Peter Singer's ethics: A critical appraisal*. Nova.

Baier, A. (1991). *A progress of sentiments: Reflections on Hume's treatise*. Harvard University Press.

Bentham, J. (1996). *The collected works of Jeremy Bentham: Introduction to the principles of morals and legislation* (J. H. Burns & H. L. A. Hart, Eds.). Clarendon Press. (Original work published 1781)

Bentham, J. (n.d.). BrainyQuote.com. Retrieved March 2, 2024, from https://www.brainyquote.com/quotes/jeremy_bentham_389252

Brandt, R. (1959). *Ethical theory*. Prentice Hall Press.

Broad, C. D. (2012). *Ethics* (C. Lewy, Ed.). Nijhoff Publishers.

Bulley, C. A., Braimah, S. M., & Achiriga, V. (2022). Ethics in marketing: The quest for equity, diversity, and inclusion. In A. Gbadamosi (Ed.), *Critical perspectives on diversity, equity, and inclusion in marketing* (pp. 265–285). IGI Global. https://doi.org/10.4018/978-1-6684-3590-8.ch016

Butler, J. (2009). *Fifteen sermons preached at the rolls chapel in British moralists* (D. D. Raphael, Ed.). Dodo Press. (Original work published 1726)

Chen, X. (2021). *The essentials of Habermas*. Springer. https://doi.org/10.1007/978-3-030-79794-2_3

Corcoran, T., & Bennett, P. (2015). Thinking critically about professional ethics. In A. Williams, T. Billington, D. Goodley, & T. Corcoran (Eds.), *Critical educational psychology* (pp. 79–87). https://doi.org/10.1002/9781394259243.ch7

Crisp, R. (2006). Hedonism reconsidered. *Philosophy and Phenomenological Research, 73*(3), 619–645. https://doi.org/10.2307/40041013.

Downie, R. S. (1987). Moral philosophy. In J. Eatwell, M. Milgate, & P. Newman (Eds.), *The new Palgrave dictionary of economics. Palgrave Macmillan* (pp. 1–8). https://doi.org/10.1057/978-1-349-95121-5_841-1

Feinberg, J. (1999). Psychological egoism. In R. Shafer-Landam (Ed.), *Reason and responsibility* (pp. 493–505). Wadsworth.

Felzmann, H. (2017). Utilitarianism as an approach to ethical decision making in health care. In P. A. Scott (Ed.), *Key concepts and issues in nursing ethics* (pp. 29–41). http://doi.org/10.1007/978-3-319-49250-6_3

Fulmer, R. (2022, September 25). *Why Adam Smith said, 'Virtue is more to be feared than vice'*. FEE Stories. Retrieved February 14, 2024, from https://fee.org/articles/why-adam-smith-said-virtue-is-more-to-be-feared-than-vice/

Hardin, R. (2001). Utilitarianism: contemporary applications. In N. J. Smelser & P. B. Baltes (Eds.), *International encyclopedia of the social & behavioral sciences,* (pp. 16111–16113). Pergamon. https://doi.org/10.1016/B0-08-043076-7/01244-4.

Hewitt, S. (2010). What do our intuitions about the experience machine really tell us about hedonism? *Philosophical Studies, 151,* 331–349. https://doi.org/10.1007/s11098-009-9440-4

Kao, Y. S. (2017). What's in it for me? On egoism and social contract theory. In G. Matthews, (Ed.), *Introduction to philosophy: Ethics* (pp. 38–46). Creative Commons.

Machiavelli, N. (2003). *The Prince: Niccolo Machiavelli.* Penguin Classics. (Original work published 1532)

May, J. (n.d.). *Psychological egoism.* Internet Encyclopedia of Philosophy (IEP). Retrieved October 22, 2024 from https://iep.utm.edu/psychological-egoism/#:~:text=Psychological%20egoism%20is%20the%20thesis,can%20have%20ultimately%20altruistic%20motives.

Merleau-Ponty, M. (n.d.). Quotefancy. Retrieved March 11, 2024, from https://quotefancy.com/maurice-merleau-ponty-quotes

Mill, J. S. (2014). *On liberty* (L. Kahn, Ed.). Broadview Press. (Original work published 1859)

Mill, J. S. (2014). *Utilitarianism.* Cambridge University Press. (Original work published 1864)

Mill, J. S. BrainyQuote.com. Retrieved March 2, 2024, from https://www.brainyquote.com/authors/john-stuart-mill-quotes

Parfit, D. (1984). *Reasons and persons.* Oxford University Press

Rand, A. (1957). *Atlas shrugged.* Generic.

Rand, A. (1964). *The virtue of selfishness.* Penguin.

Sidgwick, H. (2010). *The methods of ethics.* Kessinger Publication. (Original work published 1874)

Singer, P. (2011). *Practical ethics* (3rd ed.). Cambridge University Press. (Original work published 1979)

Singer, P. (n.d.). BrainyQuote.com. Retrieved March 2, 2024, from https://www.brainyquote.com/authors/peter-singer-quotes

Smith, A. (2010). *The theory of moral sentiments*. Penguin Classics. (Original work published 1759)

Smith, A. (2018). *The wealth of nations*. CreateSpace Independent Publishing Platform (Original work published 1776)

Smith, A. (n.d.) BrainyQuote.com. Retrieved March 2, 2024, from https://www.brainyquote.com/quotes/adam_smith_387353

Troyer, J. (2003). *The classical utilitarians*. Hackett Publishing.

Wolf, S. (1982). Moral saints. *The Journal of Philosophy, 79*(8), 419–439. https://doi.org/10.2307/2026228

Zweig, M. B. (1971). Wilhelm Reich's theory: Ethical implications. *American Imago, 28*(3), 268–286. http://www.jstor.org/stable/26302675

Part III Meta-Ethics

"Ethics" can be a complex and multifaceted topic, and individuals may interpret and define it differently based on their cultural, philosophical, and personal perspectives. Ethical discussions require precision and clarity to convey complex ideas and concepts accurately. Language plays a crucial role in ethical discourse, and the use of certain words interchangeably can indeed lead to confusion or misunderstandings. Using words interchangeably can blur distinctions and obscure important nuances, leading to confusion among participants. Words may have different connotations or implied meanings, even if they are technically synonymous. Using one word instead of another can inadvertently convey unintended implications or associations, altering the message being communicated.

For centuries, philosophers have been trying to find answers to fundamental questions such as "Do moral concepts such as 'good,' 'bad,' 'right,' and 'wrong,' have an objective basis or are they just the constructs of human language and thought?" without really resolving them. Philosophers and most recently neuro-ethics attempted to seek answers to those metaethical questions and examine how we make ethical decisions. By investigating the workings of the brain and its relationship to complex ethical questions, neuro-ethics contributes valuable insights to the field of metaethics, which explores the nature, origins, and justification of ethical principles. Neuroscientific research on the brain's mechanisms involved in decision-making examines the nature of free will. By investigating whether the human moral sense is innate, or "hardwired" in the brain, neuro-ethics provide some invaluable insights to the field of metaethics.

Metaethics, by definition, is a branch of moral philosophy that focuses on understanding the nature of moral language, moral knowledge, and moral truth. It seeks to comprehend the meaning and validation of moral claims, as well as the resolution of moral disagreements. It examines the essence and status of moral claims and the nature of moral facts rather than specific moral issues. It aims to grasp moral truth, knowledge, and the phenomenon of moral disagreement. By engaging with questions such as "How do I know what is good and what is bad?",

"What is the nature of moral truth?" or "How do we acquire moral knowledge?", we can understand the different perspectives on the nature of morality and how people shape their understanding of ethical principles and judgments.

There are three distinct areas in meta-ethics as described by Garner and Rosen (1967):

1. *Moral semantics.* This area focuses on the meanings of moral terms and judgments used in moral philosophy. It seeks to determine the semantics of terms such as "good," "bad," "right," and "wrong." Moral semantics delves into questions about the language and concepts we use to express moral ideas and principles.
2. *Moral ontology.* Moral ontology explores the nature of moral judgments and principles. It investigates whether moral judgments are unconditional or conditional, and it examines the differences in moral principles between individuals or societies. The concepts of absolutism and relativism are central to discussions in moral ontology, as they pertain to the universality or contextuality of moral principles.
3. *Moral epistemology.* This area concerns itself with how we come to know moral truths or make moral judgments. Moral epistemology asks questions about the validity and verifiability of moral claims, as well as the nature of moral knowledge. It explores whether moral claims can be verified through empirical evidence, reasoned argumentation, intuition, or other means. Concepts such as skepticism, truth, reason, and perception are central to discussions in moral epistemology.

Overall, these three areas of meta-ethics are concerned about examining the substance of morality (i.e., language, nature, and knowledge of morality) but not really concerned about whether a person or an act is moral. The question of the foundation of moral values is complex and multifaceted, and different ethical theories offer different explanations. There is no consensus among philosophers on this matter, and it remains a topic of philosophical inquiry and discussion. The essence of moral values and principles has been a subject of philosophical debate for centuries, and there is no one definitive answer. People's perceptions of ethical stance can vary widely due to a combination of factors, including cultural background, personal experiences, religious beliefs, education, and individual values and different ethical theories propose various sources for moral values.

Questions to Ask (from a Metaethical Standpoint)

Here are some important questions you might ask yourself about the original source of moral knowledge and the ways in which people's perceptions of ethical stance may differ.

- Is the moral truth objective and exists independently of human beliefs and opinions or are they subjective and dependent on individual or cultural perspectives?
- Are ethical statements or moral claims objectively true or false and relate to the objective world or are they there to express something more than or other than factual truth?
- Do emotions play a fundamental role in shaping moral judgments and are they integral to ethical considerations?
- Can moral claims be rationally justified, or can we reasonably argue for the superiority of one claim over others?
- How do we as humans come to know and understand moral principles and values?
- Are moral claims grounded in factors such as reason, emotion, culture, religion, intuition, or some other source or is there a universal foundation or framework?
- Is there a universal foundation for ethics that can ground ethical principles and values across diverse cultures and belief systems?
- What does it mean to be a 'good' person?
- Are moral concepts natural or invented?
- Is moral motivation intrinsic or extrinsic?

Often when we think about ethics, we generally think about *normative ethics* which deals with determining what actions are right or wrong, good or bad, and morally permissible or impermissible. Examples of normative ethical questions include whether it is acceptable to lie, steal, or kill, as well as statements such as "Lying is bad" and "It is good to give to charity." These types of statements are called moral claims. When we take a step back and we can also inquire about the underlying assumptions, principles, and implications of moral terms and claims. and meta-ethics seeks to clarify and analyze these diverse perspectives. It is like a foreign language, one must learn to understand how different individuals may have different understandings of what it means for something to be "good" or "right". Examining intentions behind a moral claim is also very important in meta-ethics. By examining the underlying assumptions and implications of moral claims and the intentions that inform moral reasoning, and exploring how moral claims are understood and interpreted by different individuals or cultures, meta-ethics aims to enhance our understanding of morality and provide a foundation for ethical inquiry and discourse.

Table 4 is a modest attempt to achieve a conceptual clarification for the major theories in the field of metaethics. There are two main categories in meta-ethics based on whether moral claims are considered truth-apt or non-truth-apt. Truth-apt moral claims are those that can be evaluated as true or false. They assert propositions about moral reality or moral facts that are capable of being true or false. The nature of moral language is a central concern in meta-ethics. Different philosophical positions offer contrasting views on whether moral claims are truth-apt or non-truth-apt. Some meta-ethical theories, such as moral realism, argue that moral claims are truth-apt, meaning they can be evaluated as true or false. According to moral realism, moral statements assert objective facts about moral reality that exist independently of individual beliefs or attitudes. Other meta-ethical theories, such as emotivism, posit that moral claims are non-truth-apt. Instead of expressing objective truths, moral statements are seen as expressions of emotions, attitudes, or prescriptions. From this perspective, moral claims do not have truth values but rather convey the speaker's subjective attitudes or preferences. For example, consider that your moral claim was "Lying is wrong". The interpretation of the moral claim "Lying is wrong" depends on one's philosophical perspective on the nature of moral language. Let's consider two possible interpretations: From a truth-apt perspective, the claim "Lying is wrong" would be understood as asserting a proposition about the truth or falsity of lying. In this view, the claim implies that lying possesses a property of being morally wrong, similar to how a factual statement asserts a property about the world. Under this interpretation, "Lying is wrong" would be making a truth-apt claim about the moral status of lying. Alternatively, from a non-truth-apt perspective, the claim "Lying is wrong" would be seen as expressing the speaker's disapproval or condemnation of lying rather than making a truth-apt assertion about its moral status. In this view, moral claims are understood as expressions of attitudes, emotions, or prescriptions rather than statements of objective fact. Under this interpretation, "Lying is wrong" would be expressing a negative attitude toward lying rather than making a truth-apt claim about its moral status.

In summary, the interpretation of the claim "Lying is wrong" as either truth-apt or non-truth-apt depends on one's philosophical stance on meta-ethics and the nature of moral language. Each interpretation offers a distinct understanding of the function and meaning of moral claims, highlighting the complexities involved in ethical discourse.

Table 4. A Modest Attempt to Achieve a Conceptual Clarification in Meta-Ethics

Non-Cognitivism (Moral anti-realism)	Cognitivism (Moral Realism)
Expressivism	Moral Absolutism
Emotivism	Moral naturalism
Universal prescriptivism	Moral non-naturalism
Moral Skepticism	Moral Relativism
Moral nihilism	Moral Constructivism
Error theory	Moral Subjectivism
Moral fictionalists	Cultural Relativism
	Divine Command Theory
	Moral Pluralism

Reference

Garner, R. T., & Rosen, B. (1967). *Moral philosophy: A systematic introduction to normative ethics and meta-ethics.* Macmillan.

Chapter 7 Non-Cognitivism (Moral Anti-Realism)

Non-cognitivism is a meta-ethical theory that denies that moral statements express propositions with truth values. Instead, non-cognitivists argue that moral statements are expressions of attitudes, emotions, preferences, or commands, and therefore are not capable of being true or false (Van Roojen, 2004). Non-cognitivists reject the idea that moral statements have truth conditions because they believe that moral language serves a different function than descriptive or factual language (Blome-Tillmann, 2009; Goodwin, & Darley, 2010). Instead of making claims about the world, moral statements are seen as expressions of the speaker's personal attitudes, preferences, or emotive responses to certain actions or behaviors.

One of the main theories within non-cognitivism is emotivism, which holds that moral statements express the speaker's emotions or attitudes toward particular actions or situations. For example, when a person declares, "lying is wrong", emotivists argue that that person is not actually making a claim about the truth or falsity of lying being wrong, but rather expressing their disapproval or condemnation of lying. Another theory within non-cognitivism is prescriptivism, which posits that moral statements function as commands or prescriptions for action. According to this view, when someone makes a moral statement such as "lying is wrong," s/he is not making a claim about the objective moral truth about lying but merely expressing his/her disapproval or condemnation of telling a lie (emotivism). It may not only express disapproval of lying but also serve as a command not to lie (prescriptivism).

Overall, non-cognitivism challenges the conventional view that moral claims are objective and truth-apt (Wedgwood, 1997). Instead, it emphasizes the subjective and expressive nature of moral language, focusing on the attitudes, emotions, or prescriptions conveyed by moral statements rather than their truth conditions (Marturano, n.d.). Non-cognitivists deny that moral claims have truth conditions and express propositions with truth values. Instead, they view moral language as expressing emotions, attitudes, or commands, rather than factual assertions. Expressivist within the realm of non-cognitivism typically argue that moral claims do not have truth values because they do not express propositions (Zolotar, 2013). Therefore, the question of proving or disproving their truth value is irrelevant from this perspective, as moral statements are seen as proclamation of personal choices and emotions rather than factual assertions about the world. So, depending on what you mean and intend to communicate when you are making the moral claims, you have two options within expressivism:

- if you interpret your claim as an imperative, then you are a universal prescriptivist;
- if you interpret your claim as an emotive claim, then you are an emotivist.

Moral anti-realism also rejects that moral claims can be proved true and can be verified (moral skepticism). If you believe that even if there might be some objective moral facts or properties that exist independently of human beliefs, we simply have no capacity to find such ways or discover those facts, then you are a moral skeptic. Depending on your belief on the verifiability of the moral claims, you have several options within moral skepticism:

- If you believe that there is either no objective moral fact or properties that exist independently of human beliefs, you are a nihilist (Zolotar, 2013).
- If you believe that moral statements do not express objective truths but moral discourse can be pragmatically useful or meaningful within certain contexts; then you are a moral fictionalists.
- Even if you believe objective moral facts or properties exist independently of human beliefs, but you think there is no sort of robust ontological method way to prove their existence or discover them, then you are an error theorist.

Expressivism

Moral expressivism is a metaethical theory that suggests moral statements are expressions of attitudes, emotions, or prescriptions rather than assertions of objective truths. Unlike cognitivist theories, which hold that moral statements have truth values and describe the world, expressivism argues that moral language serves primarily to convey the speaker's feelings, preferences, or commands. Expressivists deny that moral statements have cognitive content or truth values. Instead, moral language is seen as non-cognitive, meaning it does not aim to describe the world but rather to express the speaker's attitudes or commitments (Bevir, 2010). Expressivists often draw analogies between moral language and other forms of expressive discourse, such as expressions of emotion or aesthetic judgments. They argue that just as saying "I am happy" expresses a feeling of happiness, saying "lying is wrong" expresses a moral attitude.

Overall, moral expressivism provides a distinctive account of moral language and judgment, emphasizing the expressive and prescriptive functions of moral discourse while denying the existence of objective moral truths. It offers a way to understand the role of moral language in communication and social interaction without committing to moral realism or cognitivism.

Emotivistism (Ayer & Stevenson)

Ayer (1971) argues that moral facts do not exist and the presence of an ethical element in a claim does not add to its factual content. Ayer (1971) argues that the meaning of a moral claim depends on the intention of the speaker. According to Ayer (1971) ethical dilemmas are merely disagreements in attitudes not in facts. Stevenson (1937) argues that moral claims do not only express our attitude to a situation, but they are made to evoke the same attitude in others. Ayer (1971) also argues that moral claims arouse feelings and emotions, but with different strengths of command and functions with different intensity. For instance, implying a duty and saying something like that "one 'ought' to do something" is of course stronger than merely stating that something is good or bad.

Rachels (1999) argues against Ayer's emotivist theory, which reduces the role of moral language to the mere expression of emotions or subjective attitudes. Ayer famously likened moral judgments to expressions of subjective preferences or emotional responses, such as saying, "Lying is wrong" is akin to saying, "Boo to lying" or "I disapprove of lying". Rachels (1999) challenges this reductionist view by highlighting the substantive differences between moral judgments and mere expressions of emotions or preferences. He argues that moral language serves a distinct function and cannot be equated with non-moral expressions of emotion.

Ask yourself: Even if we cannot prove an ethical claim, does it make the moral discourse meaningless, irrelevant, or redundant? Or how would we make moral choices or set rules and laws? The inability to definitively prove an ethical claim does not render moral discourse meaningless, irrelevant, or redundant. Instead, moral discourse serves several essential functions in human societies, even in the absence of absolute proof or certainty. Here are some reasons why moral discourse remains valuable. While we may not have absolute certainty about the correctness of moral claims, ethical principles and values help us navigate complex moral dilemmas and guide our actions towards what we perceive as morally right or good. Through dialogue and debate, people can explore different perspectives, challenge assumptions, and refine their understanding of moral issues. This process of reflection promotes intellectual growth and moral development. In summary, while ethical claims may not always be provable in the same way as empirical claims, moral discourse remains meaningful and relevant for guiding human behavior, shaping social norms, promoting justice, and fostering ethical decision-making. By engaging in moral dialogue and deliberation, individuals and societies can navigate moral complexity, address ethical challenges, and strive towards a more just and ethical world.

Universal Prescriptivism (Hare)

Hare's ethical framework, known as prescriptivism, offers an interesting perspective on moral language and judgment. Ethical language, according to Hare (1919–2002), is prescriptive. This means that ethical statements prescribe or recommend certain courses of action, indicating what ought to be done. Hare (1952) argues that ethical statements do not aim to describe objective facts about the world but rather to express our preferences, desires, or prescriptions regarding moral matters. Hare (1952) emphasizes the use of terms like "good" and "ought" in ethical discourse. When we use these terms, we commend. Additionally, saying someone ought to do something implies that we ourselves ought to do it as well. While ethical statements are universalizable, Hare (1952) argue that they are not objective truths but merely expressions of personal opinions and preferences. Hare (1952) suggests that ethical statements express universal moral standards and are not contingent on individual preferences or subjective beliefs. Hare (1952) asserts that ethical judgments stem from individual preferences and cannot be objectively compared or ranked. Hare (1952) also suggests that moral agents cannot be hypocritical. This means that individuals should be consistent in their application of moral principles and preferences. Hare (1952) compares learning to drive with the process of modifying moral principles over time. Just as one learns to adapt driving rules based on different road conditions and scenarios, individuals modify their moral principles in response to various situations and experiences. However, unlike driving habits, moral habits require constant evaluation and attention because moral conditions and contexts can change. Moral principles may need to be reassessed due to shifts in societal norms, cultural changes, new information or perspectives, evolving personal values, or unexpected circumstances. Relying solely on habit without ongoing reflection and evaluation can lead to moral stagnation or inconsistency.

Overall, Hare's prescriptivism offers a distinctive approach to understanding ethical language and moral judgment, emphasizing the prescriptive nature of ethical statements while acknowledging their subjective and non-factual character. It encourages a recognition of the universality of moral standards while also highlighting the inherent subjectivity of ethical discourse. By applying the universalizability principle, individuals are encouraged to consider whether their preferences and actions could be consistently adopted by others in similar circumstances, thus promoting a more impartial and objective approach to moral reasoning.

Moral Skepticism

Moral skepticism, in its various forms, casts doubt on the possibility of objective moral knowledge or the existence of objective moral truths (Dancy, 2004; Sinnott-Armstrong, 2019). Skepticism raises doubts about our capacity to access or justify moral facts independently of individual perspectives or cultural contexts (Long, 1992). Moral skepticism refers to a range of metaethical positions that cast doubt on or deny certain aspects of moral knowledge, objectivity, or truth. Moral skeptics generally question the possibility of knowing objective moral facts, the actuality of moral properties, or the validity of ethical claims. Various forms of moral skepticism exist, and philosophers who hold these views may differ in their specific positions. Some notable categories and philosophers associated with moral skepticism include moral nihilism, moral perspectivism, error theory, and moral fictionalists.

Moral Nihilism

Moral nihilism is a branch of moral skepticism, which denies the existence of objective morality altogether (Krellenstein, 2017). Nihilists argue that there are no objective moral truths or values (Kagan, 2023). Moral nihilism is a metaethical position that rejects the idea that there is an external, mind-independent moral reality (Hussain, 2012). Moral nihilists reject the existence of inherent meaning, purpose, or value in the universe, and argue that moral statements lack objective truth conditions. Different forms of moral nihilism exist, ranging from the denial of moral facts to the rejection of moral language altogether. Philosophers may approach moral nihilism from different angles. Some moral skeptics emphasize the absence of objective moral facts or truths, while others may focus on the absence of inherent moral values or critique the limitations of moral language in capturing the complexity of ethical phenomena. It's important to note that moral nihilism is a controversial and minority position in ethics. Some philosophers associated with moral nihilism include:

> *Richard Garner* (2014), in his book "Beyond Morality," argues for a form of moral nihilism that denies the objective reality of moral values. Garner (2014) contends that moral judgments lack truth conditions and are expressions of individual attitudes or preferences.

Jean-Paul Sartre, an existentialist philosopher, is often associated with moral nihilism due to his rejection of inherent moral values. In "Existentialism is a Humanism" Sartre (2007) argues that without a transcendent source of values, morality is subjective and created by individuals through their choices.

Moral Perspectivism

Nietzsche (1883/1961), another existentialist philosopher, is often associated with moral nihilism due to his rejection of inherent moral values and declaration that "God is dead". Nietzsche's response to the death of God was not a celebration of nihilism but a call for the "overcoming" of nihilism. Instead, Nietzsche (1883/1961) was concerned that the rejection of traditional values without a replacement could lead to nihilism -a state where individuals might feel a sense of meaninglessness, purposelessness, and a loss of moral direction. He proposed the idea of creating new values, embracing individual creativity, and affirming life without relying on traditional religious foundations (Nietzsche, 1883/1961). Existentialism offers a unique perspective on ethics by emphasizing individual responsibility, authenticity, and freedom in the face of life's existential challenges. Nietzsche (1883/1961) criticized the traditional Christian moral values and the notion of an objective, unchanging moral order. Instead, Nietzsche argued that moral values are human creations that have evolved over time and are contingent upon cultural, historical, and psychological factors. He questioned the concept of inherent moral truths that apply universally and was critical of the idea that all values are equally valid or that any belief can be justified without scrutiny Nietzsche (1886/1997).

Nietzsche adopts a perspectivist view in the realm of skepticism, which acknowledges the role of individual perspectives and experiences in shaping moral judgments (Doyle, 2012). From this perspective, moral truths are seen as relative to the perspectives or standpoints of individuals, and there is no single privileged standpoint from which objective moral facts can be discerned. Such a questioning has significant implications for how we approach ethical discourse and moral decision-making. It challenges the notion of a single, universally applicable moral standard and highlights the diversity of moral perspectives and values across different cultures and societies. This perspective encourages critical reflection on the foundations of our moral beliefs and the limitations of our moral knowledge.

Error Theory

Error theorists argue that moral discourse is fundamentally flawed (Joyce, 2022), because it is based on false assumptions about the existence of objective moral facts or values (Barry, 2014). According to error theorists like Mackie, our moral language presupposes the existence of objective moral properties or laws that do not actually exist (Gerritsen, 2023). When individuals make moral claims, they often implicitly assume the existence of objective moral laws or values (Lossau, 2022). For example, saying "It was wrong for you to lie to me" suggests not only that lying is morally prohibited but also that there are objective moral laws governing such behavior. Mackie (1990) critiques the implicit ontological presuppositions underlying moral discourse, particularly the assumption that moral values and obligations exist as objective features of the world. He also argues that all these presuppositions are mistaken (Mackie, 1990). Therefore, he argues that moral claims based on these presuppositions are fundamentally flawed, do not withstand philosophical scrutiny, and suggests that moral language is systematically misleading. This leads to confusion and error in moral discourse. Mackie (1990) argues that moral values and obligations are invented or constructed by humans rather than discovered as objective features of the world. Overall, Mackie's moral error theory provides a radical critique of moral realism and challenges commonly held assumptions about the objectivity of morality. By highlighting the systematic misleadingness of moral language, Mackie invites readers to reconsider the foundations of our moral beliefs and consider alternative perspectives on ethics.

Moral Fictionalists

Moral fictionalism is a philosophical position that aligns with moral skepticism, particularly in rejecting the existence of objective moral truths or properties (Nolan, 2012). Fictionalists argue that moral statements do not express objective facts about the world, but rather serve a fictional or expressive purpose, thus they engage in moral thinking purely for its instrumental value (Gerritsen, 2023). From this perspective, moral judgments lack truth-value in the same way as empirical claims (Kalderon, 2005). Despite denying the existence of objective moral truths, moral fictionalists do not simply dismiss moral discourse as meaningless or devoid of value either. Instead, moral fictionalists suggest that moral discourse can be pragmatically useful or meaningful within specific social and interpersonal contexts, even if moral statements are not considered to be objectively true (Kalderon, 2005). Moral fictionalists suggest that moral language can be used to express attitudes, preferences, and social norms, as well as to guide behavior and facilitate cooperation within communities (Joyce, 2001). They often employ fictionalist strategies to understand moral discourse. They may view moral statements as akin to assertions made within a fictional narrative or framework, where moral claims are treated as if they were true for the sake of practical or rhetorical effectiveness (Gerritsen, 2023; Joyce, 2005)

By highlighting the pragmatic and contextual nature of moral discourse, moral fictionalists challenge the notion of moral objectivity. In summary, moral fictionalism offers a nuanced perspective on moral discourse, recognizing its pragmatic value while rejecting the existence of objective moral truths. It provides a way to engage with moral language and norms without committing to a realist understanding of morality.

References

Ayer, A. J. (1971). *Language, truth and logic* (6th ed.). Dover.

Barry, P. (2014). In defence of morality: A response to a moral error theory. *International Journal of Philosophical Studies, 22*(1), 63–85, https://doi.org/10.1080/09672559.2013.860613

Bevir, M. (2010). *Encyclopedia of political theory*. Sage Publication

Blome-Tillmann, M. (2009). Moral non-cognitivism and the grammar of morality. *Proceedings of the Aristotelian Society, 109*, 279–309. http://www.jstor.org/stable/20619410

Dancy, J. (2004). *Ethics without principles*. Oxford University Press.

Doyle, T. (2012). 'Nietzsche's perspectival theory of knowledge', Nietzsche on epistemology and metaphysics: *The world in view*. Edinburgh Scholarship Online. https://doi.org/10.3366/edinburgh/9780748628070.003.0002

Garner, R. (2014). *Beyond morality*. Echo Point Books & Media.

Gerritsen, E., (2023). The second revolution of moral fictionalism. *Ergo an Open Access Journal of Philosophy, 9*(20), 537–555. https://doi.org/10.3998/ergo.2276

Goodwin, G. P., & Darley, J. M. (2010). The perceived objectivity of ethical beliefs: psychological findings and implications for public policy. *Review of Philosophy and Psychology, 1*, 161–188. https://doi.org/10.1007/s13164-009-0013-4

Hare, R. M. (1952). *The language of morals*. Clarendon Press.

Hussain, N. J. Z. (2012). Metaethics and nihilism in reginster's the affirmation of life. *The Journal of Nietzsche Studies, 43*(1):99–117 https://doi.org/10.1353/nie.2012.0024

Joyce, R. (2001). *The myth of morality*. Cambridge University Press.

Joyce, R. (2005). Moral fictionalism. In M. E. Kalderon (Ed.), *Fictionalism in Metaphysics*, (pp. 287–313). Oxford University Press.

Joyce, R. (2022). *Moral anti-Realism*. In E. N. Zalta & U. Nodelman (Eds.), The Stanford Encyclopedia of Philosophy. https://plato.stanford.edu/archives/win2022/entries/moral-anti-realism

Kagan, S. (2023). *'Nihilism', answering moral skepticism*. Oxford Academic. https://doi.org/10.1093/oso/9780197688977.003.0004

Kalderon, M. E. (2005). *Moral fictionalism*. Clarendon Press.

Krellenstein, M. (2017). Moral nihilism and its implications. *The Journal of Mind and Behavior, 38*(1), 75–90. http://www.jstor.org/stable/44631529

Long, D. C. (1992). The self-defeating character of skepticism. *Philosophy and Phenomenological Research, 52*(1), 67–84. https://doi.org/10.2307/2107744

Lossau, T. (2022). Mackie and the meaning of moral terms. *Journal of the History of Analytical Philosophy, 10*(1), 1–13. https://doi.org/10.15173/jhap.v10i1.4786

Mackie, J. J. (1990). *Ethics: Inventing right and wrong*. Penguin Books.

Marturano, A. (n.d.). *Non-cognitivism in ethics*. The Internet Encyclopedia of Philosophy (IEP). https://iep.utm.edu/non-cogn

Nietzsche, F. (1961). *Thus spoke Zarathustra: A book for everyone and no one*. (R. J. Hollingdale, Trans.), Penguin Classics. (Original work published 1883)

Nietzsche, F. (1997). *Beyond good and evil* (H. Zimmern, Trans.), Courier Dover Publications. (Original work published 1886)

Nolan, D. (2012). *Moral fictionalism*. Routledge Encyclopedia of Philosophy.

Rachels, J. (1999). *The elements of moral philosophy* (3rd ed.). McGraw-Hill College

Sartre, J. P. (2007). *Existentialism and humanism*. Methuen Publishing Ltd.

Sinnott-Armstrong, W. (2019). Moral Skepticism. In E. N. Zalta & U. Nodelman (Eds.), *The Stanford encyclopedia of philosophy*. https://plato.stanford.edu/archives/sum2019/entries/skepticism-moral

Stevenson, C. L. (1937). The emotive meaning of ethical terms. *Mind, 46*(181), 14–31.

Van Roojen, M. (2004). Moral cognitivism vs. non-cognitivism. In E. N. Zalta & U. Nodelman (Eds.), *The Stanford encyclopedia of philosophy*. https://plato.stanford.edu/archives/win2023/entries/moral-cognitivism

Wedgwood, R. (1997). Non-cognitivism, truth and logic. *Philosophical Studies: An International Journal for Philosophy in the Analytic Tradition, 86*(1), 73–91. http://www.jstor.org/stable/4320746

Zolotar, M. (2013). *Internal accommodation in moral irrealism* (Publication No. MS26587). [Master's thesis, University of Victoria]. ProQuest Dissertations & Theses Global. https://www.proquest.com/dissertations-theses/internal-accommodation-moral-irrealism/docview/1520449122/se-2

Chapter 8 Cognitivism (Moral Realism)

Cognitivism is a philosophical position within metaethics that holds that moral judgments convey beliefs about the world, rather than merely expressing emotions, attitudes, or preferences (Van Roojen, 2004). In contrast to non-cognitivism, cognitivists argue moral judgments make claims about the world and can be evaluated in terms of their truth-value (Sayre-McCord, 2015). For example, when someone says "lying is wrong," a cognitivist would interpret this statement as asserting a proposition about the moral status of lying, which can be objectively assessed for its truth value (Glassen, 1959).

Cognitivism holds the view that there are objective moral facts and properties that exist independently of individual perspectives or attitudes and certain courses of behaviors are objectively right or wrong, regardless of personal opinions or cultural norms and moral discourse is a matter of discovering or uncovering these truths (Dimmock, & Fisher, 2017). Cognitivism allows for the rational evaluation and justification of moral claims (Tudela, 2004). Cognitivists believe that moral judgments can be subjected to logical analysis, empirical investigation, and reasoned debate to determine their truth or falsity (Svavarsdottir, 1999). This contrasts with non-cognitivism, which denies the cognitive status of moral judgments and therefore does not view them as subject to rational evaluation in the same way.

Moral Objectivism

If you think that moral facts are independent of individual beliefs, opinions, or cultural norms and moral truths are the same for everyone, then you are a moral absolutist (also a moral objectivist). Moral absolutists assert that certain actions are inherently right or wrong, regardless of context or subjective interpretation (Brown, 1984). If you are a moral objectivist, questions about how we interact with moral truths and gain evidence about them are essential to consider. "Do we discover those moral facts empirically just as one does in science or do these facts reduce to or fit with the natural facts?" If the answer is "yes". Then, you are a naturalist! On the other hand, if you endorse the idea that we know or discover those moral facts in a way that cannot be explained but known only, then you are a non-naturalist just as famous Greek philosopher Plato.

Moral Naturalism

Ethical naturalism is a metaethical position that seeks to understand and explain moral truths in terms of naturalistic concepts, without appealing to supernatural or non-natural entities (Frank, 2014). Ethical naturalism asserts that moral truths can be understood and explained in naturalistic terms, similar to how scientific truths are understood (Lutz, 2023). Ethical statements are seen as expressing propositions that are provable as true or false, based on empirical evidence and rational analysis. When an ethical naturalist claims that "lying is wrong" or "honesty is good," they are suggesting that these statements can be understood in terms of natural features or consequences of lying and honesty (Copp, 2003, Sinclair, 2006). For example, the statement "lying causes suffering and distress" can be used to substitute the concept of "wrongness" with a natural feature that is observable and empirically provable. Ethical naturalists believe that moral statements have a truth value that can be verified through observation and analysis of empirical data. They argue that observable phenomena, such as human well-being, social cooperation, or evolutionary processes, can provide evidence for moral truths and values. Ethical naturalists argue that ethical values are a distinctive kind of property, different from those studied by the physical sciences but possibly studied by the social sciences, such as psychology or sociology (Fink, 2006). They contend that ethical values are reducible to natural properties and can be investigated using empirical methods.

While ethical naturalism offers a framework for understanding moral truths in terms of naturalistic concepts, the exact definition of "nature," "natural," and "natural law" can vary depending on the specific ethical theory being considered. Each perspective within naturalism approaches the challenge of defining goodness and natural law differently, drawing on various sources of evidence and interpretation to support their ethical claims. If you define goodness as pleasure or happiness just as utilitarians do, then you would look for empirical evidence of the consequences of actions to determine their moral value. If you would describe goodness as whatever God commands, then you would search for evidence in religious texts or divine revelations. If you would define goodness in terms of eudaimonia or flourishing, which involves realizing human excellence and fulfilling one's function in life just as a virtue ethicist, you would look to examples of virtuous behavior and the cultivation of moral virtues as evidence of ethical goodness. To sum up, different ethical theories within ethical naturalism approach the challenge of defining "nature", "natural", and "natural law" from various perspectives. Here's how different ethical perspectives within naturalism might approach this challenge:

Theologian Naturalist (Aquinas)

Thomas Aquinas, a theologian and philosopher, is associated with a form of ethical naturalism that integrates natural law theory with theological principles (Lisska, 2013). According to Aquinas (1998), moral truths are grounded in the natural order established by God. He argues that humans can discern moral principles through reason and observation of the natural world, guided by divine revelation. For Aquinas, ethical norms are derived from the inherent purposes or telos inherent in natural beings, with human flourishing (eudaimonia) understood as the ultimate goal. Therefore, ethical truths are rooted in both natural facts and theological premises.

His influential work, "Summa Theologica" reflects his commitment to harmonizing faith and reason, combining insights from theology and natural philosophy (Aquinas, 1998). Aquinas engaged in natural theology, which involves using reason and empirical observation to explore aspects of the divine order and God's existence. His famous Five Ways are arguments for the existence of God based on observations of the natural world. While not a strict naturalist in the contemporary sense, Aquinas (1998) incorporated teleological principles into his natural law theory. He argued that the natural order reflects God's purpose, and humans can discern moral principles by observing the inherent tendencies and purposes within nature. His approach to ethics involves a synthesis of reason and faith. Aquinas sought to reconcile faith and reason, emphasizing that both are sources of knowledge. He believed that truths derived from revelation (faith) and truths discovered through natural reason (philosophy) could coexist harmoniously.

Aquinas (1998) believed that human nature, created by God, has inherent capacities and purposes. Virtuous living, according to Aquinas, involves aligning one's actions with the natural inclinations and purposes bestowed by God. Aquinas's theologian naturalism emphasizes the inherent dignity of human beings. He argues that humans, created in the image of God, possess reason and free will, enabling them to participate in moral decision-making and pursue virtue.

In summary, Aquinas's theologian naturalism involves the integration of Christian theology and natural philosophy. It emphasizes the compatibility of faith and reason, the use of reason to explore aspects of the divine, and the recognition of God's order in the natural world. Aquinas's synthesis of Aristotelian philosophy with Christian theology has had a lasting impact on the philosophy of religion and the relationship between faith and reason.

Aretaic Naturalism

Aristotle's ethical theory, known as virtue ethics, aligns with ethical naturalism in several key aspects. Aristotle argues that ethical virtues are rooted in human nature and the natural order of the world. He believes that humans have a natural capacity for moral excellence, which can be cultivated through virtuous behaviors that are conducive to human well-being. According to Aristotle, virtues such as kindness, honesty, and fairness are natural dispositions that lead to eudaimonia when cultivated and practiced (Jacobs, 2017). Thus, ethical truths in Aristotle's framework are derived from an understanding of human nature and the natural world, with eudaimonia as the ultimate aim.

Aristotle argued that we can tell what is good by observing functions in the natural world instead of relying on an abstract form. According to MacIntyre (2007), every type of item that can be considered good, whether it be persons or actions, has a specific purpose or function. He suggests that moral goodness is tied to the fulfillment of human purposes or ends. Thus, if you refer to a particular action as good or right, you in fact make a factual claim, and also imply that it is what a good man should do in similar situations (MacIntyre, 2007). MacIntyre (2007) argues that moral statements, including judgments of goodness and justice, are factual in nature. This implies that when we make moral claims, we are asserting something about the world that can be objectively evaluated or verified.

Bradley (1988) highlighted the importance of self-realization within the community and the fulfillment of one's role or function within society. He argued that this involves learning from and engaging with one's family and community, adopting societal values, and understanding one's duties and responsibilities within the social framework. He rejected the idea of moral autonomy detached from social context, instead emphasizing the interdependence of individuals within communities and the importance of contributing to the common good. He also rejected purely individualistic approaches to ethics, such as hedonism, which prioritize personal pleasure, and Kantian deontology, which emphasizes abstract principles of duty divorced from social context.

Natural Moral Law

Both Locke and Rousseau contribute to the development of natural law theory, and their emphasis on the recognition and deduction of certain moral principles as discernible through reason align them with ethical naturalism. Ethical rationalism, in the context of natural law, posits that moral principles can be deduced from the nature of humanity or the natural order by reason (Chiassoni, 2014). It contrasts with intuitionism, which holds that moral truths are self-evident and not necessarily derived from reason (Collao, 2018).

Natural moral law theory, associated with philosophers like John Locke and Jean-Jacques Rousseau, posits that moral principles are grounded in human nature and natural order (Murphy, 2019). According to this view, humans possess inherent rights and duties that are discoverable through reason and observation of the natural world. Locke (1689/2018), for example, argues that individuals have natural rights to life, liberty, and property, which are derived from their status as rational beings. Rousseau similarly emphasizes the natural goodness of humans and the importance of social contracts based on mutual consent. In both cases, ethical truths are understood to be based on natural facts about human beings and their social interactions.

Locke's natural law theory, articulated in his work "Two Treatises of Government (1689/2018)" is based on the idea that individuals possess natural rights derived from the law of nature. While Locke (1689/2018) doesn't explicitly develop a detailed moral theory, his emphasis on reason and natural law suggests a rationalistic approach. Locke (1689/2018) argues that individuals, guided by reason, can discern and abide by the laws of nature, which include principles such as self-preservation and respect for others' property. Rousseau's approach to morality, on the other hand, is more complex, as he emphasizes the concept of the "general will" and the idea of a social contract. While Rousseau (1762/1913) acknowledges a sense of conscience or moral sentiment, his views are not strictly intuitionist. Rousseau (1762/1913) argues for the formation of a collective will through a social contract, and individuals are to act in accordance with this general will, which is guided by reason and the common good.

Utilitarian Ethical Naturalism

Utilitarianism is a form of ethical naturalism, particularly in its emphasis on deriving moral principles from empirical and observable aspects of human experience (pleasure and pain). The ultimate standard for evaluating actions is grounded in the observable experiences of individuals.

Utilitarianism holds that ethical principles are derived from the consequences of actions and their impact on human well-being or happiness. According to utilitarianism, the right action is the one that maximizes overall utility or happiness for the greatest number of people. This perspective views ethical truths as grounded in natural facts about human desires, pleasures, and pains, with the goal of maximizing overall well-being.

Bentham, considered the founder of utilitarianism, formulated the principle of utility. According to Bentham, actions are morally right to the extent that they maximize pleasure or happiness and minimize pain or suffering (Troyer, 2003). Bentham (1781/1996) sought to ground ethics on a quantifiable and empirical basis, emphasizing the measurement and calculation of pleasure and pain as the foundation for determining the morality of actions. Mill who built upon Bentham's utilitarianism, introduced qualitative distinctions in pleasures in his work "Utilitarianism." Mill (1864/2014) argued that not all pleasures are equal and that higher or more intellectual pleasures have greater moral worth than lower, sensory pleasures (Troyer, 2003). While still rooted in the principle of utility, Mill's version of utilitarianism incorporates a nuanced understanding of pleasure and happiness.

In summary, Bentham and Mill, as proponents of utilitarianism, contribute to ethical naturalism through their emphasis on empirical foundations, consequentialist evaluation of actions, and the quantifiable aspects of pleasure and happiness in determining moral principles.

Moral Non-Naturalism

Non-naturalism, within the realm of metaethics, is the philosophical position that moral properties exist independently of natural properties and are not reducible to them. Thus, attempts to reduce goodness to natural properties or facts commit the naturalistic fallacy by conflating different kinds of properties. It holds that moral facts are objective and normative, yet they cannot be described in naturalistic terms and moral facts and values are distinct from empirical facts about the natural world. Moore (1903/2018) criticizes ethical naturalism for attempting to define "Good" in terms of natural properties or facts. He labels this attempt the "naturalistic fallacy." According to Moore (1903/2018), it is a mistake to identify "Good" with any natural property, such as pleasure, because "Good" is a distinct and non-natural property. Moore (1903/2018) argues that "Good" is a simple concept, akin to "yellow," and cannot be further decomposed or defined in terms of other properties. Moore (1903/2018) maintains that "Good" does not consist of parts that can be substituted in our minds, and it cannot be fully explained to someone who does not already understand it. In summary, Moore's critique of ethical naturalism focuses on its attempt to define moral concepts in terms of natural properties, which he argues is mistaken due to the non-natural, irreducible nature of moral properties. This critique is encapsulated in his famous naturalistic fallacy, which highlights the distinction between natural and moral properties.

Within non-naturalism, there can be interpretations that lean towards either consequentialist intuitionism or deontologist intuitionism (Shafer-Landau, 2003; Huemer, 2005). Whether non-naturalist consequentialist intuitionism or non-naturalist deontologist intuitionism is more compelling depends on the specific ethical intuitions and commitments of the philosopher in question. Both perspectives maintain the objectivity of moral truths while differing in their emphasis on either consequences or intrinsic duties as the foundation of morality.

Consequentialist Intuitionism

In this perspective, moral truths are understood to be apprehended through intuition, but the emphasis is on the consequences of actions (Railton, 2014). Non-naturalist consequentialist intuitionism would assert that individuals intuitively recognize moral truths that are grounded in the consequences of actions, rather than in intrinsic duties or principles (Audi, 2004; Huemer, 2005; Shafer-Landau, 2003). These moral intuitions guide individuals towards actions that lead to the best overall consequences, such as maximizing happiness or minimizing suffering, without relying on naturalistic descriptions of these moral properties.

Plato's ethical philosophy, particularly as articulated in his later dialogues, resonates more closely with consequentialist intuitionism. While Plato's theory of forms emphasizes the existence of objective standards of goodness, he also explores the idea that moral actions lead to certain consequences for the soul, both in this life and in the afterlife (Dutra, 2022). In works like "The Republic" Plato discusses the concept of the philosopher-king ruling for the greater good of society, suggesting a concern for the consequences of ethical decisions (Plato, 2007). Additionally, Plato's emphasis on the importance of reason and intuition in apprehending the forms and pursuing knowledge could be seen as compatible with the idea of intuitively recognizing moral truths that lead to beneficial outcomes. Plato (2007) asserts that goodness is a simple, unanalyzable quality that is self-evident and apprehended through intuition.

Haidt (2001) presents a perspective that can be interpreted as consequentialist intuitionism within the realm of non-naturalism. His approach suggests that moral judgments are primarily driven by intuitive emotional responses rather than deliberate reasoning. Haidt (2001) explains that emotive responses are often rooted in unconscious processes and are triggered spontaneously in response to moral dilemmas or situations, whereas cognitive reasoning requires mental effort and involves analytical thinking, logical deduction, and deliberative reflection. He argues that people make moral judgments quickly and automatically, based on gut feelings or intuitions, and then use reasoning post hoc to justify these judgments. Haidt's definition of moral intuition highlights the spontaneous and affective nature of moral judgments, emphasizing the role of automatic cognitive processes in shaping moral behavior. This perspective challenges traditional models of moral decision-making that prioritize conscious reasoning and underscores the importance of understanding the complex interplay between emotion and cognition in moral psychology.

Within the framework of non-naturalism, Haidt's approach can be interpreted as consequentialist intuitionism because it emphasizes the significance of intuitive responses in moral judgement, rather than adherence to fixed moral principles or duties. In this view, moral intuitions are shaped by the consequences of actions and their impact on individuals' emotional well-being or social harmony. Haidt's approach does not rely on the existence of objective moral truths or natural properties but instead suggests that moral judgments arise from our advanced psychological systems that have been evolved by natural selection over the course of human evolution. These intuitions guide individuals towards actions that promote social cohesion or individual well-being, without appealing to external moral principles or duties.

Overall, Haidt's social intuitionist approach which is often characterized by its reliance on evolutionary psychology can be seen as a form of consequentialist intuitionism within the realm of non-naturalism, as it emphasizes the importance of intuitive emotional responses and the consequences of actions in moral judgment, without grounding morality in objective moral truths or natural properties.

Deontological Intuitionism

Alternatively, within non-naturalism, there is a deontologist intuitionist interpretation where moral truths are considered to be apprehended through intuition, but the emphasis is on intrinsic moral duties or principles (Audi, 2004; Huemer, 2005). Non-naturalist deontologist intuitionism posits that individuals intuitively recognize objective moral principles or duties that are not reducible to natural properties (Shafer-Landau, 2003). These principles guide moral decision-making independent of consequences, focusing instead on the inherent rightness or wrongness of actions.

Socrates' ethical inquiries, as depicted in Plato's dialogues, often revolve around questions of justice, piety, and the nature of a good life. His famous method of dialectics involved questioning assumptions and seeking definitions of moral concepts, suggesting a concern for moral absolutes rather than contingent outcomes. Moreover, he emphasizes the importance of moral principles, and the pursuit of virtue as ends in themselves, rather than merely as means to achieve desirable consequences (Dutra, 2022). This emphasis on moral duties and principles aligns with the core tenets of deontological intuitionism, which asserts that moral truths are objective and intuitively apprehended.

Prichard's ethical philosophy is best understood within the framework of deontological intuitionism. He emphasizes the existence of objective moral principles apprehended through intuition, which are binding regardless of their consequences. His ethical theory, as outlined in works like "Moral Obligation" and "Duty and Ignorance of Fact" emphasizes the existence of moral principles that are self-evident and intuitively known. Prichard (2003a, 2003b) argues that moral obligations are fundamental and irreducible, not contingent upon consequences or empirical facts. According to him, certain moral principles, such as the duty to keep promises or refrain from harming others, are apprehended through intuition and are binding regardless of their outcomes. This aligns closely with deontological intuitionism, which asserts that moral truths are objective and intuitive, rather than dependent on the consequences of actions.

Prichard (2003a) distinguishes between duty and other kinds of reasons for action, such as prudential or instrumental reasons. He argues that duty carries a unique force that cannot be overridden by competing considerations, emphasizing the absolute nature of moral obligations. This emphasis on the primacy of duty and the intuitive recognition of moral principles aligns with deontological intuitionism rather than consequentialist intuitionism. Prichard (2003a) argues that the word "ought" cannot be precisely defined or reduced to a set of criteria. Instead, he suggests that the concept of "ought" is inherently intuitive and resistant to formal definition. Despite this, Prichard contends that individuals possess an innate understanding of when they ought to do certain actions, even if they cannot articulate a precise definition of the term. Prichard (2003a) distinguishes between two modes of moral thinking: reason and intuition. Reason involves a rational analysis of the facts and considerations relevant to a moral situation, while intuition involves an immediate, intuitive sense of what one ought to do. Prichard suggests that both reason and intuition play important roles in moral decision-making, but intuition often takes precedence in guiding action. Prichard acknowledges that individuals may have different moral intuitions due to variations in upbringing, culture, and personal experiences. As a result, what one person intuitively feels is morally right may differ from what another person believes. Prichard cautions against using individual intuitions alone to establish the intrinsic goodness of an action, emphasizing the importance of considering the moral obligations inherent in a particular situation.

Ross, a prominent British philosopher of the early 20th century, is often associated with a form of deontological intuitionism known as pluralistic deontology. Ross's (1930/2002) ethical theory, as outlined in his seminal work "The Right and the Good" combines elements of both deontological and consequentialist reasoning. According to Ross's concept of prima facie duties there are prima facie duties, which are moral obligations and duties that are intuitively apprehended and carry moral weight but can be overridden in certain circumstances by other, more pressing duties (Ross, 1930/2002). He also added that a "mature mind" would recognize these prima facie duties in any given situation as they become apparent at first appearance for a "mature mind".

While Ross (1930/2002) acknowledges the importance of consequences in moral decision-making, he maintains that certain duties are intrinsically binding regardless of their outcomes. This aligns with deontological intuitionism, which asserts the existence of objective moral principles that are intuitively apprehended and do not depend solely on consequences. However, Ross's theory also incorporates consequentialist elements in the sense that he recognizes that moral decision-making often involves weighing competing prima facie duties and considering the overall consequences of actions. In situations where duties conflict, individuals must use practical reasoning to determine which duty has greater weight in the given circumstances, considering both the intrinsic value of the duties and the likely consequences of different courses of action.

In summary, Ross's ethical theory can be understood as a form of deontological intuitionism, given its emphasis on the existence of objective moral principles apprehended through intuition. However, Ross also incorporates consequentialist considerations by recognizing the importance of consequences and practical reasoning in moral decision-making, leading to a nuanced approach that balances both deontological and consequentialist concerns.

Moral Non-Objectivism

If you think that moral facts are not independent of individuals' beliefs, perspectives, or cultural contexts, then you are a moral non-objectivist. Moral non-objectivism suggests that moral facts, such as what is morally right or wrong, good, or bad, are contingent upon individuals' beliefs or subjective perspectives (Harman, 1977). In other words, moral truths are not objective or universal but are instead shaped by individual attitudes, beliefs, and cultural norms (Joyce, 2006; Mackie, 2011). So, the next question to be asked becomes "whose values determine the rightness or wrongness of moral claims?" You have four main options within the realm of standard meta-ethics: human agency and reason (moral constructivism), individual subjectivity (moral subjectivity), society (cultural relativism), or God (divine command theory).

Moral Constructivism

If you think that even if moral claims can be proved true, their truth capacity does not hold a value, because those discovered moral facts are no more important than your justified, constructed moral facts, then you are a moral constructivist. While moral constructivism doesn't necessarily deny the existence of moral facts, it just does not care whether it is possible to obtain those fact, because it typically places the source of morality in human construction, and human processes of agreement, or consensus. Moral constructivism is a metaethical theory that suggests that moral truths or principles are constructed by individuals or societies rather than being discovered as objective facts (Korsgaard, 2008; Street, 2008).

There are different forms of moral constructivism, and various philosophers have contributed to its development. Korsgaard (1996), for example, developed a Kantian version of moral constructivism and argued that moral principles are products of practical reason, and social agreement, constructed through rational deliberation.

John Rawls (1999), in his influential work "A Theory of Justice," presents a form of moral constructivism known as "reflective equilibrium." He argues that moral principles arise through a process of reflective equilibrium, where individuals balance and adjust their moral intuitions to achieve a coherent and justifiable moral framework.

Hilary Putnam's contribution to moral constructivism includes his work on the fact/value dichotomy (2004). He argues against a strict separation between factual and evaluative claims, suggesting that values are inextricably intertwined with our descriptions of the world.

Jürgen Habermas is known for his discourse ethics, a form of moral constructivism that emphasizes the role of rational discourse in constructing moral principles. He argues that moral norms must be justifiable through a process of rational deliberation among free and equal participants (Rehg, 2011).

Shelly Kagan has explored moral constructivism in his work, particularly in the context of contractualism. Kagan (1991) argues that moral principles are constructed through a hypothetical social contract, where individuals agree on principles that would govern their interactions.

These philosophers represent various strands of moral constructivism, each offering unique perspectives on how moral principles are constructed. While they may differ in their approaches, moral constructivists generally share the view that morality is a human construct and that moral principles are not discovered but rather created through rational deliberation, agreement, or reflective equilibrium.

Moral Subjectivism

This perspective holds that moral judgments are grounded in individual subjectivity. In other words, what is considered morally right or wrong varies from person to person based on their personal beliefs, attitudes, or emotions (Harman, 1975; Mackie, 1990). Under this view, moral truths are not objective but are instead relative to the individual making the judgment. So, the statement "mercy is good" is true when that person says it but may not be true for a different person who believes that mercy is merely good for people who need them (e.g., slaves). While moral subjectivism acknowledges the diversity of moral beliefs among individuals, it struggles to provide a satisfactory account of moral disagreement, particularly when confronted with extreme cases like those involving psychopathy. The belief that murder is morally permissible may seem deeply troubling to many people, challenging the coherence of moral subjectivism. The existence of individuals who hold morally reprehensible beliefs raises important ethical questions about how societies should respond. While moral subjectivism recognizes the diversity of moral perspectives, it does not necessarily provide a framework for evaluating or justifying these perspectives. It merely endorses that moral truths are relative to each individual.

Existentialism is a philosophical movement which is often associated with moral subjectivism as it emphasizes individual existence, freedom, and choice. Existentialist thinkers such as Jean-Paul Sartre and Friedrich Nietzsche focus on the individual's responsibility in creating their own values and meaning in life. Existentialism can be associated with individualism in the sense that it prioritizes individual autonomy and self-determination. They all argue that the truth of a moral claim depends on the beliefs of the person making the claim.

Hume's ethical philosophy is often associated with subjectivism, a view that emphasizes the role of individual sentiments and feelings in the formation of moral judgments. Hume's subjectivism is a key component of his broader empiricist and skeptical approach to philosophy. Hume (1739) argues that moral distinctions arise not from reason but from sentiments or passions. He contends that moral judgments are expressions of approval or disapproval that result from the individual's emotional responses to certain actions or qualities. He proposes that moral concepts and distinctions have their origins in human sentiments and are shaped by individual and collective experiences. Hume (1739) challenges the traditional view that reason alone can be the source of moral distinctions. He famously states that "reason is and ought only to be the slave of passions," suggesting that moral judgments are not deduced through reason but are guided by emotions and sentiments. Hume (1739) acknowledges the diversity of moral practices and norms across different cultures. Hume (1739) attributes these variations to differences in sentiments, customs, and habits. This recognition of cultural diversity aligns with a subjectivist stance that allows for varying moral judgments.

Cultural Relativism

Cultural relativism is a perspective in ethics that asserts that cultural norms and values shape individuals' perceptions of what is morally right, or wrong (Herskovits, 1948). According to this view, right action is merely what the law and customs of one's society require. Unlike moral subjectivism, which focuses on individual beliefs, cultural relativism emphasizes the influence of cultural context on moral judgments and highlights the importance of understanding moral beliefs and practices within their cultural context and encourages respect for cultural diversity (Pojman, & Fieser, 2016). While it acknowledges the variability of moral norms across cultures, cultural relativism also sparks debate about the existence of universal moral principles and the ethical implications of cultural diversity.

Cultural relativism recognizes that different cultures have distinct sets of norms, values, and practices (Rachels, 2015). What is considered morally acceptable or unacceptable can vary widely across different cultures and societies. According to cultural relativism, there are no universal or objective standards for morality that apply to all cultures (Benedict, 1934). Moral judgments are understood within the specific cultural context in which they arise. Cultural relativism encourages individuals to suspend judgment of other cultures based on their own cultural norms (Wong, 2018). It opposes ethnocentrism, which is the tendency to evaluate other cultures according to the standards of one's own culture. Cultural relativism promotes respect for cultural diversity and the recognition that different cultures may have valid reasons for their moral beliefs and practices. Cultural relativism raises important ethical questions about how to navigate moral diversity and cultural differences. It prompts individuals and societies to engage in cross-cultural dialogue and reflection on the values and norms that shape moral judgments.

From a relativistic perspective, what is considered morally right or wrong is determined by the prevailing attitudes and customs of a particular society at a given time. Therefore, you might worry that moral relativism undermines the notion of moral progress by suggesting that moral judgments are ultimately arbitrary and contingent upon cultural relativism. Moreover, moral relativism may lead to moral skepticism or indifference, as it denies the possibility of moral truths that transcend cultural boundaries. Critics also argue that there are universal moral principles that should apply regardless of cultural context. For instance, practices that violate human rights or lead to harm, such as female genital mutilation or slavery should never be justified. Critics of moral relativism contend that certain moral principles, such as respect for human rights and the prevention of harm, should be regarded as universal and non-negotiable. They argue that these principles provide a basis for ethical judgments that transcend cultural differences and serve as a moral compass for individuals and societies worldwide.

Divine Command Theory

Divine command theory is a metaethical position which asserts that the foundation of morality is based on the decrees or desires of a divine being or deity (Adams, 1999). According to this perspective, moral obligations and values are determined by God's commands (Quinn, 1979). God is seen as the origin and regulator of morality. According to divine command theory, moral truths are objective and absolute and grounded on God's will. What is morally right or wrong is determined by divine commands and is independent of human beliefs or cultural norms. Actions are morally right if God commands them, and they are morally wrong if God prohibits them. Compliance with divine commands is seen as a requirement of God's omnipotence and moral perfection (Wierenga, 1983). It asserts that moral principles are derived from the commands or will of a divine being, such as God (Cudworth, 1996[1731]). Actions are considered morally right if they align with the divine commands, and they are morally wrong if they go against these commands. The duty to follow divine commands takes precedence over the consequences of the actions. The demands of Christian ethics, e.g., include a level of mercy, forgiveness, and love that go beyond the other person's rights, beyond what the other person deserves. There is the teaching of Jesus to love your enemies, which entails more than what they have a right to. On the other hand, such things may be regarded as honoring God's rightful claims on us. The essence of divine command theory is that what determines the rightness or wrongness of an action is whether God commands it or forbids it. The golden rule, or the ethics of reciprocity -the moral principle of all Abrahamic religions and a precept in the Gospel of Matthew (7:12) which calls upon people to treat others the way you would like to be treated. It emphasizes empathy and reciprocity in moral interactions and suggests that individuals should treat others with the same kindness, respect, and consideration that they would wish to receive themselves. This principle is often seen as a foundational aspect of many moral traditions and is based on the idea of promoting mutual understanding and cooperation.

Ethics of selflessness often align with religious teachings and moral philosophies and posits that one is moral only to the extent s/he sees herself/himself fundamentally as a servant, sacrificing one's own interests for the sake of God's commands or more moderately, to the extent one acts primarily with regard to God's commands. One thing that severely differs Kantian deontology from divine command theory is that while Kant considers people as a rational being and relies on their rationality of people to ensure the universality of moral laws, divine command states that the moral laws are universal because it's the laws of God and decreed by God.

We can praise the divine command theory for its simplicity. When you do not know what to do, ask God and find the answer in the holy book. According to the Christian faith, the Bible sets out the essential rules from God that tell Christians how to live a good life and dispense our relationships with God and other human beings, or Qur'an that tells Muslims how to lead a life with dignity or Torah (the Hebrew Bible) that tells Jewish people how to lead a fulfilling life and please God now and forever. Although, this seems very straightforward and simple, it is not. Here are some common critiques of Divine Command Theory:

First of all, which book? – Torah, Quran, or Bible? For example, although the Quran and Bible are basically the same story told different way, they are not the same. For example, the Quran tells us that a newborn baby is innocent like an angel. Yet, as s/he grows up s/he becomes sinful. The Holy Bible, on the other hand, argues that we are born sinful. Indeed, this belief is the essence of the baptism- an act of purification. Yet, in Islam a ritual washing is performed on corpse as an act of purification to prepare corpse for a final prayer. So, in one religion while you need to be purified after birth, in the other you need to be purified before your death ceremony, because in one religion you are sinful upon birth, but in the other one, you become sinful while living.

Second, all those books need some kind of interpretation. So even religious people are bothered by uncertainty and moral conflict as all of those texts need interpretation. Moral commandments, such as "Thou shall not kill" or "Thou shall not bear false witness against thy neighbor," are subject to interpretation based on various factors, including cultural context, religious tradition, and ethical reasoning. Different individuals and religious communities may interpret these commandments differently, leading to diverse perspectives on their meaning and application. Moral principles often need to be understood in light of specific circumstances and contexts. For example, while the commandment "Thou shall not kill" may be interpreted as prohibiting the taking of innocent lives, there may be exceptions in cases of self-defense or just wars. Similarly, the prohibition against bearing false witness may be understood as condemning dishonesty, but there may be situations where deception is deemed permissible or even necessary. Some religious thinkers have indeed proposed that lying may be acceptable or even morally praiseworthy in certain situations, particularly if it serves a higher purpose or furthers the interests of a religious community. For example, the use of deceit, deception, and lies in police interrogation are necessary for law enforcement officers to obtain crucial information and trick suspects into confession, particularly in cases involving serious crimes or national security threats. The question of whether certain types of lies, such as white lies or lies told for benevolent purposes, are morally justifiable is another topic of ethical debate. White lies are typically considered to be harmless or trivial falsehoods told to avoid hurting someone's feelings or to maintain social harmony. For example, telling someone they look good in an outfit when you don't genuinely believe it could be considered a white lie. Some argue that these lies are necessary for maintaining polite social interactions and preventing unnecessary conflict or discomfort. Similarly, lies told in situations where someone's safety or well-being is at risk, such as during wartime or to protect someone from harm, are often seen as morally defensible. For instance, if someone asks you where your child is hiding to avoid capture by an aggressor, lying to protect your child could be seen as a morally justifiable act. All commandments often require careful consideration of specific circumstances and contexts. It is for this reason why two believing Christians can read the same scripture and reach different conclusions regarding its meaning and application and it is exactly the reason that why religious traditions, such as Judaism, Christianity, Islam, Buddhist, and Confucian traditions has produced commentaries upon commentaries. Thus, moral reasoning and thoughtful reflection are essential for clergy and religious leaders when addressing ethical dilemmas and guiding their communities. Simply applying pre-formed answers or offering superficial responses may not adequately address the complexities of moral issues faced by individuals and communities. Otherwise, we would end up like the politician who listened to the first citizen and said, "You're right", then to the second and said, "You're right." When someone overheard the conversation and asked, "You said both were right, but if one is right the other cannot be right" The politician replied, "You're right, too"!

Third, none of those books sufficiently address our contemporary worries. It is often inconsistent with our autonomy, free-will and our rationality -perhaps because our rationality is bounded by our limited intelligence and existing knowledge, but most importantly divine commands may sometimes be inconsistent within itself -of course according to our limited rationality (Hare, 2012). The most notable and striking example of it is the God's command to Abraham, to sacrifice his son Isaac. One interpretation suggests that God's command was a test of Abraham's faith rather than an actual directive to kill Isaac. In this view, God never intended for Isaac to be harmed, but rather sought to demonstrate Abraham's unwavering trust and obedience. However, this interpretation does not entirely resolve the ethical dilemma presented by the story. If God's command was indeed a test, it raises questions about the morality of testing someone's faith in such a drastic and morally troubling manner. It also challenges conventional understandings of truthfulness and honesty, as God's command could be seen as intentionally deceptive if it was not meant to be carried out literally.

Another objection is that God's commands are often to particular people, like Abraham or Mohammed, at particular times and particular places and they are not easily deducible (Hare, 2012). This raises questions about the universality and accessibility of divine commands, especially if they are not easily deducible or applicable beyond the specific circumstances in which they were given. The objection highlights the potential limitations of human rationality in understanding divine commands. If divine commands are ultimately beyond human comprehension, then individuals may be required to exercise faith and trust in God's wisdom and guidance, even when they cannot fully understand or deduce the reasons behind specific commands.

Moral Pluralism

Moral pluralism is indeed a position in metaethics that recognizes the existence of diverse and conflicting moral views, values, and judgments within society (Kekes, 1997). Unlike moral absolutism, which asserts that there is only one correct moral answer or standard, and moral relativism, which suggests that moral judgments are relative to individuals or cultures and thus, "there is no wrong answer", moral pluralism acknowledges the complexity and diversity of moral perspectives and endorse finding a moderate position between moral absolutism and moral relativism (Biasucci & Prentice, 2018).

Forsyth's classification of ethical perspectives into four dichotomized categories based on the dimensions of relativism and idealism provides a framework for understanding different approaches in moral pluralism (see Figure 8).

Relativism reflects the degree to which individuals rely on situational factors and skepticism in forming their moral judgments, rather than adhering strictly to ethical principles. In other words, relativism suggests that moral judgments are contingent upon the specific circumstances and individuals involved, rather than being guided by universal or absolute moral standards (Forsyth, 1980). On the other hand, idealists believe that harming others can always be avoided by choosing the "right" action, and therefore, they would not compromise by choosing what they perceive as the lesser of two evils (Forsyth, 1980).

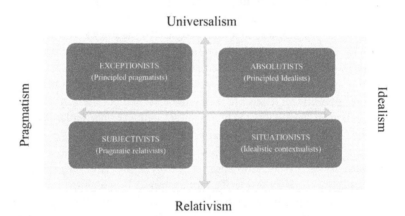

Figure 8. The "ethical ideology/ethics position" Framework Adapted from Forsyth (1980)

Absolutists (Principled Idealists)

Absolutists, or principled idealists as described by Forsyth (1980), adhere to the belief that the best outcomes can always be attained by following universal moral rules. They firmly hold that actions should strive to produce positive results for all individuals involved and are particularly sensitive to instances where actions cause harm to others or violate universal ethical principles. Similar to deontologists in ethical theory, absolutists prioritize the adherence to moral principles and rules above situational factors or consequences. They believe in the importance of upholding ethical norms and values universally, regardless of the specific circumstances or potential outcomes.

Absolutists maintain a strong commitment to moral integrity and consistency, often viewing ethical dilemmas through the lens of universal moral rules rather than subjective or pragmatic considerations. They are guided by a sense of duty to uphold moral principles and strive to ensure that their actions align with these principles, even when faced with challenging or conflicting situations.

Situationists (Idealistic Contextualists)

Situationists, also known as idealistic contextualists according to Forsyth (1980), reject the notion of universal ethical principles but still acknowledge the obligation to act in a manner that generates positive outcomes for society at large. They prioritize achieving the most beneficial consequences for all members of a group, even if it means deviating from traditional moral rules. Unlike absolutists, situationists advocate for a contextual and individualized approach to ethical decision-making, emphasizing the importance of analyzing each situation independently rather than adhering strictly to overarching moral standards. They prioritize minimizing harm and maximizing positive outcomes, even if it requires departing from conventional moral norms.

Situationists' ethical outlook is characterized by ethical skepticism or value pluralism, suggesting that the morality of an action is contingent upon the consequences it produces in a given situation. This perspective allows for flexibility and adaptability in ethical decision-making, as it recognizes the complexity and variability of real-world circumstances. Situationists may be willing to employ tactics such as deception if they believe it will lead to the best overall results for society.

Subjectivists (Pragmatic Relativists)

Subjectivists, also referred to as pragmatic relativists according to Forsyth (1980), formulate their moral evaluations based on personal emotions and perspectives rather than adherence to universal moral principles. Unlike absolutists or situationists, subjectivists neither recognize nor prioritize behaviors aimed at generating positive outcomes for all parties involved. From the subjectivist perspective, actions that may cause harm to others could still be considered ethical if they align with personal judgments regarding winning or losing. Subjectivists acknowledge the possibility of negative consequences but prioritize individual autonomy and subjective interpretation of morality.

Subjectivists exhibit skepticism towards the idea of basing moral judgments on universal or trans-personal rules, as they believe that moral standards vary depending on individual perspectives and situational contexts. They may agree with statements suggesting that ethical norms are inherently subjective and cannot be universally resolved. Furthermore, subjectivists may adopt a relatively callous orientation towards preventing harm to others, as they do not strongly endorse the principle of "do no harm" and prioritize personal interests or desires over the well-being of others. Examples of subjectivist perspectives include ethical egoism, amoralism, and act-utilitarianism.

Exceptionists (Principled Pragmatists)

Exceptionists, characterized as principled pragmatists by Forsyth (1980), hold the belief that individuals should generally adhere to moral rules but remain open to pragmatic exceptions. Unlike absolutists, exceptionists acknowledge the necessity of obeying ethical principles but reject the notion of their universality. They recognize that negative consequences cannot always be avoided entirely, and their moderate level of idealism allows them to balance the positive and negative outcomes of actions pragmatically.

In essence, exceptionists view ethical principles as valuable frameworks for guiding behavior but understand that there may be circumstances where deviations from these principles are necessary to achieve the best overall outcomes. They prioritize creating positive consequences for all parties involved, even if it means personally sacrificing or facing disadvantages. For example, exceptionists may subscribe to rule-utilitarianism, which advocates following moral rules that generally lead to the greatest overall good but allows for exceptions when deviation from the rule results in better outcomes.

The findings of Forsyth et al.'s (2008) meta-analysis suggest significant cultural differences in moral philosophies, particularly in terms of idealism and relativism. Western cultures generally lean towards less idealistic moral philosophies compared to Eastern cultures. Idealism, which involves the belief in adherence to universal moral rules and principles, tends to be more pronounced in Eastern cultures. Furthermore, the analysis indicates that Eastern cultures exhibit higher levels of relativism compared to Western cultures. Relativism implies that moral judgments are influenced by situational factors and individual perspectives rather than universal principles. This suggests that Eastern cultures may be more inclined to consider contextual factors and individual perspectives when making moral judgments. In terms of specific moral philosophies, situationism, characterized by high levels of both idealism and relativism, is predominant in Eastern cultures. Situationists prioritize positive consequences for all parties involved and may be more open to pragmatic exceptions to moral rules based on situational factors. On the other hand, exceptionism, characterized by low levels of both idealism and relativism, is more prevalent in Western cultures. Exceptionists generally adhere to moral rules but remain open to pragmatic exceptions when necessary to achieve the best overall outcomes. Overall, these findings highlight the importance of considering cultural differences in moral philosophies when examining ethical decision-making processes and moral reasoning across different societies.

References

Adams, R. M. (1999). *Finite and infinite goods: A framework for ethics.* Oxford University Press.

Aquinas, T. (1998). *Summa Theologica.* Thomas More.

Aristotle. (2012). *Aristotle's Nicomachean ethics* (R. C. Bartlett, & S. D. Collins, Trans.). University of Chicago Press.

Audi, R. (2004). *The good in the right: A theory of intuition and intrinsic value.* Princeton University Press.

Benedict, R. (1934). *Patterns of culture.* Houghton Mifflin Harcourt.

Bentham, J. (1996). *The collected works of Jeremy Bentham: Introduction to the principles of morals and legislation* (J. H. Burns & H. L. A. Hart, Eds.). Clarendon Press. (Original work published 1781)

Biasucci, C., & Prentice, R. (2018). *Teaching notes.* Ethics Unwrapped. https://ethicsunwrapped.utexas.edu

Bradley, F. H. (1988). *Ethical studies.* Clarendon Press

Brown, S. R. (1984). The subjective communicability of meta-ethics: A note on fishkin's methodology. *Political Methodology, 10*(4), 465–478. http://www.jstor.org/stable/25791244

Chiassoni, P. (2014). Kelsen on natural law theory: An enduring critical affair. *Law, Logic and Morality, 23,* 135–163. https://doi.org/10.4000/revus.2976

Collao, F. (2018). Natural law moral epistemology: Naturalist, intuitionist or both? *Rechtstheorie, 49*(2), 131–154. https://doi.org/10.3790/rth.49.2.131

Copp, D. (2003). Why naturalism? *Ethical Theory and Moral Practice 6*(2), 179–200. https://doi.org/10.1023/a:1024420725408

Cudworth, R. (1996). *A treatise concerning eternal and immutable morality.* (S. Hutton, Ed.). Cambridge University Press. (Original work published 1731)

Dimmock, M., & Fisher, A. (2017). Metaethical theories. In *Ethics for A-level: For AQA philosophy and OCR religious studies* (pp. 93–120). Open Book Publishers. http://books.openedition.org/obp/4425

Dutra, J. (2022, June 12). *What did Socrates, Plato, and Aristotle think about wisdom?* The Collector. https://www.thecollector.com/socrates-plato-aristotle-wisdom/

Fink, H. (2006). Three sorts of naturalism. *European Journal of Philosophy, 14*(2), 202–221. https://doi.org/10.1111/j.1468-0378.2006.00222.x

Forsyth, D. R. (1980). A taxonomy of ethical ideologies. *Journal of Personality and Social Psychology, 39*(1), 175–184. https://doi.org/10.1037/0022-3514.39.1.175

Forsyth, D. R., O'Boyle, E. H., & McDaniel, M. A. (2008). East meets west: A meta-analytic investigation of cultural variations in idealism and relativism. *Journal of Business Ethics, 83*(4), 813–833. https://www.jstor.org/stable/25482415

Frank, L. E. (2014). *Moral motivation and the authority of morality: A defense of naturalist moral realism.* CUNY Academic Works. https://academicworks.cuny.edu/gc_etds/211

Garner, R. (2014). *Beyond morality.* Echo Point Books & Media.

Garner, R. T., & Rosen, B. (1967). *Moral philosophy: A systematic introduction to normative ethics and meta-ethics.* Macmillan.

Glassen, P. (1959). The cognitivity of moral judgments. *Mind, 68*(269), 57–72. http://www.jstor.org/stable/2251164

Haidt, J. (2001). The emotional dog and its rational tail: A social intuitionist approach to moral judgment. *Psychological Review, 108*(4), 814–834. https://doi.org/10.1037/0033-295X.108.4.814

Hare, J. E. (2012). Divine command. *Ankara Üniversitesi İlahiyat Fakültesi Dergisi, 53*(2), 187–197. https://doi.org/10.1501/Ilhfak0000001370.

Harman, G. (1975). Moral relativism defended. *The Philosophical Review, 84*(1), 3–22.

Harman, G. (1977). *The nature of morality: An introduction to ethics.* Oxford University Press.

Herskovits, M. J. (1948). *Cultural relativism: Perspectives in cultural pluralism.* Random House.

Huemer, M. (2005). *Ethical intuitionism.* Palgrave Macmillan.

Hume, D. (1739). *A treatise of human nature.* Oxford University Press. https://doi.org/10.1093/oseo/instance.0004622

Jacobs, J. (2017). Aristotelian ethical virtue: Naturalism without measure. In D. Carr, J. Arthur, & K. Kristjánsson (Eds.), *Varieties of virtue ethics* (pp. 125–142). Palgrave Macmillan. https://doi.org/10.1057/978-1-137-59177-7_8

Joyce, R. (2006). *The evolution of morality.* MIT Press.

Kagan, S. (1991). *The limits of morality.* Clarendon Press.

Kekes, J. (1997). Moral pluralism: The concept of diversity. In S. Luper-Foy (Ed.), *The possibility of knowledge: Nozick and his critics* (pp. 293–312). Rowman & Littlefield.

Korsgaard, C. (1996). *The sources of normativity.* Cambridge UP.

Lisska, A. J. (2013). Right reason in natural law moral theory: Thomas Aquinas and William of Ockham. In J. A. Jacobs (Ed.), *Reason, religion, and natural law: From Plato to Spinoza* (pp. 155–174). Oxford Academic. https://doi.org/10.1093/acprof:oso/9780199767175.003.0006

Locke, J. (2018). *Two treaties of Government.* Forgotten Books. (Original work published 1689)

Lutz, M. (2023). *Moral naturalism.* In E. N. Zalta & U. Nodelman (Eds.), *The Stanford encyclopedia of philosophy.* https://plato.stanford.edu/archives/fall2023/entries/naturalism-moral

MacIntyre, A. (2007). *After virtue* (3rd ed.). University of Notre Dame Press. (Original work published 1981)

Mackie, J. J. (1990). *Ethics: Inventing right and wrong.* Penguin Books.

Mackie, J. L. (2011). *Ethics: Inventing right and wrong* Penguin.

Mill, J. S. (2014). *Utilitarianism.* Cambridge University Press. (Original work published 1864)

Moore, G. E. (2018). *Principia ethica.* Independently Published. (Original work published 1903)

Murphy, M. (2019). The natural law tradition in ethics, In E. N. Zalta & U. Nodelman (Eds.), *The Stanford Encyclopedia of Philosophy.* https://plato.stanford.edu/archives/sum2019/entries/natural-law-ethics

Nietzsche, F. (1961). *Thus Spoke Zarathustra: A book for everyone and no one.* (R. J. Hollingdale, Trans., Ed.). Penguin Classics. (Original work published 1883)

Plato. (2007). *The republic* (D. Lee, Trans.). Penguin Classics.

Pojman, L. P., & Fieser, J. (2016). *Ethics: Discovering right and wrong.* Cengage Learning.

Prichard, H. A. (2003a). Duty and ignorance of fact. In J. MacAdam, (Ed.), *Moral writings* (pp. 84–101). Oxford Academic. https://doi.org/10.1093/0199250197.003.0006

Prichard, H. A. (2003b). Moral obligation. In J. MacAdam (Ed.), *Moral writings* (pp. 163–225). Oxford Academic. https://doi.org/10.1093/0199250197.003.0009

Putnam, H. (2004). *The collapse of the fact/value dichotomy and other essays.* Harvard University Press

Quinn, P. L. (1979). Divine command ethics: A causal theory. In W. A. Frankena (Ed.), *Divine commands and moral requirements* (pp. 68–86). Oxford University Press.

Rachels, J. (2015). *The elements of moral philosophy.* McGraw-Hill Education.

Railton, P. (2014). Moral learning and moral progress: Mapping the terrain. In H. Cappelen, T. S. Gendler, & J. Hawthorne (Eds.), *The Oxford handbook of philosophical methodology* (pp. 447–476). Oxford University Press.

Rawls, J. (1999). *A theory of justice* (2nd ed.). Belknap Press.

Rehg, W. (2011). *Discourse ethics*. In B. Fultner (Ed.), *Jürgen Habermas: Key concepts* (pp. 115–139). Acumen Publishing.

Ross (2002). *The right and the good* (P. Stratton-Lake, Ed.). Oxford University Press. (Original work published 1930)

Rousseau, J. J. (1913). *On the social contract* (G. D. H. Cole, Trans.). Chump Change. (Original work published 1762)

Sartre, J. P. (2007). *Existentialism and humanism*. Methuen Publishing Ltd.

Sayre-McCord, G. (2015). *Moral realism*. In E. N. Zalta & U. Nodelman (Eds.), *The Stanford encyclopedia of philosophy*. https://plato.stanford.edu/archives/win2023/entries/moral-realism

Shafer-Landau, R. (2003). *Moral realism: A defence*. Oxford University Press.

Sinclair, N. (2006). Two kinds of naturalism in ethics. *Ethical Theory and Moral Practice, 9*(4), 417–439.

Svavarsdottir, S. (1999). Moral cognitivism and motivation. *The Philosophical Review, 108*(2), 161–219. https://doi.org/10.2307/2998300

Troyer, J. (2003). *The classical utilitarians*. Hackett Publishing.

Tudela, P. (2004). Cognitivism. In C. D. Spielberger (Ed.), *Encyclopedia of Applied Psychology* (pp. 393–401). Elsevier. https://doi.org/10.1016/B0-12-657410-3/00967-3

Van Roojen, M. (2004). Moral cognitivism vs. non-cognitivism. In E. N. Zalta & U. Nodelman (Eds.), *The Stanford Encyclopedia of Philosophy*. https://plato.stanford.edu/archives/win2023/entries/moral-cognitivism

Wierenga, E. (1983). A defensible divine command theory. *Noûs, 17*(3), 387–407. https://doi.org/10.2307/2215256

Wong, D. B. (2018). Moral relativity. In E. N. Zalta & U. Nodelman (Eds.), *The stanford encyclopedia of philosophy*. Stanford University.

Part IV Applied Ethics

The demand for employees and employers adhering to ethical standards keeps rising. Applied ethics plays a crucial role in addressing moral dilemmas and guiding decision-making processes in various fields. As advancements in medicine, technology, and other domains present new ethical challenges, applied ethics provides a framework for analyzing and resolving these complex issues. In the realm of healthcare, for example, applied ethics helps healthcare professionals navigate difficult decisions regarding patient care, medical research, and end-of-life treatment. It addresses questions about the allocation of scarce resources, patient autonomy, and the ethical implications of emerging medical technologies. In education, applied ethics informs discussions about academic integrity, student rights, and ethical conduct in research and teaching. It guides educators in promoting values such as honesty, fairness, and respect within educational institutions. Similarly, in technology and engineering, applied ethics considers the ethical implications of innovations such as artificial intelligence, genetic engineering, and biotechnology. It aims to ensure that technological developments are aligned with ethical principles and respect human rights and dignity. In the military and law enforcement, applied ethics help personnel navigate complex moral dilemmas related to warfare, use of force, and treatment of prisoners. It emphasizes principles of justice, proportionality, and respect for human rights in decision-making processes. In business and finance, applied ethics addresses issues such as corporate social responsibility, fair competition, and ethical decision-making in financial transactions. It promotes ethical leadership, transparency, and accountability in business practices.

While individuals may not always consciously apply moral theories in their daily decision-making, they inevitably encounter situations where the ethical implications of their actions become apparent. This recognition often arises when professionals in different industries confront the real-world consequences of their work on individuals, communities, and broader society. For instance, healthcare professionals may realize the ethical complexities involved in allocating scarce medical resources during a pandemic, prompting them to consider principles of distributive justice and patient autonomy. Similarly, engineers and technologists may grapple with the ethical implications of developing and deploying new technologies that have the potential to impact privacy, autonomy, and social equity.

In business and finance, professionals may confront ethical dilemmas related to corporate governance, environmental sustainability, and fair labor practices, prompting them to consider principles of corporate social responsibility and ethical leadership. In education, educators may reflect on the ethical dimensions of grading policies, student-teacher relationships, and academic integrity, prompting them to consider principles of fairness, respect, and integrity. Across these and other fields, the realization of the ethical dimensions of one's work often leads to a deeper engagement with applied ethics. Professionals recognize the need for more reflection, consideration, and ethical deliberation to evaluate the consequences of their actions and decisions. They understand that their choices can have significant impacts on individuals, communities, and society as a whole, and they strive to act in ways that promote the common good and uphold ethical principles.

Applied ethics plays a crucial role in bridging the gap between theoretical ethical frameworks and real-world decision-making in professional settings. By translating abstract ethical theories and principles into practical guidelines and approaches, applied ethics equips individuals with the tools and perspectives needed to navigate complex moral dilemmas in their respective fields. One of the key contributions of applied ethics is its ability to simplify moral reasoning without sacrificing depth or rigor. In professional contexts where time and resources may be limited, it is essential to provide practitioners with accessible frameworks and decision-making processes that enable them to address ethical challenges effectively. Applied ethics achieves this by distilling ethical theories and principles into actionable guidelines and strategies that professionals can apply in their daily work. Moreover, applied ethics emphasizes the importance of context-specific considerations, recognizing that ethical decision-making is often contingent upon the unique circumstances and dynamics of particular situations. By grounding ethical analysis in real-world contexts, applied ethics enables practitioners to identify relevant factors, assess potential consequences, and make informed judgments that align with ethical principles. Furthermore, applied ethics fosters a mindset of moral decision-making in workplaces by promoting ethical awareness, sensitivity, and responsibility among professionals. By encouraging individuals to reflect on the ethical dimensions of their actions and decisions, applied ethics helps cultivate a culture of ethical behavior and integrity within organizations.

Overall, applied ethics serves as a valuable resource for professionals across various fields, offering practical guidance and support for navigating ethical challenges in the workplace. By integrating ethical considerations into professional practice, individuals can contribute to ethical decision-making, promote accountability and integrity, and uphold the values of justice, fairness, and respect in their interactions with others. In this part, we will delve into three commonly used approaches in applied ethics to guide ethical decision-making: Principlism, case-based reasoning and ethical codes.

Chapter 9 Principlism (Principle-Based Ethics)

Principlism, as advocated by Beauchamp and Childress (2019), offers a practical and widely used framework for ethical decision-making in various professional contexts, particularly in the field of biomedical ethics. This approach aims to provide a structured and systematic method for addressing ethical dilemmas by relying on a set of core principles that are considered fundamental to ethical practice. The four prima facie principles proposed by Beauchamp and Childress - respect for autonomy, nonmaleficence, beneficence, and justice- serve as foundational ethical values that guide moral reasoning and decision-making. Let's briefly examine each of these principles:

Respect for autonomy: This principle emphasizes the importance of respecting individuals' right to make autonomous decisions about their own lives and health care. It requires healthcare professionals to obtain informed consent from patients before proceeding with medical interventions and to recognize patients' right to refuse treatment or make decisions that align with their values and preferences.

Nonmaleficence: The principle of nonmaleficence dictates that healthcare professionals must strive to avoid causing harm to patients. This entails minimizing the risk of harm associated with medical interventions, preventing foreseeable harm, and refraining from actions that may result in unnecessary suffering or injury to patients.

Beneficence: Beneficence entails a duty to promote the well-being and welfare of patients. Healthcare professionals are expected to act in ways that benefit patients, enhance their health outcomes, and contribute to their overall quality of life. This may involve providing effective treatments, offering support and compassion, and prioritizing patients' best interests.

Justice: The principle of justice pertains to the fair and equitable distribution of resources, benefits, and burdens within society. In healthcare contexts, justice requires that healthcare resources and services be distributed fairly, without discrimination or bias, and that individuals receive the care they need based on relevant criteria such as medical need, urgency, and effectiveness.

By applying these four principles, healthcare professionals can systematically analyze ethical dilemmas, weigh competing interests and values, and arrive at ethically defensible decisions that uphold the principles of respect, beneficence, nonmaleficence, and justice. Principlism provides a flexible and adaptable framework that accommodates the complexity and diversity of real-world ethical challenges encountered in clinical practice, research, and healthcare policy.

The scope of principlism extends beyond the realm of biomedical ethics to various industries and professional contexts, encompassing workplace ethics, quality-based ethics, and corporate social responsibility (CSR). Let's explore each of these dimensions:

Workplace Ethics

Principlism guides ethical conduct within the workplace by promoting values such as integrity, respect, fairness, and accountability among colleagues, superiors, peers, and subordinates. This entails adhering to ethical principles in interpersonal relationships, communication, decision-making, conflict resolution, and professional conduct. Workplace ethics are fundamental for fostering trust, morale, and cooperation among employees, as well as for maintaining the organization's reputation and sustainability. Workplace ethics encompass the moral principles that guide interactions and behaviors within the organization. Workplace ethics encompass issues such as moral autonomy, integrity, justice, respect, compliance, confidentiality, and responsibility. While all those principles may seem to be self-explanatory, they are still worth extra attention. Here's a closer look at what process-based workplace ethics principles entail:

> *Moral autonomy* is a very critical principle, and it refers to the ability and habit of thinking rationally and choosing the right without outside pressure. This principle urges professionals to recognize and resolve moral dilemmas at any time at the workplace and achieve moral autonomy. Moral autonomy emphasizes individuals' ability to make moral decisions freely and independently. It refers to the capacity of individuals to make moral decisions and take moral actions based on their own values, beliefs, and reasoning, rather than being dictated by external influences or authorities. It involves the ability to critically evaluate moral principles and to act in accordance with one's own moral judgments. The competencies associated with moral autonomy are essential for professionals to navigate ethical challenges effectively. The components of moral autonomy include:
>
> > *Moral awareness:* This competency involves professionals being honest with themselves about their values, beliefs, and biases that may influence their moral positions. By recognizing these influences, individuals can better understand their own ethical standpoint and make more informed decisions.

Moral Sensitivity: This refers to the ability to recognize moral problems and issues independently without relying solely on external guidance, and to be aware of the moral implications of one's actions and decisions. It involves sensitivity to genuine difficulties and implies being empathetic and compassionate towards others' moral struggles. This competency emphasizes the importance of being proactive and vigilant in identifying ethical dilemmas in various contexts, such as teaching or professional practice.

Moral Motivation: This refers to the willingness and desire to act in accordance with one's own moral judgments, even when doing so may be difficult or unpopular. It involves a genuine concern for ethical issues and a willingness to engage with them constructively, rather than avoiding or dismissing them. It also involves moral beneficence which means acting in ways that promote the well-being and interests of others and moral non-maleficence which is about avoidance of causing harm or inflicting harm on others.

Moral Integrity: This involves consistency between one's moral beliefs and one's actions, and a commitment to acting in accordance with one's moral principles, even in the face of pressure or temptation to do otherwise. It requires individuals to have the strength of character to stand up for what is right, even in the face of adversity. It involves having the courage to confront moral issues, challenge unethical behavior, and advocate for ethical principles, even when it may be difficult or unpopular. Moral integrity also urges professionals not to rob the credit of others, not to shift the blame on others wrongfully, or not make false accusations.

Moral Judgment: This involves the ability to make moral decisions based on one's own values and beliefs, rather than simply following rules or guidelines set by others. This competency highlights the ability to express one's moral views clearly and confidently without depending on external validation or support. It emphasizes the importance of being able to articulate and defend one's ethical positions using a common ethical language.

Moral Agency: This refers to the capacity of the agent to take moral actions and be responsible for the consequences of those actions. It involves recognizing one's power to make a difference in the world through his/her moral choices. It also involves a sense of moral responsibility towards others and society as a whole. It implies recognizing the impact of one's actions on others and taking accountability for the consequences. This includes acknowledging mistakes, addressing harm caused by unethical behavior, and actively working to prevent future wrongdoing.

Moral Development: This involves the process of developing and refining one's moral reasoning, judgment, and motivation over time, through experience, reflection, and learning from others. Critical reflection is crucial for assessing and evaluating moral arguments and perspectives, including those that differ from one's own. Professionals need to develop skills in analyzing, clarifying, and critically evaluating moral issues to arrive at well-informed and reasoned conclusions. Collaboration involves being open to alternative perspectives and creative solutions to ethical challenges. It emphasizes the importance of seeking consultation and engaging with others in ethical decision-making processes to consider diverse viewpoints and potential solutions.

Moral Reasoning: This involves the ability to think critically about moral issues, to weigh different moral principles and values, and to make reasoned judgments about what is morally right or wrong. This competency encompasses the ability to make ethical decisions that are consistent, comprehensive, and based on relevant facts and considerations. Professionals need to weigh the implications of different options carefully and arrive at decisions that align with their values and ethical principles.

Integrity is a fundamental principle in applied ethics. It involves more than just following rules and regulations; it requires individuals to have a strong moral compass and the courage to act ethically, even when faced with challenges or temptations to do otherwise. It emphasizes upholding honesty, transparency, and consistency in all business dealings and compels individuals to raise their voice when faced with a wrongdoing. Here's a breakdown of the key aspects of integrity in business ethics:

Honesty: Integrity involves being truthful and straightforward in all business interactions, whether with customers, employees, suppliers, or other stakeholders. This includes accurately representing products or services, providing honest feedback, and disclosing relevant information, even when it may be uncomfortable or inconvenient.

Transparency: Transparency is essential for building trust and credibility in business relationships. It entails openness and clarity in communication, ensuring that stakeholders have access to relevant information to make informed decisions. Transparency also involves disclosing potential conflicts of interest, financial dealings, and other relevant details that may impact stakeholders.

Consistency: Integrity also requires consistency in behavior and decision-making, regardless of the circumstances. It means adhering to ethical principles and values even when faced with pressure or temptation to compromise. Consistency builds trust and reliability, demonstrating that individuals can be counted on to uphold their moral commitments.

Informing Authorities: In cases where wrongdoing or unethical behavior is observed, integrity compels individuals to responsibly confront moral issues and to take appropriate action which may include informing authorities or relevant stakeholders. This helps to prevent harm, promote accountability, and uphold ethical standards within the organization and the broader community.

By upholding integrity in all business dealings, professionals demonstrate their commitment to ethical behavior and contribute to a culture of trust, respect, and accountability. Integrity is not only essential for individual reputation and success but also for the long-term sustainability and reputation of businesses and organizations.

Justice, as a principle in business ethics, revolves around ensuring fairness and equity in the distribution of benefits and burdens within the organization and making decision-making processes free from bias, favoritism, or discrimination. This principle is foundational for creating an ethical and harmonious workplace environment. It is a fundamental principle in business ethics that emphasizes ensuring impartiality and equity in decision-making processes, policies, and treatment of employees. It is essential for creating a workplace environment where employees feel valued, respected, and motivated to contribute their best. Fair treatment demands that all individuals within the organization are treated fairly and impartially. Impartiality ensures that decisions are made fairly and transparently, instilling confidence and trust among employees. This includes aspects such as hiring, promotion, compensation, performance evaluation, and disciplinary actions. Decisions related to these areas should be based on objective criteria, such as qualifications, merit, and performance rather than subjective factors like personal relationships or biases. In addition to fair treatment, justice emphasizes equity in the allocation of resources and opportunities. This includes opportunities for hiring promotion, training, compensation, benefits, and recognition. Equity recognizes that individuals may have different needs and circumstances and aims to address these differences to ensure that everyone has an equal chance to succeed based on their abilities and contributions. This may involve implementing policies and practices that promote diversity, inclusion, and equal access to advancement opportunities. Here's a deeper look at what justice entails:

Procedural Justice: Procedural justice focuses on the fairness and transparency of decision-making processes within the organization (Greenberg, 1990). It ensures that procedures for making decisions are clear, consistent, and free from bias. This means communicating openly and honestly with employees about the criteria, standards, and rationale behind decisions that affect them. Transparency helps to build trust, credibility, and accountability within the organization and ensures that employees understand the basis for organizational policies and practices. Employees should have a voice in decision-making processes that affect them, and procedures should be implemented in a manner that is perceived as fair by all parties involved. It involves applying policies and procedures consistently and uniformly to all employees. Consistency ensures that similar situations are treated similarly, regardless of individual differences or circumstances. By maintaining consistency in decision-making, organizations demonstrate their commitment to fairness and avoid perceptions of favoritism or unfair treatment. For example, in a legal setting, procedural justice might involve ensuring that all parties have equal access to information, that hearings are conducted fairly, and that decisions are based on evidence and the law.

Distributive Justice: Distributive justice concerns the fair distribution of rewards, benefits, and burdens within the organization (Moorman, 1991). This includes aspects such as wages, bonuses, benefits, work assignments, and responsibilities. Distributive justice ensures that rewards and burdens are allocated in a manner that is perceived as fair and equitable by employees, taking into account factors such as contribution, effort, and need. For example, in a legal setting, distributive justice might involve ensuring that the penalties imposed on people who are found guilty of crimes are proportionate to the severity of their offenses. It also entails providing opportunities for employees to voice their concerns, provide feedback, and participate in decision-making processes that affect them. This includes mechanisms such as grievance procedures, employee surveys, and forums for open dialogue and discussion. Employee voice helps to ensure that decisions are made with consideration for the perspectives and interests of those affected by them, enhancing fairness and inclusivity in the workplace.

Informational Justice: This is about the fairness and transparency of the information that is available to people. It's about ensuring that people have access to the information they need to understand the decisions that are being made and to participate effectively in the decision-making process. For example, in a legal setting, informational justice might involve ensuring that all parties have access to relevant evidence and legal arguments.

Interpersonal Justice: This refers to the fairness and respectfulness of the interactions between people (Bies & Moag, 1986). It's about ensuring that people are treated with dignity and respect in their interactions with others. For example, in a legal setting, interpersonal justice might involve ensuring that all parties are treated respectfully and given the opportunity to be heard.

By prioritizing fairness in decision-making processes, policies, and treatment of employees, organizations can create a positive and supportive work environment where employees feel valued, respected, and motivated to contribute their best. Fairness not only promotes employee satisfaction and engagement but also contributes to organizational success, productivity, and reputation in the long run. They are all important aspects of justice, and they can all contribute to people's perceptions of whether a decision or process is fair. Overall, justice in the workplace is essential for maintaining employee morale, motivation, and trust in organizational leadership. Organizations that prioritize justice not only create a positive work environment but also foster a culture of fairness, integrity, and respect, which are critical for long-term success and sustainability.

Respect is a fundamental principle in business ethics that emphasizes treating all individuals with dignity, fairness, and empathy. Fostering a workplace culture grounded in respect contributes to creating an environment where everyone feels valued, included, and empowered to contribute their best. Here's a closer look at what respect entails:

Respecting moral autonomy: It means respecting individuals' right to make their own decisions and choices freely and independently without any external pressure.

Dignity: Respect involves recognizing and honoring the inherent worth and value of every individual, regardless of their role, background, or status within the organization. It means treating people with courtesy, kindness, and consideration, and acknowledging their rights to autonomy, privacy, and personal expression.

Fairness: Respect requires treating people fairly and without discrimination or prejudice. This includes providing equal opportunities for advancement and development, regardless of factors such as race, gender, religion, age, disability, or sexual orientation. Fair treatment ensures that everyone has an equal chance to succeed based on their abilities and contributions.

Empathy: Respect entails understanding and empathizing with the perspectives, feelings, and experiences of others. It involves active listening, compassion, and sensitivity to the needs and concerns of colleagues, customers, and stakeholders. Empathy fosters stronger relationships, better communication, and a greater sense of connection and belonging within the workplace.

Inclusivity: Respect involves creating an inclusive and welcoming workplace culture where all individuals feel valued, respected, and included. This means embracing diversity and celebrating the unique backgrounds, talents, and perspectives that each person brings to the table. Inclusive practices promote collaboration, creativity, and innovation by harnessing the full potential of a diverse workforce.

Professionalism: Respect also encompasses professionalism in all interactions and communications within the workplace. This includes maintaining a positive attitude, showing integrity and honesty, and adhering to ethical standards and organizational values. Professional behavior fosters trust, credibility, and mutual respect among colleagues and stakeholders.

By prioritizing respect in the workplace, organizations can cultivate a culture that values diversity, promotes collaboration, and fosters mutual trust and respect among employees. A respectful workplace not only enhances employee satisfaction and engagement but also contributes to organizational success, innovation, and sustainability in the long run.

Compliance is a critical aspect of business ethics that involves adhering to legal and regulatory requirements, industry standards, and internal policies to maintain ethical conduct within an organization. Here's a breakdown of what compliance entails:

Legal and Regulatory Requirements: Compliance with laws and regulations is essential for ensuring that the organization operates within the bounds of the law. This includes adhering to laws at the local, national, and international levels, as well as regulations specific to the industry in which the organization operates. Examples of legal and regulatory areas that require compliance include labor laws, environmental regulations, consumer protection laws, antitrust laws, and data privacy regulations.

Industry Standards: In addition to legal requirements, compliance also involves adhering to industry standards and best practices. Industry standards may be established by professional organizations, trade associations, or regulatory bodies within a particular sector. Compliance with industry standards helps organizations maintain competitiveness, build trust with stakeholders, and demonstrate commitment to quality and excellence in their products or services.

Internal Policies and Procedures: Organizations often have internal policies and procedures in place to govern various aspects of their operations, such as human resources, finance, information technology, and risk management. Compliance with internal policies and procedures ensures consistency, accountability, and efficiency in organizational practices. Internal policies may include codes of conduct, employee handbooks, and guidelines for ethical decision-making.

Risk Management: Compliance also plays a crucial role in risk management by helping organizations identify, assess, and mitigate legal and ethical risks. By proactively addressing compliance requirements, organizations can minimize the likelihood of legal violations, financial penalties, reputational damage, and other adverse consequences associated with non-compliance.

Ethical Conduct: While compliance primarily focuses on meeting legal and regulatory requirements, it is important to note that ethical conduct goes beyond mere compliance. Ethical conduct involves making decisions and taking actions that are morally right and consistent with ethical principles and values. While compliance provides a framework for legal behavior, organizations should also strive to promote a culture of ethics and integrity that guides behavior beyond minimum legal requirements.

Overall, compliance is essential for organizations to operate ethically, maintain trust with stakeholders, and mitigate legal and reputational risks. By prioritizing compliance with legal requirements, industry standards, and internal policies, organizations can demonstrate their commitment to ethical conduct and responsible business practices.

Confidentiality is a crucial principle in business ethics that involves safeguarding sensitive information and respecting the privacy rights of employees, customers, and other stakeholders. It is essential for building trust, maintaining confidentiality, and upholding ethical standards within the organization. Here's a deeper look at what confidentiality entails:

Safeguarding Sensitive Information: Confidentiality requires organizations to establish and maintain robust safeguards to protect sensitive information from unauthorized access, use, or disclosure. This includes implementing secure data storage systems, encryption technologies, access controls, and confidentiality agreements to prevent data breaches and unauthorized disclosures.

Respecting Privacy Rights: Confidentiality also involves respecting the privacy rights of individuals and stakeholders by limiting access to their personal information and using it only for legitimate purposes. This includes obtaining consent before collecting, storing, or sharing personal data and providing individuals with control over their own information, such as the right to access, correct, or delete their data.

Legal and Regulatory Compliance: Confidentiality requires organizations to comply with relevant laws, regulations, and industry standards governing the protection of sensitive information and privacy rights.

Ethical Considerations: Confidentiality also involves ethical considerations beyond legal requirements, such as respecting the confidentiality of sensitive information even when not explicitly mandated by law. This includes honoring confidentiality agreements, maintaining professional discretion, and exercising judgment and discretion in handling confidential information to protect the interests and privacy of individuals and stakeholders.

Trust and Reputation: Confidentiality is essential for building trust and maintaining the reputation of the organization. When individuals and stakeholders trust that their sensitive information will be kept confidential and their privacy rights respected, they are more likely to engage with the organization and share information openly. Conversely, breaches of confidentiality can damage trust, tarnish the organization's reputation, and lead to legal and financial consequences.

By prioritizing confidentiality and respecting the privacy rights of employees, customers, and other stakeholders, organizations can demonstrate their commitment to ethical conduct, build trust, and protect sensitive information from unauthorized access or disclosure. Confidentiality is not only a legal requirement but also a fundamental ethical principle that contributes to organizational integrity, credibility, and success.

Responsibility is a core principle in business ethics that entails accepting accountability for actions and decisions, including addressing the social and environmental impact of business operations. It reflects an organization's commitment to ethical conduct, sustainability, and corporate citizenship. Here's a closer look at what responsibility entails:

Accountability: Responsibility involves holding oneself and others accountable for their actions and decisions. This means acknowledging mistakes, taking ownership of outcomes, and being willing to accept the consequences, whether positive or negative. Accountability fosters transparency, trust, and integrity within the organization and promotes a culture of accountability at all levels.

Ethical Conduct: Responsibility encompasses ethical conduct in all aspects of business operations, including interactions with stakeholders, compliance with laws and regulations, and adherence to ethical principles and values. It requires making decisions and taking actions that are morally right and consistent with ethical standards, even when faced with challenges or competing interests. Ethical conduct builds trust, credibility, and reputation for the organization and contributes to long-term success and sustainability.

Social Impact: Responsibility includes considering and addressing the social impact of business operations on stakeholders, communities, and society at large. This may involve initiatives to promote social welfare, such as corporate philanthropy, community engagement, diversity and inclusion programs, and responsible sourcing practices. Organizations have a responsibility to contribute positively to society and mitigate any adverse social impacts resulting from their operations.

Environmental Impact: Responsibility also entails recognizing and mitigating the environmental impact of business activities on the planet. This includes efforts to reduce carbon emissions, conserve natural resources, minimize pollution, and promote sustainable practices throughout the supply chain. Organizations have a responsibility to protect the environment and minimize their ecological footprint to preserve natural resources for future generations.

Stakeholder Engagement: Responsibility involves engaging with stakeholders to understand their concerns, interests, and expectations and incorporating their input into decision-making processes. This includes employees, customers, suppliers, investors, communities, and other stakeholders who may be affected by or have an interest in the organization's activities. By actively engaging with stakeholders, organizations can build trust, foster collaboration, and address issues proactively, enhancing their social license to operate.

All these competencies are essential for fostering moral autonomy and ethical competence in professionals across various fields. By developing these skills, individuals can enhance their ability to navigate complex ethical dilemmas responsibly, and professionally with integrity. Overall, responsibility is essential for organizations to operate ethically, sustainably, and responsibly in today's complex and interconnected world. By embracing responsibility and integrating ethical, social, and environmental considerations into their business practices, organizations can create value for all stakeholders, contribute to the greater good, and achieve long-term success and prosperity.

Quality-Based Ethics

Ethics related to the quality of work focus on ensuring excellence, integrity, and adherence to ethical standards in the products, services, or outputs delivered by the organization. This dimension focuses on the quality of the organization's work and its commitment to meeting or exceeding ethical expectations. Ethics related to the quality of work are essential for building customer trust, loyalty, and satisfaction, as well as for upholding the organization's reputation and competitiveness in the marketplace. Let's explore key considerations in quality-based workplace ethics in more detail:

Fiduciary duty refers to the legal and ethical obligation of individuals or entities to act in the best interests of another party, often referred to as the beneficiary. Fiduciary relationships are characterized by trust, loyalty, and a high standard of care owed by the fiduciary to the beneficiary (Valsan, 2021). Common examples of fiduciary relationships include those between trustees and beneficiaries, attorneys and clients, financial advisors and clients, and directors and shareholders. For example, lawyers owe a fiduciary duty to their clients to represent their interests diligently and ethically. Similarly, Physicians have a fiduciary duty to prioritize the well-being and best interests of their patients in providing medical care. Likewise, Financial advisors, trustees, and investment managers have fiduciary duties to manage assets prudently and in the best interests of their clients or beneficiaries. Another example is that directors and officers of corporations have fiduciary duties to act in the best interests of shareholders and the company.

Fiduciaries must have undivided loyalty and act solely in the best interests of those they serve and avoid conflicts of interest. Fiduciaries are expected to exercise diligence, competence, and skill in carrying out their responsibilities. Fiduciaries must fully disclose any conflicts of interest that may affect their ability to fulfill their duties impartially. Fiduciaries are obligated to maintain the confidentiality of information entrusted to them by their clients, patients, beneficiaries, or stakeholders. Violating fiduciary duties, whether intentionally or accidentally, is considered unethical and may have legal consequences. Breaches of fiduciary duty can result in lawsuits, financial penalties, loss of professional licenses, and damage to reputation.

Fiduciaries must respect the autonomy of beneficiaries by prioritizing their wishes and preferences. For example, financial advisors should provide clients with relevant information and respect their investment goals and risk tolerance. Fiduciaries have a duty to act in the best interests of beneficiaries, aligning with the principle of beneficence. This involves making decisions and taking actions that maximize the well-being and interests of those they serve. Fiduciaries must avoid actions or decisions that could harm beneficiaries, consistent with the principle of nonmaleficence. This includes refraining from conflicts of interest, self-dealing, or negligence that could adversely affect the beneficiaries' interests. Fiduciaries are obligated to treat beneficiaries fairly and equitably, in accordance with the principle of justice. This may involve ensuring equal access to resources, avoiding discrimination, and upholding the rights of all parties involved.

Accountability is a critical principle in business ethics that involves holding professionals and organizations responsible for the quality and impact of their products, services, or deliverables. It reflects a commitment to transparency, integrity, and ethical conduct in business operations. Here's a closer look at what accountability entails:

Quality Assurance: Accountability involves ensuring that products, services, or deliverables meet or exceed established standards of quality, reliability, and performance. This includes implementing quality assurance processes, conducting regular evaluations and assessments, and continuously improving processes to enhance the quality of outcomes. Accountability for quality ensures customer satisfaction, builds trust, and enhances the reputation of the organization.

Impact Assessment: Accountability also entails assessing the impact of products, services, or deliverables on stakeholders, communities, and the environment. This includes considering both intended and unintended consequences of business activities and taking responsibility for any negative impacts that occur. Impact assessment helps organizations identify opportunities for improvement, mitigate risks, and make informed decisions that align with ethical and sustainable practices.

Compliance and Ethics: Accountability requires ensuring compliance with relevant laws, regulations, and industry standards governing business operations. It also involves upholding ethical principles and values in all aspects of decision-making and conduct. This includes promoting integrity, honesty, fairness, and respect for stakeholders' rights and interests. Compliance with legal and ethical standards demonstrates a commitment to responsible business practices and helps prevent legal and reputational risks.

Transparency and Disclosure: Accountability involves being transparent and open about business practices, performance, and outcomes. This includes providing clear and accurate information to stakeholders about products, services, pricing, terms, and conditions. Transparency fosters trust, credibility, and accountability and enables stakeholders to make informed decisions and hold the organization accountable for its actions.

Responsiveness to Feedback: Accountability includes being responsive to feedback, complaints, and concerns from stakeholders. This involves listening to stakeholders' perspectives, addressing issues promptly and effectively, and taking corrective actions when necessary. Responsiveness demonstrates a commitment to continuous improvement, customer satisfaction, and stakeholder engagement.

Overall, accountability is essential for organizations to operate ethically, sustainably, and responsibly. By holding professionals and organizations accountable for the quality and impact of their products, services, or deliverables, stakeholders can trust that their interests are being protected, and organizations can maintain their reputation, credibility, and long-term success. Professionalism: Upholding high standards of quality, reliability, and accuracy in products, services, or deliverables and maintaining high standards of expertise, competence, and ethical conduct in all aspects of work, including adherence to professional codes of conduct.

Customer satisfaction is a foundational principle in business ethics that emphasizes prioritizing the needs, expectations, and satisfaction of customers or clients. It involves ensuring the delivery of value-added products or services that meet or exceed customer expectations. Here's a closer look at what customer satisfaction entails:

Understanding Customer Needs: Customer satisfaction begins with understanding the needs, preferences, and expectations of customers. This involves listening to customers, conducting market research, and gathering feedback to gain insights into their wants and desires. By understanding customer needs, organizations can tailor their products or services to meet customer expectations effectively.

Quality Products or Services: Customer satisfaction requires delivering high-quality products or services that meet or exceed customer expectations. This includes ensuring reliability, durability, functionality, and performance in the products or services offered. Quality products or services not only satisfy immediate needs but also build long-term customer loyalty and trust.

Value Addition: Customer satisfaction involves adding value to products or services by providing additional benefits or features that enhance their utility or appeal. Value addition may include offering competitive pricing, warranties, after-sales support, customization options, or complementary services. By providing value-added solutions, organizations can differentiate themselves from competitors and enhance customer satisfaction.

Responsive Customer Service: Customer satisfaction depends on responsive and effective customer service that addresses customer inquiries, concerns, and feedback promptly and courteously. This includes providing multiple channels for customer communication, such as phone, email, chat, and social media, and ensuring that customer service representatives are knowledgeable, helpful, and empathetic in their interactions with customers.

Continuous Improvement: Customer satisfaction is an ongoing process that requires continuous improvement and innovation. This involves regularly evaluating customer feedback, analyzing customer satisfaction metrics, and identifying areas for improvement in products, services, and processes. By continuously striving to enhance customer satisfaction, organizations can adapt to changing customer needs and preferences and maintain their competitive edge in the market.

Building Customer Relationships: Customer satisfaction extends beyond individual transactions to building long-term relationships with customers. This involves nurturing trust, loyalty, and satisfaction through personalized communication, loyalty programs, and engagement initiatives. By investing in customer relationships, organizations can foster repeat business, referrals, and positive word-of-mouth marketing, which are essential for sustainable growth and success.

Overall, customer satisfaction is essential for business success and sustainability. By prioritizing customer needs, delivering quality products or services, adding value, providing responsive customer service, continuously improving, and building lasting relationships, organizations can create positive customer experiences, drive customer loyalty, and achieve long-term success in the marketplace.

Corporate Social Responsibility (CSR)

Corporate Social Responsibility (CSR) is a concept that has been subject to various interpretations and debates over the years. Two prominent views on CSR are those presented by Milton Friedman and Archie Carroll.

Milton Friedman's Shareholder View: Friedman (1972), an economist and Nobel laureate, argued that the primary responsibility of a corporation is to its shareholders. According to this view, the sole purpose of a business is to generate profits within the framework of the law, and any activities beyond this narrow objective are considered illegitimate (Friedman, 1972). Friedman believed that managers should act as agents of shareholders and make decisions that maximize shareholder wealth. He argued that engaging in CSR activities, such as philanthropy or environmental initiatives, could undermine this goal by diverting resources away from profit-maximizing activities. In essence, Friedman's shareholder view suggests that businesses should focus solely on economic outcomes and that any social or environmental concerns should be addressed through government regulation or individual philanthropy rather than corporate action. Shareholder view advocates that every penny, energy or time spent from shareholders' investment for the causes other than making profit should be seen as a betrayal to shareholder's trust.

Archie Carroll's Stakeholder View: Archie Carroll, a management scholar, proposed a broader view of CSR that takes into account the interests of multiple stakeholders beyond just shareholders. He developed the "CSR Pyramid," which outlines four categories of responsibilities that businesses have towards society: economic, legal, ethical, and philanthropic (Carroll, 2016). According to Carroll's stakeholder view (2016), businesses have a responsibility to not only generate profits but also to comply with laws and regulations, act ethically, and contribute to the well-being of society through philanthropic activities. Carroll argued that businesses operate within a broader social context and are accountable to various stakeholders, including employees, customers, suppliers, communities, and the environment. Therefore, they should consider the impacts of their decisions and actions on all stakeholders and strive to create value for society as a whole. The stakeholder view of CSR emphasizes the importance of considering the interests of all stakeholders affected by a company's operations, not just shareholders. This perspective recognizes that businesses impact and are impacted by a wide range of stakeholders, including employees, customers, suppliers, communities, and the environment. According to the stakeholder view, businesses have a moral and ethical responsibility to balance the interests of all stakeholders and to make decisions that take into account the broader social and environmental implications of their actions. This view advocates for a more holistic approach to CSR that goes beyond simply maximizing shareholder wealth and considers the long-term sustainability and well-being of the organizations and society as a whole.

In summary, Friedman's shareholder view emphasizes the primacy of profit maximization and the interests of shareholders, while Carroll's stakeholder view advocate for a more inclusive approach to CSR that considers the interests of all stakeholders and the broader societal context in which businesses operate.

Environmental and social responsibility are integral principles in business ethics that involve integrating ethical considerations into business practices. This includes ethical marketing and advertising, implementing sustainability initiatives, corporate social responsibility (CSR) programs, and ethical sourcing practices to minimize negative impacts on the environment and society while maximizing positive contributions. Here's a closer look at what environmental and social responsibility entail:

Ethical marketing and advertising are essential components of business ethics that prioritize honesty, transparency, and integrity in all marketing practices. This includes avoiding deceptive or manipulative tactics that could mislead consumers or exploit their trust. By prioritizing honesty, transparency, integrity, respect for consumer rights, social responsibility, and compliance with regulations, organizations can engage in ethical marketing and advertising practices that build trust, enhance brand reputation, and contribute to long-term success and sustainability. Ethical marketing not only benefits consumers but also strengthens the organization's relationships with stakeholders and reinforces its commitment to ethical conduct and corporate citizenship. Here's a closer look at what ethical marketing and advertising entail:

Honesty: Ethical marketing and advertising require honesty in all communications with consumers. This means providing accurate and truthful information about products or services, including their features, benefits, limitations, and pricing. Avoiding misleading or exaggerated claims helps to build trust and credibility with consumers and avoids potential legal and reputational risks.

Transparency: Transparency is essential in ethical marketing and advertising to ensure that consumers have access to relevant information to make informed decisions. This includes disclosing any material information that could affect consumers' purchasing decisions, such as product ingredients, terms and conditions, and potential risks or side effects. Transparent marketing practices help to build trust, foster long-term relationships with consumers, and enhance brand reputation.

Integrity: Ethical marketing and advertising require integrity in all interactions with consumers and stakeholders. This involves adhering to ethical principles and values, even when faced with pressure to engage in unethical or questionable practices. Maintaining integrity builds credibility, fosters goodwill, and strengthens the reputation of the organization and its brands.

Respect for Consumer Rights: Ethical marketing and advertising respect the rights and dignity of consumers. This includes avoiding intrusive or deceptive advertising practices that could infringe on consumers' privacy or manipulate their emotions. Respecting consumer rights helps to build trust and loyalty with consumers and promotes a positive brand image.

Social Responsibility: Ethical marketing and advertising consider the broader social and environmental impacts of marketing activities. This includes avoiding marketing tactics that could harm individuals, communities, or the environment and actively promoting socially responsible behaviors, such as sustainability, diversity, and inclusivity. Socially responsible marketing practices contribute to the well-being of society and enhance the organization's reputation as a responsible corporate citizen.

Compliance with Regulations: Ethical marketing and advertising comply with relevant laws, regulations, and industry standards governing marketing practices. This includes laws related to truth in advertising, consumer protection, data privacy, and marketing to vulnerable populations. Compliance with regulations helps to mitigate legal risks and ensures that marketing activities are conducted ethically and responsibly.

Sustainability Initiatives: Environmental responsibility involves implementing sustainable practices that minimize the ecological footprint of business operations. This includes reducing energy and water consumption, minimizing waste and pollution, promoting recycling and reuse, and adopting renewable energy sources. Sustainability initiatives aim to protect natural resources, mitigate climate change, and preserve ecosystems for future generations.

Corporate Social Responsibility (CSR) Programs: Social responsibility involves engaging in activities that benefit society and improve the well-being of communities. CSR programs encompass initiatives related to philanthropy, volunteerism, community development, and social impact investing. This may include donating to charitable organizations, sponsoring community events, supporting education and healthcare initiatives, and addressing social and economic inequalities. CSR programs demonstrate a commitment to corporate citizenship and contribute to positive social outcomes.

Ethical Sourcing Practices: Social and environmental responsibility also extends to the supply chain through ethical sourcing practices. This involves ensuring that products and materials are sourced responsibly, taking into account social, environmental, and ethical considerations. Ethical sourcing practices may include fair labor practices, labor rights protections, environmental sustainability criteria, and transparency in the supply chain. By sourcing ethically, organizations can minimize risks related to human rights violations, labor exploitation, and environmental degradation, while also supporting responsible suppliers and promoting ethical standards throughout the industry.

Stakeholder Engagement: Environmental and social responsibility entail engaging with stakeholders, including employees, customers, suppliers, investors, and communities, to understand their concerns, interests, and expectations. This includes involving stakeholders in decision-making processes, soliciting feedback, and collaborating on initiatives to address environmental and social issues. Stakeholder engagement builds trust, fosters collaboration, and ensures that business practices align with stakeholder needs and values.

Transparency and Accountability: Environmental and social responsibility require transparency and accountability in reporting on progress and outcomes. This includes disclosing information about environmental and social performance, including goals, metrics, and impacts, in a clear and transparent manner. Accountability involves holding the organization accountable for its commitments, actions, and results, and addressing any shortcomings or areas for improvement. Transparency and accountability build credibility, trust, and confidence among stakeholders and demonstrate a commitment to responsible business practices.

By integrating environmental and social responsibility into business practices, organizations can create value for society, minimize risks, enhance reputation, and contribute to long-term sustainability and success. Environmental and social responsibility not only benefits the environment and society but also strengthens relationships with stakeholders and reinforces the organization's commitment to ethical conduct and corporate citizenship.

References

Beauchamp, T. L., & Childress, J. F. (2019) *Principles of biomedical ethics* (8th ed.). Oxford University Press.

Bies, R. J., & Moag, J. F. (1986). Interactional justice: Communication criteria of fairness. In R. J. Lewicki, B. H. Sheppard, & M. H. Bazerman (Eds.), *Research on negotiations in organizations*, (pp. 43–55). JAI Press.

Carroll A. B. (2016). Carroll's pyramid of CSR: Taking another look. International *Journal of Corporate Social Responsibility, 1*(1), 1–8. https://doi.org/10.1186/s40991-016-0004-6

Friedman M. (1972). *An economist's protest: Columns in political economy.* Thomas Horton and Company.

Greenberg, J. (1990). Organizational justice: Yesterday, today and tomorrow. *Journal of Management, 16*(3), 399–432. https://doi.org/10.1177/01492063900160020

Moorman, R. H. (1991). Relationship between organizational justice and organizational citizenship behaviors: Do fairness perceptions influence employee citizenship? *Journal of Applied Psychology, 76*(6), 845–855. https://doi.org/10.1037/0021-9010.76.6.845

Valsan, R. (2021). Fiduciary duties. In A. Marciano & G. B. Ramello (Eds.), *Encyclopedia of law and economics* (pp. 1–8). Springer. https://doi.org/10.1007/978-1-4614-7883-6_698-2

Chapter 10 Case-Based Reasoning (CBR)

Case-based reasoning (Casuistry) involves the use of specific cases, examples or scenarios to inform ethical decision-making. Instead of relying solely on abstract principles or theories, practitioners analyze real-life cases and draw insights from previous experiences to guide their ethical judgments (Lozano, 2003). This approach recognizes the complexity and context-dependence of ethical dilemmas and emphasizes the importance of practical wisdom and judgment (Lozano, 2003). By examining previous cases, precedents, and relevant examples, individuals can better understand the complexities of ethical dilemmas, recognize patterns, and develop practical strategies for resolving similar situations in the future. Case-based reasoning complements principlism by providing concrete illustrations of how ethical principles can be applied in diverse contexts. Case-based reasoning (CBR) is a problem-solving paradigm that involves solving new problems based on the solutions of similar past problems. It is often used in legal contexts, where lawyers and judges examine previous cases, precedents, and relevant examples to inform their decisions.

Features: Case-based reasoning considers the unique circumstances of each case, taking into account factors such as the individuals involved, the cultural context, and the potential consequences of different courses of action. It involves identifying relevant similarities and differences between the current case and past cases to inform ethical decision-making.

Application: Case-based reasoning is widely used in various fields, including medicine, law, business ethics, and engineering. In medical ethics, for example, clinicians often rely on case studies and clinical experiences to navigate complex ethical issues in patient care, such as end-of-life decisions or informed consent. One example of CBR in legal contexts is the use of case law, which involves examining previous court decisions to determine how similar cases were resolved. For example, if a lawyer is preparing a case involving a dispute over property rights, they may research previous cases involving similar disputes to see how they were resolved and to identify any relevant legal principles or precedents. Another example of CBR in legal contexts is the use of legal databases and research tools, which allow lawyers and judges to search for relevant cases and precedents based on keywords and other criteria. These tools can help lawyers and judges find relevant examples and precedents quickly and efficiently, which can be especially useful in complex or time-sensitive cases. Overall, CBR can be a valuable tool in legal contexts, as it allows lawyers and judges to draw on the knowledge and expertise of previous cases and precedents to inform their decisions and solve new problems.

Benefits: Case-based reasoning provides concrete examples and practical insights that can help individuals develop moral sensitivity and ethical judgment. By examining real-world cases, practitioners can learn from past experiences and apply ethical principles in specific contexts.

Limitations: While case-based reasoning offers valuable insights into practical ethics, it may lack the systematic approach and generalizability of frameworks like principlism. Additionally, the interpretation of cases and the application of ethical principles may vary depending on individual perspectives and biases.

In summary, case-based reasoning complements approaches like principlism and ethical codes by providing practical insights and real-world examples that inform ethical decision-making in applied contexts. By analyzing specific cases and drawing on relevant experiences, practitioners can navigate complex ethical dilemmas and uphold ethical standards in their professional endeavors.:

For example, we can teach *ethics to AI* using Case-Based Reasoning (CBR). CBR can be a valuable approach in teaching ethics to AI. CBR is a problem-solving paradigm that involves solving new problems based on solutions to similar past problems. Here's how CBR can be used to teach ethics to AI:

Identifying Similar Cases: The first step in teaching ethics to AI using CBR is to identify similar cases where ethical decisions were made. This could involve analyzing a database of past ethical dilemmas and their solutions or using a knowledge base of ethical principles and guidelines.

Analyzing Ethical Principles: Next, the AI would analyze the ethical principles that are relevant to the situation, such as fairness, transparency, and the duty to act in the best interests of stakeholders.

Applying Precedents: The AI would then apply the solutions from similar cases to the current situation, taking into account the relevant ethical principles and guidelines.

Evaluating the Solution: Finally, the AI would evaluate the proposed solution based on its adherence to ethical principles and guidelines, and its potential impact on stakeholders.

By using CBR to teach ethics to AI, we can help ensure that AI systems make ethical decisions that are consistent with human values and principles. This approach can also help AI systems learn from past ethical dilemmas and improve their ability to make ethical decisions in the future. Shortly, in the context of AI ethics, CBR can be used to analyze and address ethical dilemmas by comparing them to similar cases where ethical decisions were made. Moreover, CBR can be a useful tool for reasoning about the ethical implications of any act. Let us consider some scenarios that we may employ CBR:

For example, in the context of *a golden parachute and conflict of interest,* CBR can be used to analyze and address potential ethical conflicts that may arise when an executive is offered a golden parachute. The term "golden parachute" typically refers to a financial arrangement between a company and an executive that provides significant financial benefits to the executive if they are terminated or if the company is taken over by another company (Johnsen, 1985). It is a form of severance payment, but it is often much more generous than a typical severance package. Golden parachutes can include a variety of benefits, such as cash payments, stock options, and other perks. The terms of the golden parachute are usually outlined in the executive's employment contract or in a separate agreement.

The "golden parachute" is designed to provide executives with a financial cushion in the event that they lose their job or are forced to leave the company due to a change in control, such as a merger or acquisition. The idea is to incentivize executives to stay with the company and work towards its success, knowing that they will be financially protected if they are let go.

Critics of golden parachutes argue that they can encourage executives to prioritize their own financial interests over the long-term success of the company (Shapiro, 2003). They also argue that golden parachutes can create a moral hazard, where executives are less motivated to work hard and make difficult decisions if they know they will be financially rewarded regardless of the outcome (Machlin et al., 1993).

Supporters of golden parachutes argue that it is necessary to attract and retain top executive talent, particularly in industries where competition for talent is fierce, and offering golden parachutes to hire top executive talent is a way to do so (Fich et al., 2013). They also argue that golden parachutes can provide a measure of stability and security for executives, which can be important for their mental well-being and job performance (Wade et al., 1990).

Overall, the use of golden parachutes is a controversial topic, and different companies and industries have different views on their appropriateness and effectiveness. Let us consider a hypothetical scenario and use CBR to address potential ethical conflicts that may arise when an executive is offered a golden parachute.

Scenario: A company is considering offering a golden parachute to its CEO, who is responsible for negotiating a potential merger with another company. The CEO's compensation package includes a substantial golden parachute in the event of a change in control, such as a merger.

CBR Analysis: Similar Cases: The first step in a CBR analysis would be to identify similar cases where executives were offered golden parachutes in the context of a potential merger.

Ethical Principles: Next, the CBR analysis would examine the ethical principles that are relevant to the situation, such as fairness, transparency, and the duty to act in the best interests of the company and its shareholders.

Precedents: The analysis would then look at the outcomes of similar cases to determine how ethical conflicts were addressed and whether any ethical principles were violated.

Relevant Examples: The analysis would also look for relevant examples of best practices and guidelines for addressing ethical conflicts in similar situations.

CBR Application: Based on the analysis of similar cases, ethical principles, and relevant examples, the company could develop a plan for addressing potential ethical conflicts in the CEO's compensation package. This plan might include measures such as: (1) Ensuring that the CEO's compensation package is fair and transparent, and that it aligns with the best interests of the company and its shareholders; (2) establishing a committee of independent directors to oversee the negotiation process and ensure that the CEO's compensation package does not unduly influence their decisions. (3) Providing transparency to shareholders and stakeholders about the CEO's compensation package and the potential ethical conflicts it may create. (4) Seeking input from ethical experts and stakeholders to ensure that the CEO's compensation package complies with relevant ethical principles and guidelines.

Conclusion: By using CBR for moral decision-making, the company can develop a plan that balances the interests of the CEO, shareholders, and other stakeholders. This approach can help to ensure that the CEO's compensation package is ethical, transparent, and in the best interests of the company.

For example, in the context of *cooptation and corporate governance*, CBR for moral decision-making could be used to analyze and address potential conflicts of interest that may arise when a union representative is offered a position on the board of directors.

Cooptation, in the context of organizations and governance, refers to the process of bringing in individuals or groups from outside the organization or governance structure into positions of power or influence within the organization or governance structure. This is often done in an attempt to gain support, legitimacy, or expertise from these individuals or groups. In the context of corporate governance, cooptation can refer to the practice of appointing independent directors to boards of directors to improve corporate governance and oversight. These independent directors are expected to bring an outside perspective and provide oversight of management, but they may also face conflicts of interest and challenges in maintaining their independence. Cooptation can also be seen as a way to manage opposition as it can be seen as a form of manipulation or co-option of dissenting voices, rather than a genuine attempt to address their concerns or incorporate their perspectives (Trumpy, 2008). In the context of organizations or governance structures, cooptation of opposition can be used to maintain or consolidate power, prevent fragmentation or splintering of the group, and create an appearance of inclusivity or diversity of thought. However, it can also lead to coopted individuals or groups losing their original purpose or principles, as they become aligned with the interests of those in power (Zaman et al., 2021). So, it is quite a controversial issue. Cooptation can take various forms, such as:

Inclusion in Decision-Making: Bringing external stakeholders, such as community representatives or industry experts, into decision-making bodies or committees.

Hiring External Consultants or Advisors: Engaging external consultants or advisors to provide expertise or guidance on specific issues or projects.

Appointing External Members to Boards: Adding individuals from outside the organization or governance structure to boards of directors or advisory boards.

Collaboration and Partnerships: Forming partnerships or collaborations with external organizations or groups to achieve common goals.

Managing oppositions: Forming partnerships or collaborations with dissenting voices to gain their support or weaken their opposition to certain policies or decisions.

Cooptation can be seen as a way to broaden perspectives, bring in fresh ideas, and build relationships with external stakeholders. However, it can also raise concerns about conflicts of interest, loss of independence, and the potential for undue influence from external parties. Overall, cooptation is a complex and multifaceted concept that can have both positive and negative implications depending on the specific context and how it is implemented. For example, cooptation as a way to manage opposition refers to a strategy used by individuals or groups in power to neutralize or incorporate dissenting voices or opposition into their own ranks. This can be done in various ways, such as offering positions of influence or power, providing incentives, or co-opting the language or symbols of the opposition to appear more aligned with their goals. It can also lead to conflicts of interest, as coopted individuals or groups may be expected to prioritize the interests of those in power over their original constituents or principles. For example, in political contexts, cooptation can involve offering positions in government or political parties to members of opposition groups, thereby weakening their ability to challenge the status quo. In corporate contexts, cooptation can involve bringing in representatives from labor unions or community organizations onto boards of directors or advisory boards, to gain their support or neutralize their opposition to certain policies or decisions. Cooptation, particularly in the context of governance or organizational leadership, can present several ethical problems:

Loss of Independence: Individuals or groups that are coopted may lose their independence and become aligned with the interests of those in power. This can compromise their ability to represent the interests of their original constituents or principles.

Conflicts of Interest: Coopted individuals or groups may face conflicts of interest, as they may be expected to prioritize the interests of those in power over their original constituents or principles.

Manipulation and Control: Cooptation can be seen as a form of manipulation or co-option of dissenting voices, rather than a genuine attempt to address their concerns or incorporate their perspectives.

Lack of Transparency: Cooptation can lead to a lack of transparency and accountability, as coopted individuals or groups may not be fully transparent about their relationship with those in power.

Fragmentation and Division: Cooptation can lead to fragmentation or division within opposition groups, as some members may be coopted while others remain independent or opposed to those in power.

Here are some potential measures that a company could take to address potential ethical conflicts in managing opposition via cooptation:

Transparency and Disclosure: The company should be transparent about its cooptation efforts and disclose any potential conflicts of interest that may arise. This can help to build trust with stakeholders and mitigate concerns about manipulation or co-option of dissenting voices.

Fair and Inclusive Process: The company should ensure that its cooptation efforts are fair and inclusive, and that all stakeholders have a voice in the decision-making process. This can help to ensure that cooptation is not seen as a form of manipulation or co-option, but rather as a genuine attempt to address concerns and incorporate diverse perspectives.

Consultation and Engagement: The company should engage with stakeholders and seek their input and feedback on cooptation efforts. This can help to ensure that cooptation is aligned with the interests and values of stakeholders, and that it is seen as a collaborative and inclusive process.

Ethical Guidelines and Oversight: The company should establish ethical guidelines and oversight mechanisms to ensure that cooptation efforts are consistent with ethical principles and guidelines. This can include establishing a committee or board to oversee cooptation efforts and ensure that they are transparent, fair, and inclusive.

Evaluation and Accountability: The company should regularly evaluate its cooptation efforts and hold itself accountable for their outcomes. This can help to ensure that cooptation is effective in addressing concerns and incorporating diverse perspectives, and that it is seen as a legitimate and ethical approach to managing opposition.

Overall, cooptation can present several ethical problems, particularly when it involves the cooption of dissenting voices or opposition groups. It can lead to conflicts of interest, loss of independence, manipulation and control, lack of transparency, and fragmentation or division within opposition groups. Based on the analysis of similar cases, ethical principles, and relevant examples, CBR could help identify similar cases where conflicts of interest were successfully managed and develop a plan for addressing potential conflicts of interest in this situation.

When it comes to **whistleblowing**, CBR can be a useful tool for reasoning about the ethical implications of whistleblowing in a specific context. For example, if an employee is considering blowing the whistle on their employer for unethical behavior, they could use CBR to compare their situation to similar past cases of whistleblowing and to consider the ethical principles and values that were applied in those cases. CBR can help individuals to reason about the potential risks and consequences of whistleblowing, as well as the potential benefits and the potential harm that may be prevented. It can also help individuals to consider alternative courses of action and to weigh the potential impact of their decision on themselves and others. Ultimately, CBR can be a valuable tool for reasoning about the ethical implications of whistleblowing and for making informed ethical decisions in complex and challenging situations.

Whistleblowing is the act of exposing wrongdoing or unethical behavior within an organization, typically by an employee or former employee (Near & Miceli, 1985). Whistleblowers may report misconduct to their employer, to a regulatory agency, or to the media, depending on the nature of the wrongdoing and the laws and policies in place. Whistleblowing can be a complex and challenging decision for individuals to make. On one hand, whistleblowers play a crucial role in holding organizations accountable and preventing harm to individuals, communities, and the environment. Whistleblowing can also be a way for individuals to uphold their professional and ethical responsibilities. On the other hand, whistleblowers may face significant risks and consequences for speaking out. They may face retaliation from their employer, including termination, demotion, or harassment. They may also face legal and financial consequences, including lawsuits and loss of income.

The ethics of whistleblowing are complex and often debated. Some argue that whistleblowing is a moral imperative, particularly when the wrongdoing is significant and the potential harm is great. They argue that whistleblowers have a duty to protect the public interest and to hold organizations accountable for their actions. Others argue that whistleblowing should be a last resort and used only when all other options have been exhausted (Park & Blenkinsopp, 2009). Individuals should first try to address their concerns through internal channels within the organization.

The ethics of whistleblowing depend on the specific context and circumstances of each case. It's important to consider the potential risks and consequences of whistleblowing, as well as the potential benefits and the potential harm that may be prevented.

References

Fich, E. M., Tran, A. L., & Walkling, R. A. (2013). On the importance of golden parachutes. *The Journal of Financial and Quantitative Analysis, 48*(6), 1717–1753. http://www.jstor.org/stable/43303859

Johnsen, K. C. (1985). Golden parachutes and the business judgment rule: Toward a proper standard of review. *The Yale Law Journal, 94*(4), 909–928. https://doi.org/10.2307/796290

Lozano, A. J. (2003). A historical perspective of casuistry and its application to contemporary biomedical ethics. *The Linacre Quarterly, 70*(1), https://epublications.marquette.edu/lnq/vol70/iss1/5

Machlin, J. C., Choe, H., & Miles, J. A. (1993). The effects of golden parachutes on takeover activity. *The Journal of Law & Economics, 36*(2), 861–876. http://www.jstor.org/stable/725810

Near, J. P., & Miceli, M. P. (1985). Organizational dissidence: The case of whistleblowing. *Journal of Business Ethics, 4*, 1–16. https://doi.org/10.1007/BF00382668

Park, H., & Blenkinsopp, J. (2009). Whistle-blowing as planned behavior – A survey of South Korean police officers. *Journal of Business Ethics, 85*(4), 545–556. https://doi.org/10.1007/s10551-008-9788-y

Shapiro, S. P. (2003). Bushwhacking the ethical high road: Conflict of interest in the practice of law and real life. *Law & Social Inquiry, 28*(1), 87–268. http://www.jstor.org/stable/1215767

Trumpy, A. J. (2008). Subject to negotiation: The mechanisms behind co-optation and corporate reform. *Social Problems, 55*(4), 480–500. https://doi.org/10.1525/sp. 2008.55.4.480

Wade, J., O'Reilly, C. A., & Chandratat, I. (1990). Golden parachutes: CEOs and the exercise of social influence. *Administrative Science Quarterly, 35*(4), 587–603. https://doi.org/10.2307/2393510

Zaman, R., Atawnah, N., Baghdadi, G. A., & Liu, J. (2021). Fiduciary duty or loyalty? Evidence from co-opted boars and corporate misconduct. *Journal of Corporate Finance, 70*(102066). https://doi.org/10.1016/j.jcorp fin.2021.102066

Chapter 11 Ethical Codes

What is morally sound behavior in any industry, profession, or organization? Ethical codes are sets of guidelines or rules established by professional organizations or regulatory bodies to govern the behavior of individuals within specific professions or industries. These codes outline expected standards of conduct, professional responsibilities, and ethical norms for practitioners. Ethical codes typically cover areas such as confidentiality, honesty, integrity, respect for diversity, and the welfare of clients or stakeholders. They serve as practical tools for promoting ethical behavior and ensuring accountability within professional settings.

A code of ethics serves as a foundational document that codifies the standards of conduct expected within a profession or organization. It provides clear guidelines for professionals regarding acceptable behavior and ethical standards and ensures transparency by explicitly outlining the moral responsibilities and expectations associated with membership in a professional organization. Codes of ethics often reflect universal ethical principles that transcend cultural or legal boundaries. They establish a common framework for ethical behavior, promoting consistency and coherence in decision-making across diverse contexts. By establishing a set of ethical principles and standards, a code of ethics holds professionals accountable for their actions. It provides a framework for evaluating behavior and can be used to address ethical breaches through disciplinary measures or exclusion from the organization. It stimulates important conversations and promotes awareness of ethical considerations within the profession or industry. They encourage individuals to reflect on their own roles in ethical decision-making and assert their moral standpoint on various issues. By identifying behaviors and actions that are inherently wrong (malum in se), ethical codes help prevent harm and mitigate risks associated with unethical conduct. This proactive approach can safeguard individuals, organizations, and stakeholders from potential harm or damage.

Codes of ethics play a crucial role in guiding behavior and decision-making by clearly defining what is considered inherently wrong, regardless of any regulations or laws in place. This distinction between malum in se (wrong in itself) and malum prohibitum (wrong because prohibited) is essential for promoting ethical conduct, particularly in rapidly evolving domains such as the digital space. In dynamic and fast-paced environments like the digital space, ethical codes provide a flexible framework that can adapt to evolving challenges and emerging ethical dilemmas. They enable individuals to apply ethical principles to new contexts and technologies, ensuring relevance and effectiveness over time. Adherence to ethical codes enhances professionalism and fosters trust among stakeholders, including clients, customers, partners, and the public. By upholding ethical principles, individuals and organizations demonstrate integrity, reliability, and commitment to ethical conduct.

Overall, a well-written and inclusive code of ethics serves as an educational tool, especially for individuals who may not be well-versed in ethical considerations. It helps professionals understand their ethical obligations and guides them in navigating complex moral dilemmas. A code of ethics helps identify and prioritize key areas with moral implications within the profession or organization. It highlights ethical challenges and fosters a culture of responsibility by creating awareness of ethical issues that may have been overlooked. While a code of ethics may not immediately bring about significant change, it serves as an important first step towards promoting ethical behavior and organizational culture. It lays the foundation for ongoing discussions and initiatives aimed at improving ethical standards and practices. Some examples of professions with established ethical codes include medicine (e.g., the Hippocratic Oath), law, journalism, and engineering.

Digital Ethics

Digital ethics refers to the moral principles and guidelines that govern the use of digital technologies, data, and information. Digital ethics is an evolving field, and new ethical challenges and dilemmas continue to emerge as technology advances. It is important for individuals, organizations, and policymakers to consider these ethical issues and work together to develop ethical guidelines and standards for the responsible use of digital technology. It encompasses a wide range of topics, including privacy, security, transparency, accountability, fairness, and the impact of technology on society and the environment. Digital ethics is concerned with ensuring that the use of digital technologies is aligned with ethical values and norms, and that the benefits of technology are maximized while minimizing potential harms. Some key principles of digital ethics include:

Privacy: Protecting individuals' personal information and ensuring that it is used only for legitimate purposes.
Security: Ensuring that digital systems and data are secure from unauthorized access, breaches, and cyberattacks.

Transparency: Providing clear and understandable information about how digital technologies and algorithms work, and how they are being used.

Accountability: Holding individuals and organizations responsible for their actions and decisions related to digital technologies.

Fairness: Ensuring that digital technologies are used in a way that is fair and equitable, and that they do not perpetuate or exacerbate existing inequalities.

Impact on society and the environment: Considering the broader social, economic, and environmental impacts of digital technologies, and working to minimize negative effects.

Media Ethics or Journalism Ethics

Journalist ethics, also known as media ethics or journalism ethics, refers to the moral principles and standards that guide the conduct of journalists in their professional practice. These ethics are essential for upholding integrity, credibility, and accountability in journalism. Key principles and considerations in journalist ethics include:

Truth and Accuracy: Journalists have a duty to report truthfully and accurately, striving to present information that is factually correct and verified to the best of their ability. They should verify the accuracy of sources, corroborate information from multiple sources when possible, and clearly distinguish between facts, opinions, and speculation.

Independence and Objectivity: Journalists should strive to maintain independence and objectivity in their reporting, avoiding bias, undue influence, or conflicts of interest that may compromise their integrity. They should resist pressure from external parties, such as advertisers, sources, or political interests, and remain impartial in their coverage.

Fairness and Balance: Journalists should seek to present a balanced and fair representation of events, issues, and viewpoints, providing context and allowing for diverse perspectives to be heard. They should avoid sensationalism, distortion, or manipulation of facts that could mislead or unfairly influence audiences.

Privacy and Sensitivity: Journalists should respect individuals' privacy rights and exercise sensitivity when reporting on personal or sensitive matters, especially involving victims, minors, or vulnerable groups. They should obtain consent, when necessary, protect confidential sources, and avoid unnecessary intrusion into private lives.

Accountability and Transparency: Journalists should be accountable for their work and transparent about their methods, sources, and potential conflicts of interest. They should be open to feedback, corrections, and criticism from the public and adhere to established editorial standards and codes of conduct.

Public Interest: Journalists have a responsibility to serve the public interest by providing information that is relevant, valuable, and contributes to an informed citizenry. They should prioritize issues of significance, hold those in power accountable, and promote transparency and accountability in public affairs.

Professional Conduct: Journalists should conduct themselves in a professional manner, respecting ethical standards and professional codes of conduct established by their organizations or professional associations. They should avoid plagiarism, fabrication, conflicts of interest, and other unethical practices that undermine the credibility of journalism.

Overall, journalist ethics provide a framework for responsible and ethical journalism, ensuring that journalists uphold the highest standards of integrity, accuracy, and accountability in their pursuit of informing the public and serving as watchdogs of democracy.

Medical Ethics (Bioethics or Healthcare Ethics)

Medical ethics, also known as bioethics or healthcare ethics, refers to the moral principles and values that guide the conduct of healthcare professionals, researchers, and organizations in the field of medicine. It addresses the ethical dilemmas and considerations that arise in clinical practice, biomedical research, healthcare policy, and the delivery of healthcare services. Key principles and topics in medical ethics include:

Autonomy: Respect for patient autonomy is a fundamental principle in medical ethics (Crane et al., 2005). It involves recognizing patients' rights to make their own healthcare decisions based on informed consent, free from coercion or undue influence (Kelly, 2003). Healthcare professionals should provide patients with relevant information about their medical condition, treatment options, risks, and benefits, empowering them to make autonomous decisions about their care.

Beneficence: The principle of beneficence emphasizes the obligation of healthcare professionals to act in the best interests of patients, promoting their well-being and health outcomes (Bester, 2020). Healthcare providers should strive to maximize benefits and minimize harm in their clinical decisions and interventions, prioritizing the welfare and interests of patients.

Nonmaleficence: Nonmaleficence entails the duty of healthcare professionals to do no harm to patients, avoiding actions or omissions that could cause unnecessary suffering, injury, or harm. Healthcare providers should carefully assess the risks and potential harms of medical interventions and take steps to mitigate or prevent adverse outcomes (Bester, 2020).

Justice: The principle of justice emphasizes fairness, equity, and the allocation of healthcare resources in a just and equitable manner. Healthcare professionals and institutions should ensure fair access to healthcare services, address disparities in healthcare delivery, and advocate for social justice in health policy and practice.

Confidentiality: Respect for patient confidentiality is essential for maintaining trust and privacy in the patient provider relationship. Healthcare professionals have a duty to safeguard patients' confidential information and only disclose it with the patient's consent or when required by law or ethical considerations.

Professional Integrity: Healthcare professionals are expected to adhere to high standards of professional conduct, honesty, integrity, and accountability in their interactions with patients, colleagues, and the public. They should uphold ethical principles and values in their clinical practice, research endeavors, and involvement in healthcare policy and decision-making.

End-of-Life Care and Palliative Care: Ethical considerations in end-of-life care and palliative care involve respecting patients' wishes, providing compassionate and supportive care, and addressing issues such as advance care planning, euthanasia, and withdrawal of life-sustaining treatment (Akdeniz et al., 2021). Healthcare professionals should engage in open and honest communication with patients and their families, ensuring that their preferences and values are respected at the end of life.

Medical ethics provides a framework for addressing ethical dilemmas, navigating complex moral issues, and promoting ethical conduct in healthcare practice, research, and policy. It ensures that healthcare professionals uphold the highest standards of integrity, compassion, and professionalism in their interactions with patients and the broader community.

War Ethics (also Known as the Ethics of War or Just War Theory)

War ethics, also known as the ethics of war or just war theory, is a branch of applied ethics that deals with moral principles and considerations related to armed conflict and warfare. It provides a framework for evaluating the morality of going to war (jus ad bellum) and the conduct of war (jus in bello). Key principles and concepts in war ethics include:

1. *Jus ad Bellum (Justice in Going to War):*

Just Cause: War is considered morally justifiable only if it is waged for a righteous cause, such as self-defense against aggression, defense of innocent civilians, or the restoration of justice (Davenport, 2011).

Last Resort: War should only be initiated after all peaceful means of resolving conflicts, such as diplomacy, negotiation, or sanctions, have been exhausted (Lango, 2009).

Proportionality: The anticipated benefits of going to war must outweigh the expected harm and costs, both in terms of human lives and other consequences (Hurka, 2005).

Legitimate Authority: War must be authorized and declared by a legitimate governing authority, such as a recognized state or international organization, in accordance with established legal and constitutional procedures (Zuo & Yunpeng, 2007).

2. *Jus in Bello (Justice in Conducting War):*

Civilians vs non-combatants discrimination: Parties engaged in war must distinguish between combatants and non-combatants, targeting only military objectives and avoiding harm to civilians and non-combatants (Swiney, 2005).

Proportionality: The use of force must be proportional to the military objective and necessary to achieve legitimate military goals, avoiding excessive or indiscriminate violence (Gardam, 1993).

Military Necessity: The use of force must be necessary to achieve military objectives and should be limited to what is militarily necessary to accomplish those goals.

Humanitarian Treatment: Combatants must adhere to principles of humanity, treating prisoners of war and captured enemies with dignity and respect, and providing medical care to the wounded and sick (Hongsheng, 2006).

3. Other Ethical Considerations:

Preventive War: The ethics of preventive war, or preemptive strikes, involves complex moral considerations about the justification for initiating hostilities based on anticipated future threats or aggression (Lango, 2005). Use of Weapons: Ethical considerations also extend to the use of specific weapons and tactics in warfare, such as chemical weapons, nuclear weapons, landmines, and drones, weighing their military effectiveness against their potential harm to civilians and the environment (Rizzo, 1982). Post-War Justice: War ethics also address issues of post-war justice, including the prosecution of war crimes, reconciliation and reconstruction efforts, and the establishment of peace and stability in the aftermath of conflict (Loyle & Appel, 2017).

War ethics provides a moral framework for assessing the legitimacy, conduct, and consequences of armed conflict, aiming to minimize the harm and suffering caused by war and promote principles of justice, humanity, and peace.

Military Ethics

Military ethics refers to the moral principles, values, and codes of conduct that guide the behavior and decision-making of military personnel in the armed forces. It encompasses a range of ethical considerations specific to the military context, including the conduct of warfare, the treatment of combatants and non-combatants, and the responsibilities of military leaders. Key principles and concepts in military ethics include:

Loyalty and Obedience: Military personnel are expected to demonstrate loyalty to their country, their unit, and their fellow service members. They are also obligated to obey lawful orders from their superiors, provided those orders are consistent with moral and legal norms (Yakovleff, 2007).

Professionalism and Integrity: Military professionals are expected to uphold high standards of professionalism, honesty, and integrity in their conduct, both on and off duty (Yakovleff, 2007). They must adhere to ethical codes of conduct and maintain the trust and confidence of the public.

Respect for Human Dignity: Military ethics emphasize the importance of respecting the inherent dignity and rights of all individuals, including enemy combatants, prisoners of war, and civilians. Military personnel are expected to treat others with dignity, fairness, and respect, even in the heat of battle (Hongsheng, 2006).

Adherence to Laws and Rules of War: Military operations must be conducted in accordance with national and international laws, treaties, and conventions governing the conduct of warfare, such as the Geneva Conventions. This includes principles of proportionality, distinction, and military necessity.

Accountability and Responsibility: Military leaders and personnel are accountable for their actions and decisions, including those made in combat situations. They must take responsibility for the consequences of their actions and ensure that they are consistent with moral and legal standards.

Protection of Civilians and Non-Combatants: Military personnel have a duty to minimize harm to civilians and non-combatants during armed conflict, taking precautions to avoid targeting civilian populations and infrastructure and to prevent collateral damage (Swiney, 2005).

Ethical Leadership: Military leaders are expected to demonstrate ethical leadership, setting a positive example for their subordinates and fostering a culture of integrity, accountability, and respect within their units. They must make ethical decisions that prioritize the welfare of their personnel and the mission.

Continuous Professional Development: Military personnel are encouraged to engage in ongoing training and education to enhance their ethical awareness, decision-making skills, and understanding of the ethical principles that govern their profession.

Military ethics plays a crucial role in maintaining the morale, discipline, and effectiveness of the armed forces, as well as in promoting adherence to ethical standards in the conduct of military operations and the treatment of all individuals affected by armed conflict. By upholding principles of integrity, respect, and responsibility, military personnel contribute to the ethical conduct of warfare and the protection of human rights and dignity.

Environmental Ethics

Environmental ethics is a branch of ethics that focuses on the moral principles and values that guide human interactions with the natural world. It addresses ethical issues related to the environment, including the rights of non-human entities, the responsibilities of humans toward nature, and the moral implications of environmental policies and practices. Key principles and concepts in environmental ethics include:

Intrinsic Value of Nature: Environmental ethics asserts that nature has inherent value and worth apart from its utility to humans (Anthony & Essien, 2018). This principle recognizes the intrinsic value of ecosystems, species, and individual organisms, irrespective of their instrumental value to human beings.

Anthropocentrism vs. Ecocentrism: Anthropocentrism places humans at the center of moral consideration, viewing nature primarily in terms of its usefulness to human interests and well-being (Samuelsson, 2013). Ecocentrism expands moral consideration to include the entire ecosystem and all its components, recognizing the interconnectedness and interdependence of all living beings and natural systems (Samuelsson, 2013).

Stewardship and Responsibility: Environmental ethics emphasize humans' responsibility as stewards of the Earth, with a duty to care for and protect the environment for present and future generations (Fang et al., 2023). Stewardship involves managing natural resources responsibly, minimizing harm to ecosystems, and promoting sustainable practices that preserve the integrity and health of the environment.

Sustainability and Intergenerational Equity: Sustainability entails meeting present needs without compromising the ability of future generations to meet their own needs. Environmental ethics advocates for sustainable development practices that balance environmental, social, and economic considerations (Langhelle, 1999). Intergenerational equity requires considering the interests and rights of future generations in environmental decision-making, ensuring that they inherit a healthy and thriving planet.

Respect for Biodiversity: Biodiversity refers to the variety of life forms and ecosystems on Earth. Environmental ethics emphasizes the importance of preserving biodiversity, recognizing the intrinsic value of all species and ecosystems and the role they play in maintaining ecological balance and resilience (Oksanen, 1997).

Environmental Justice: Environmental justice addresses the disproportionate burden of environmental degradation and pollution borne by marginalized communities, including low-income neighborhoods and communities of color. It advocates for equitable distribution of environmental benefits and burdens, fair access to resources and decision-making processes, and recognition of the rights of affected communities to a clean and healthy environment (Torres, 1994).

Global Responsibility and Solidarity: Environmental ethics recognizes that environmental issues are global in nature and require collective action and cooperation at local, national, and international levels. It emphasizes the importance of solidarity among nations and communities in addressing environmental challenges, sharing resources, and promoting sustainable development worldwide.

Environmental ethics provides a framework for ethical reflection and decision-making in environmental conservation, resource management, and policy formulation. By integrating ethical principles with scientific knowledge and social values, environmental ethics seeks to promote harmonious and sustainable relationships between humans and the natural world.

Educational Ethics

Educational ethics refers to the moral principles, values, and standards that guide the conduct of educators, administrators, students, and other stakeholders in the field of education. It encompasses ethical considerations related to teaching, learning, research, and the overall educational environment. Key principles and concepts in educational ethics include:

Respect for Students: Educators have a responsibility to treat students with respect, dignity, and fairness, recognizing their individual needs, backgrounds, and perspectives. They should create inclusive and supportive learning environments that promote equity, diversity, and inclusion, and foster a sense of belonging for all students. Integrity and Honesty: Educators should uphold principles of academic integrity and honesty, both in their own conduct and in teaching students the importance of ethical behavior. They should model honesty and integrity in grading, assessment, research, and scholarly activities, and discourage cheating, plagiarism, and other forms of academic misconduct.

Professional Responsibility: Educators have a duty to maintain professional competence, staying abreast of developments in their field, and engaging in continuous professional development. They should adhere to ethical standards and codes of conduct established by professional organizations and educational institutions, and act in the best interests of their students and the broader community.

Confidentiality and Privacy: Educators must respect the confidentiality and privacy rights of students, protecting sensitive information and maintaining appropriate boundaries in their interactions. They should only disclose student information with consent or when required by law and take measures to safeguard student data and personal information.

Equity and Access: Educators should promote equitable access to educational opportunities and resources, addressing barriers to learning and ensuring that all students have the support they need to succeed. They should advocate for social justice and educational equity, and strive to eliminate disparities based on race, ethnicity, gender, socioeconomic status, disability, or other factors.

Professional Relationships: Educators should establish professional boundaries in their interactions with students, colleagues, parents, and other stakeholders, maintaining appropriate relationships based on trust, respect, and professionalism. They should avoid conflicts of interest, favoritism, or discriminatory behavior, and handle interpersonal conflicts and disagreements with integrity and sensitivity.

Community Engagement and Service: Educators have a role in engaging with the broader community and promoting civic responsibility, social awareness, and community service among students. They should encourage students to contribute to their communities, address local and global challenges, and become responsible and ethical citizens. Educational ethics provides a framework for ethical reflection and decision-making in all aspects of education, from curriculum development and teaching practices to student assessment and institutional governance. By upholding principles of integrity, respect, fairness, and social responsibility, educators contribute to creating positive learning environments that promote the holistic development and well-being of students.

Business Ethics

Business ethics refers to the moral principles, values, and standards that guide the conduct of individuals and organizations in the business world. It involves considering ethical considerations and responsibilities in decision-making processes and interactions with stakeholders, including employees, customers, suppliers, shareholders, and the broader community. Key principles and concepts in business ethics include:

Corporate governance refers to the system of rules, practices, processes, and structures by which a company is directed and controlled (Tirole, 2001). It encompasses the relationships between the various stakeholders involved in the company, including shareholders, management, the board of directors, employees, customers, suppliers, and the broader community. The primary goal of corporate governance is to ensure that the company operates in a transparent, ethical, and accountable manner while maximizing shareholder value and safeguarding the interests of all stakeholders. Key components of corporate governance include:

Board of Directors: The board of directors has a fiduciary duty to shareholders to run the corporation in their interest (Boatright, 1994). It typically consists of a group of individuals elected by shareholders to represent their interests. The board sets corporate objectives, approves major decisions, appoints senior management, and monitors the company's performance.

Shareholder Rights: Corporate governance seeks to protect and promote the rights of shareholders, including the right to vote on important matters, such as the election of directors, mergers and acquisitions, and changes to corporate governance structures (Tirole, 2001). Shareholders also have the right to receive timely and accurate information about the company's financial performance and strategy.

Ethical Conduct and Transparency: Corporate governance promotes ethical conduct and transparency in all aspects of business operations structures (Tirole, 2001). This includes ensuring compliance with laws and regulations, maintaining accurate financial records, disclosing relevant information to stakeholders, and upholding high standards of integrity and accountability.

Risk Management: Corporate governance involves identifying, assessing, and managing risks that could affect the company's performance or reputation. This includes implementing systems and controls to mitigate risks related to operations, finance, compliance, cybersecurity, and other areas structures (Tirole, 2001). Effective risk management helps to protect shareholder value and ensure the long-term sustainability of the company.

Stakeholder Engagement: Corporate governance encourages engagement with stakeholders to understand their concerns, interests, and expectations and to incorporate their input into decision-making processes (Greenwood, 2007). This includes communicating with employees, customers, suppliers, communities, and other stakeholders to build trust, foster relationships, and address issues proactively.

Accountability and Performance Evaluation: Corporate governance establishes mechanisms for holding management accountable for their actions and decisions. This may include performance evaluations, executive compensation structures, and mechanisms for addressing conflicts of interest or breaches of fiduciary duty (Boatright, 1994). Accountability ensures that management acts in the best interests of the company and its stakeholders.

Integrity and Honesty: Business ethics emphasizes the importance of integrity and honesty in all business dealings, including interactions with employees, customers, competitors, and the public. Organizations should strive to be truthful, transparent, and forthright *in their communications, advertising, and marketing practices.*

Fairness and Equity: Fairness and equity are central principles in business ethics, requiring organizations to treat all stakeholders with fairness, impartiality, and respect. Businesses should strive to create a level playing field for competition, avoid discrimination and favoritism, and ensure equitable treatment of employees in hiring, promotion, compensation, and decision-making.

Corporate Social Responsibility (CSR): Corporate social responsibility involves businesses taking responsibility for their impact on society, the environment, and the well-being of stakeholders beyond their financial performance (Wang et al., 2016). Organizations should consider the social, environmental, and ethical implications of their operations and seek to make positive contributions to the communities in which they operate.

Accountability and Transparency: Business ethics emphasizes the importance of accountability and transparency in organizational governance, decision-making, and reporting. Companies should be accountable for their actions and decisions, disclose relevant information to stakeholders, and maintain transparency in financial reporting, corporate governance, and ethical practices.

Respect for Stakeholders: Business ethics requires organizations to respect the rights, interests, and dignity of all stakeholders affected by their operations, including employees, customers, suppliers, shareholders, and the community. Businesses should listen to the concerns and feedback of stakeholders, engage in dialogue and collaboration, and seek to address social and environmental issues in a responsible manner.

Environmental Sustainability: Environmental sustainability involves businesses minimizing their environmental impact, conserving natural resources, and promoting sustainable practices throughout their operations and supply chain. Organizations should adopt environmentally friendly practices, reduce waste and pollution, and integrate sustainability into their business strategies and decision-making processes.

Ethical Leadership: Ethical leadership is essential for fostering a culture of integrity, trust, and ethical behavior within organizations. Leaders should lead by example, demonstrate ethical values and behaviors, and promote a culture of ethics, accountability, and responsibility throughout the organization.

Overall, effective corporate governance is essential for maintaining investor confidence, mitigating risks, promoting ethical conduct, and creating long-term value for shareholders and stakeholders. By adhering to principles of transparency, accountability, integrity, and stakeholder engagement, companies can strengthen their corporate governance practices and enhance their reputation and competitiveness in the marketplace. Business ethics provides a framework for ethical reflection and decision-making in all aspects of business operations, including corporate governance, corporate social responsibility, human resources, marketing, finance, and supply chain management. By upholding ethical principles and values, businesses can enhance their reputation, build trust with stakeholders, and contribute to sustainable and responsible business practices.

Counseling Ethics

Counseling ethics refers to the moral principles, values, and standards that guide the conduct of counselors, therapists, and mental health professionals in their professional practice. Ethical guidelines are essential in counseling to ensure the well-being, autonomy, and confidentiality of clients, as well as to maintain the integrity and professionalism of the counseling profession. Key principles and concepts in counseling ethics include:

Confidentiality: Counselors have a duty to protect the confidentiality of client information and communications, maintaining the privacy and trust of clients (Adams, 1965). They should only disclose confidential information with the client's informed consent or when required by law, such as in cases of imminent harm to the client or others.

Informed Consent: Counselors should obtain informed consent from clients before beginning therapy, explaining the nature and purpose of counseling, the counselor's qualifications and approach, the rights and responsibilities of both the counselor and client, and the limits of confidentiality (Kelly, 2003). Informed consent ensures that clients are fully informed and empowered to make autonomous decisions about their participation in counseling.

Boundaries and Dual Relationships: Counselors should establish and maintain appropriate professional boundaries with clients, avoiding dual or multiple relationships that could compromise the therapeutic relationship or create conflicts of interest (Flanagan & McGrew, 1961). They should refrain from engaging in personal, social, financial, or romantic relationships with current or former clients, and maintain objectivity and impartiality in their interactions.

Competence and Professionalism: Counselors have a responsibility to maintain high standards of competence, professionalism, and ethical conduct in their practice. They should pursue ongoing training, supervision, and professional development to enhance their knowledge, skills, and effectiveness as counselors.

Cultural Competence and Diversity: Counselors should demonstrate cultural competence and sensitivity in working with clients from diverse backgrounds, respecting their cultural, ethnic, religious, and social identities. They should strive to understand the cultural context and worldview of clients and adapt their counseling approach to meet the unique needs and preferences of each individual.

Ethical Decision-Making: Counselors should engage in ethical decision-making processes when faced with ethical dilemmas or conflicts of interest in their practice. They should consult relevant ethical guidelines, seek supervision or consultation from colleagues or ethical committees, and consider the potential consequences of their actions on clients and the counseling relationship.

Professional Relationships and Supervision: Counselors should establish supportive and professional relationships with colleagues, supervisors, and other professionals, seeking supervision and consultation when needed to enhance their ethical practice. They should collaborate with other professionals involved in the care of clients, maintain appropriate communication and referrals, and adhere to ethical guidelines in their interactions with colleagues.

Counseling ethics provides a framework for ethical reflection and decision-making in counseling practice, ensuring that counselors uphold the highest standards of integrity, competence, and professionalism in their work with clients. By adhering to ethical principles and guidelines, counselors promote the well-being and dignity of clients and contribute to the credibility and trustworthiness of the counseling profession.

Research and Publication Ethics

Research ethics refer to the moral principles and guidelines that govern the conduct of research involving human subjects, animals, and the environment. These principles are designed to protect the rights, safety, and well-being of research participants and to ensure that research is conducted in a responsible and ethical manner. Publication ethics refers to the ethical standards and principles that govern the conduct of authors, reviewers, editors, publishers, and other stakeholders involved in the process of scholarly publishing. These ethical standards aim to ensure the integrity, credibility, and reliability of published research and to maintain public trust in the academic and scientific community.

Some key principles of research ethics include:

Ethical Treatment of Subjects: Studies involving human subjects should adhere to ethical guidelines and regulations, including those related to privacy, confidentiality, and protection from harm. Studies involving animals, on the other hand, must ensure the humane treatment of animals and must be conducted in a manner that minimizes harm and suffering, and that respects the intrinsic value and welfare of animals and the environment (Regan, 2012). Researchers must obtain voluntary, informed consent from participants before involving them in research (Kelly, 2003). Informed consent means that participants must be fully informed about the purpose, procedures, risks, and benefits of the research, and they must have the capacity to understand this information and make an informed decision about whether to participate. Researchers must respect the autonomy and dignity of research participants and treat them with fairness, respect, and sensitivity (Aluwihare-Samaranayake, 2012). This includes protecting the privacy and confidentiality of participants and ensuring that they are treated with dignity and respect throughout the research process. Researchers must strive to maximize the benefits of research while minimizing any potential harm to participants (Aluwihare-Samaranayake, 2012). This includes ensuring that the risks of research are justified by the potential benefits, and that participants are not exposed to unnecessary risks. *Honesty and Integrity:* Researchers must ensure that the benefits and burdens of research are distributed fairly among participants, and that vulnerable or marginalized populations are not unfairly targeted or exploited in *research*. Researchers must conduct research with honesty, integrity, and transparency, and they must accurately report their findings and methods without falsification, fabrication, plagiarism, or other forms of research misconduct. This includes avoiding conflicts of interest and disclosing any potential conflicts or biases that could influence their objectivity or impartiality in the process. Similarly, reviewers and editors should act with integrity, providing fair and impartial evaluations of manuscripts based on their scholarly merit.

Research ethics is an evolving field, and new ethical challenges and dilemmas continue to emerge as research methods and technologies advance. It is important for researchers, institutions, and policymakers to consider these ethical issues and work together to develop ethical guidelines and standards for the responsible conduct of research.

References

Adams, J. F. (1965). Ethical responsibilities of the counselor. *The School Counselor, 12*(4), 197–205. http://www.jstor.org/stable/23909701

Akdeniz, M., Yardımcı, B., & Kavukcu, E. (2021). Ethical considerations at the end-of-life care. *SAGE Open Medicine, 9.* https://doi.org/10.1177/2050312121 1000918

Aluwihare-Samaranayake, D. (2012). Ethics in qualitative research: A view of the participants' and researchers' world from a critical standpoint. *International Journal of Qualitative Methods, 11*(2), 64–81. https://doi.org/10.1177/1609406 91201100208

Anthony, G. B., & Essien, C. K. (2018). Sustainable management of solid waste in Nigerian urban centres. *LWATI: A Journal of Contemporary Research, 15*(3), 1–10.

Bester, J. C. (2020). Beneficence, interests, and wellbeing in medicine: What it means to provide benefit to patients. *The American Journal of Bioethics, 20*(3), 53–62. https://doi.org/10.1080/15265161.2020.1714793

Boatright, J. R. (1994). Fiduciary duties and the shareholder-management relation: Or, what's so special about shareholders? *Business Ethics Quarterly, 4*(4), 393–407. https://doi.org/10.2307/3857339

Crane, M. K., Wittink, M., & Doukas, D. J. (2005). Respecting end-of-life treatment preferences. *American Family Physician, 72*(7), 1263–1268. https://doi.org/10.1007/978-981-19-4234-1_6

Davenport, J. J. (2011). Just war theory, humanitarian intervention, and the need for a democratic federation. *The Journal of Religious Ethics, 39*(3), 493 555. http://www.jstor.org/stable/23020002

Fang, W. T., Hassan, A., & LePage, B. A. (2023). *Living environmental education. Sustainable Development goals series.* Springer. https://doi.org/10.1007/978-981-19-4234-1_6

Flanagan, M. M., & McGrew, D. R. (1961). A suggested code of ethics for school counselors. *The School Counselor, 8*(4), 136–141. http://www.jstor.org/stable/45133974

Gardam, J. G. (1993). Proportionality and force in international law. *The American Journal of International Law, 87*(3), 391–413. https://doi.org/10.2307/2203645

Greenwood, M. (2007). Stakeholder engagement: Beyond the myth of corporate responsibility. *Journal of Business Ethics, 74*(4), 315–327. http://www.jstor.org/stable/25075473

Hongsheng, S. (2006). The evolution of law of war. *The Chinese Journal of International Politics, 1*(2), 267–301. https://www.jstor.org/stable/48615600

Hurka, T. (2005). Proportionality in the morality of war. *Philosophy & Public Affairs, 33*(1), 34–66. http://www.jstor.org/stable/3557942

Kelly, A. (2003). Research and the subject: The Practice of informed consent. *Political and Legal Anthropology Review, 26*(2), 182–195. http://www.jstor.org/stable/24497629.

Langhelle, O. (1999). Sustainable development: Exploring the ethics of "our common future". *International Political Science Review 20*(2), 129–149. http://www.jstor.org/stable/1601572

Lango, J. W. (2005). Preventive wars, just war principles, and the united nations. *The Journal of Ethics, 9*(1/2), 247–268. http://www.jstor.org/stable/25115823

Lango, J. W. (2009). Before military force, nonviolent action: An application of a generalized just war principle of last resort. *Public Affairs Quarterly, 23*(2), 115–133. http://www.jstor.org/stable/40441521

Loyle, C. E., & Appel, B. J. (2017). Conflict recurrence and postconflict justice: Addressing motivations and opportunities for sustainable peace. *International Studies Quarterly, 61*(3), 690–703. https://www.jstor.org/stable/48539044

Oksanen, M. (1997). The moral value of biodiversity. *Ambio, 26*(8), 541–545. http://www.jstor.org/stable/4314663

Regan, T. (2012). Animal rights and environmental ethics. In D. Bergandi (Ed.). *The structural links between ecology, evolution and ethics* (pp. 117–126). Springer. https://doi.org/10.1007/978-94-007-5067-8

Rizzo, R. F. (1982). Nuclear war: The moral dilemma. *CrossCurrents, 32*(1), 71–84. http://www.jstor.org/stable/24458544

Samuelsson, L. (2013). At the centre of what? A critical note on the centrism-terminology in environmental ethics. *Environmental Values, 22*(5), 627–645. http://www.jstor.org/stable/43695715

Swiney, G. (2005). Saving lives: The principle of distinction and the realities of modern war. *The International Lawyer, 39*(3), 733–758. http://www.jstor.org/stable/40707812

Tirole, J. (2001). Corporate Governance. *Econometrica, 69*(1), 1–35. http://www.jstor.org/stable/2692184

Torres, G. (1994). Environmental burdens and democratic justice. *Fordham Urban Law Journal, 21*(3), 430–460. https://ir.lawnet.fordham.edu/ulj/vol21/iss3/2

Wang, H., Tong, L., Takeuchi, R., & George, G. (2016). From the editors: corporate social responsibility: an overview and new research directions. *The Academy of Management Journal, 59*(2), 534–544. http://www.jstor.org/stable/24758301

Yakovleff, M. (2007). The foundations of morale and ethics in the armed forces: Some revealing variations among close allies. *Inflexions, 6*, 177–197. https://doi.org/10.3917/infle.006.0177

Zuo, G., & Yunpeng, X. (2007). Just war and justice of war: Reflections on ethics of war. *Frontiers of Philosophy in China, 2*(2), 280–290. http://www.jstor.org/stable/27823293

List of Figures

List of Tables

About the Author

B. Çağla GARİPAĞAOĞLU, PhD, is currently working as an Associate Professor at the Faculty of Educational Sciences, Educational Leadership and Administration Program, Bahçeşehir University (BAU), Istanbul, Turkey. She has more than 15 years of experience in teaching and supervision of students, research, consultancy work, workshops, seminars and advisory services within and outside the university. In addition, she has four years of working experience as a school principal at Bahçeşehir College, Umraniye campus which is a home to over 1000 students in Istanbul, Turkey. She completed her undergraduate degree (1996–2001) in Teaching Mathematics department at Boğaziçi (Bosphorous) University (formerly known as Robert College), Istanbul, Turkey. Then she received her MA (2004–2005) in Educational Sciences at The University of Sydney, Sydney, Australia and PhD (2006–2012) in Business Administration at Yeditepe University, Istanbul, Turkey. So far, she has researched about management strategies, leadership styles, and organizational behavior. Dr. Garipaagaoglu has various scientific studies, book chapters, and national/international presentations about organizational leadership & behavior ad specifically interested in conflict management organizational culture and post-modern/quantum leadership.